PRO DEO, REGE ET PATRIA

For God, King and Country

STUART McDOUALL

AuthorHouse™ UK
1663 Liberty Drive
Bloomington, IN 47403 USA
www.authorhouse.co.uk
UK TFN: 0800 0148641 (Toll Free inside the UK)
UK Local: 02036 956322 (+44 20 3695 6322 from outside the UK)

Because of the dynamic nature of the Internet, any web addresses or links contained in
this book may have changed since publication and may no longer be valid. The views
expressed in this work are solely those of the author and do not necessarily reflect the
views of the publisher, and the publisher hereby disclaims any responsibility for them.

This book is printed on acid-free paper.

ISBN: 979-8-8230-9061-2 (sc)
ISBN: 979-8-8230-9063-6 (hc)
ISBN: 979-8-8230-9062-9 (e)

Library of Congress Control Number: 2024923664

Print information available on the last page.

Published by AuthorHouse   01/20/2025

authorHOUSE®

DEDICATION

For my sons Jack and Patrick who were the inspiration behind this book, Hazel Miller who did the proof reading and to Gerald Sze, the computing ace who put together all of my images in it. And, behind it all, my wife Susanna who unobtrusively kept me going through thick and thin.

FOREWORD

Some of Stuart McDouall's friends - the sporty ones – call him by his Hash House Harrier moniker McTool. That doesn't do him justice for me. He's one of those blokes who goes flat out at anything that attracts him. His energy is like a fire-hose and his enthusiasm rampant. So much so that when I first got to know him in Hong Kong, over forty years ago, I wondered if he could succeed in a bureaucratic police force. But he did make it, retiring in 2005 after a successful career spanning 35 years. No, he's not McTool. He's McTurbo.

Who's the character behind his name? Firstly he's a family man; wife Susanna, sons Jack and Patrick and daughters-in-law, Pei-chen and Carrie respectively. Next, he's a servant to the community:-

- with the police, rising to Senior superintendent and one-time commandant of the Hong Kong Police Training School;
- With scouting Stuart became head of 19 English-speaking Scout groups in Hong Kong and formed two new Scout troops.
- With freemasonry, where he holds grand rank, he's heavily involved in charity work; and
- with the church, at St. John's Cathedral, he's poured his energy into the construction of the annual fund-raising fair for many years.

Also he's a serious sportsman, chairing the popular Police Athletics Club for 14 years and running with the not so serious Kowloon Hash. there is an anecdote told of Stuart when he was out on a run with two police colleagues on Hong Kong Island's scenic Dragon's Back, near Shek O, when he spied in the bush six men having the appearance and behaviour of illegal immigrants. He and his fellow officers, unarmed, rounded them up and ran them down to the police station, under arrest.

I got to know Stuart in the '70s, both of us Hashmen, and we talked of the fun potential of a convention of the Hash House Harriers, world-wide, to be held in Hong Kong. Stuart lit the after-burners, roaring off and composing the first circular for an 'Inter-Hash'. Back came the positive response from a dozen hashes in a dozen countries; beyond all expectations. And it happened. Since then there have been numerous Inter-Hash events all over the globe. We're to blame!

Stuart's book is for everyone who is interested in travel to far-flung places like the Falkland Islands and the Far East; Hong Kong and China. It's the fusion of the enthusiasm and energy of a couple made in Hong Kong. He's from Edinburgh and Susanna is a fourth-generation Hong Konger; rather rare. They met in the mid '70s when both were police inspectors.

Susanna was taught to love Chinese history by her father; chief compositor for a respected Chinese newspaper, the *Wah Kiu Yat Bo*. In her spare time she trained as a calligrapher and played the *Er-hu* (Chinese violin). Having left the police, she became the PA to the Director of Music in the Academy for the Performing Arts. When she retired in 2011 the couple entrained for Beijing and, from their base in son Jack's flat, they spent five months touring China. Stuart, who does nothing by halves, diarized and photographed the whole trip. A year later that turned into a fabulous travel book of China.

This book is every bit as interesting.

Jethro Roger Medcalf,
Saikung, Hong Kong.

PROLOGUE

I have titled this book *Pro Deo, Rege et Patria*, meaning For God, King and Country, because that is my family motto and it aptly describes my approach to life, if not always matching those high ideals. The *raison d'etre* behind each chapter in this book is that motto. It was my great x 3 grandfather John McDouall of Glasgow, a prominent tobacco merchant in his day, who, in 1763, designed our coat of arms around our family designation 'McDouall of Freugh'. Freugh is the village *cum* district in Dumfries and Galloway, Scotland, from whence my ancestors came.

Nearly two years ago a great friend of mine, a former journalist and businessman, asked me and other contemporaries of his who lived and worked in Hong Kong, to collaborate with him in producing a book about our lives. I duly wrote eight chapters, each one dealing with different aspects of my career in the RHKP. But when the scripts from some 20 authors were sent to the publishers there was a great deal of editing done, not so much as to sanitize the content as to shorten the volume of it. When the final proofs were sent to me I was mildly irritated at the literary butchering of several of my chapters and so decided to go it alone.

This book is a collection of events, chapter by chapter, that I have been involved in, one way or another, since finishing my education. It is not an autobiography where I lay bare my life, warts and all, but rather a compendium of experiences that have been of interest to me, which have influenced me or in which I have participated. None of them are of common or general knowledge.

In my preliminary chapter about voluntary service overseas I have sought to acquaint the reader with life in the Falkland Islands circa 1969-70 and how that isolated part of the world shaped my career choice. In the remaining chapters I attempt to give readers some insight into the makeup of Hong Kong society, particularly relating to the work of the Royal Hong Kong Police in maintaining law and order.

It is only natural, given the proximity and the financial, political and social influences of mainland China with Hong Kong that I make mention of this national relationship in several chapters. I have maintained objectivity throughout, without bias, and only been subjective with my personal views.

I sincerely hope you find this book interesting reading.

Stuart McDouall

VOLUNTARY SERVICE OVERSEAS (VSO)

The Falkland Islands

VSO was founded in 1958 by Alec and Mora Dickson who wrote to The Sunday Times proposing a year-long educational experience overseas for school leavers, initially only males, before starting university. It was the forerunner of what became known as *a gap year*. Applicants for this scheme underwent a selection process; a residential extended interview in London; and, once accepted, were given their postings to either impoverished or sparsely inhabited and remote territories around the world, volunteering in unskilled work such as nature conservation, practical health and hygiene and primary school-age basic education.

In 1962 the practice of taking school leavers changed to taking university graduate volunteers. In 1968 I applied to undertake VSO, following in the footsteps of my two elder sisters who had also done VSO, one in Pakistan and the other in Tunisia. I was posted to the Falkland Islands as a school teacher for children living in isolated country or 'camp' settlements. Initially I thought that the Falklands were islands off the wild coastline of northern Scotland. It was only when I got my hands on an atlas that I discovered their location at the other end of the world, off the southern tip of South America, near stormy Cape Horn and only a couple of hundred miles from Antarctica.

I had a few month's notice of departure from England during which time I had to obtain inoculations, put travel documents in order, buy a given list of personal clothing and equipment, read a recommended text book on child education and learn to ride a horse if not yet proficient in that skill. At that time we were living in Camberley, five minutes from Sandhurst where there is a military riding school. My father, being in the army, secured me several riding lessons.

On a wet and cold day in April I took a train into London, met up with two young men of my age, Richard and Graham, at the VSO office from where the three of us were driven to Heathrow Airport and put on a flight to Montevideo, Uruguay. On arrival we were met by a British embassy official who took us to a down-town hotel booked for two nights prior to our boarding the Royal Mail Ship (RMS) Darwin bound for the Falkland Islands.

The next morning, awake early and looking out of the window, I saw an interesting street scene; a Model Ford T with the petrol tank on its roof, a horse-drawn cart and pedestrians in colourful clothes and hats. Grabbing my camera I nipped downstairs, out onto the pavement and started taking photographs. Within minutes I was apprehended by a soldier with a rifle who spoke to me in Spanish. I shrugged my shoulders, spreading my hands, and he realised I was a foreigner. He took my camera off me and, indicating with his rifle that I should walk ahead of him, off we went, my heart in my mouth.

About five minutes later we turned into a gated lane where a sentry admitted us to the forecourt of an old and grimy, stone-built, three story building. I didn't need an interpreter to discover what the wording on the plaque was, above the huge double doors, 'Departomento de Policia'. I was taken down dimly-lit stone-flagged corridors, turning into a large room with lines of benches occupied by quite a few civilians. In front was a long desk behind which sat two uniformed men, one on the 'phone and the other writing in a big book. The soldier who had arrested me indicated I should sit. He then walked to the desk, talked briefly to the writer and handed him my camera, a Yashika FX-2 35mm. A few minutes later that officer took my camera out through a door to one side, before returning empty handed. It seemed ages, while others in the room were coming and going, before I was pointed at and motioned to stand. Moments later my arresting officer took me out of that room, down a corridor and into a smaller room where three men in civilian clothes sat behind a desk. One of them talked to the arresting officer briefly then waved him away. He made a gesture for me to sit on the solitary chair in front of them.

The younger man turned out to be an interpreter in English and Spanish. The older man, wearing tinted glasses, was looking at a passport which I recognised as mine and which listed my occupation as 'Student'. He also had my wallet, tickets, VSO papers and a note pad. No camera. I realised that my room had been searched while I was waiting in the police station. Questions were asked about my reasons for being in town? Why was I taking photographs? Had I met students in Montevideo? Who was paying me? And many more. They didn't harangue me but I was scared, knowing that they believed me to be a dissident; a trouble-maker.

By this time I was squirming with the need for a toilet. The panel seemed to realise my discomfort and said something to a man standing at the back who made me follow him out of the room, back up the same corridor and into a washroom where there was an open row of smelly, dilapidated-looking urinals. Back out of there and down another corridor, I was passed to a uniformed man who locked me in a small window-less cell lit by an electric light on the wall, caged in wire. No wash basin or toilet and the only furniture was an iron-maiden bed, without mattress. Fixed to the wall beside the bed was a small wooden shelf displaying a plastic bust of a military looking person. Later I discovered that the bust was that of Jose Artigas, a Uruguayan national hero who fought for the emancipation of the River Plate delta region in the late 19th century. Left alone, cold fear returned. I didn't even have my wristwatch. There was nothing I could do but sit on the edge of the bed and wait...for what?

The door was unlocked and the gaoler handed me a grubby-white porcelain cup containing what turned out to be bitter, black coffee. He left, locking the rusty iron door behind him. I sipped the drink. It seemed to me that it was at least an hour before the door was unlocked again by the gaoler. Behind him was a suited white-man carrying a briefcase. He came forward, said 'good afternoon' with an American accent and asked my name? Satisfied, he said he was from the American embassy and that he would now escort me to the English embassy. On the way out he fumbled in his brief case and returned my passport and other possessions taken from my hotel room. And then he gave me back my camera, *sans* film. And he explained the reason for my arrest; that there had recently been anti-government unrest, sparked by university students, resulting in a partial curfew, and that students had been arrested.

"Royal Mail Ship Darwin"

Reunited with my two VSO friends I told them of my harrowing experience and, in turn, they recounted how worried they had been when they found out what had happened. After that we didn't dare leave the hotel until the following morning when it was time to board the RMS Darwin for the voyage to the Falkland Islands.

The voyage should have been completed in four days but on the last day a storm blew up from the south which practically stopped the ship in its tracks, bows to the wind and the hull rising and falling into big waves. The three of us were sick as dogs and one of the stewards helped to strap us into our bunks, we not being allowed out on deck for safety reasons. Each of us had a sick basin, wet towels and bread and water on a table between the bunks. The storm raged right through the night before it abated and our ship could make headway again. Feeling better we met up with other passengers and learned that one of the kitchen hands had died after accidentally being shut into a walk-in freezer the night before. No one found out until the morning after. There was an alarm button inside the freezer but, for some reason, it had not been activated.

The three of us were met off the boat, at the government quay in Stanley Harbour, by Mr Draycott, the Director of the education department. He drove us along the waterfront to the whitewashed government secretariat where the Union Jack and the Falkland Islands flags were flying from two flagpoles in the lawns fronting the building. In the comfort of a sitting room Mr Draycott welcomed us and handed out copies of an induction course itinerary for the next week. Seeing how tired his new VSO teachers were, he despatched us in a government land rover to a residential house three streets up from the waterfront, on a gentle slope overlooking the harbour. We introduced ourselves to widow Mrs Ada Watts, the redoubtable owner of the house; her two offspring, son Patrick, newly into his 20s and working at the FI's radio station, and daughter Rita, just out of school and learning to be a hairdresser.

At 09.00 hrs on day one, dressed in jacket and tie, we knocked on Draycott's door and then began an introductory tour of the secretariat which included meeting the Governor, Sir Cosmo Haskard, in the drawing room. Lunch was taken in the Malvinas Hotel, a short walk from the secretariat. Afterwards there was a visit to Christ Church which is the C of E cathedral of the FIs, centre piece of the waterfront. Lastly we visited the Royal Marine's base at the top end of the inner harbour. They were of platoon strength and, among their military vehicles, they had a 10 seater hovercraft to get about in.

Days two to five were in the classroom where we learned about the geography and topography of the islands, its history and politics, population statistics (1,960 long term residents), commerce and industry and the 'Who's who' of the community. On the last day we were told our teaching beats; all in 'the camp' which is everywhere except for Stanley; and given some educational tips relevant to the particular children we would each be responsible for. Part of that was a note of caution. No trysting with women that we might meet and to be wary of girls of our age, some being eager to get away from the Falklands for a life in the UK. Before leaving I asked Mr. Draycott if he could arrange for me to undertake the Duke of Edinburgh's gold award expedition, the last part of the award scheme that I had started whilst still at school. He agreed to help me.

I was given the North Arm beat of four settlements down the length of the east side of the east island which comprised Teal Inlet, Fitzroy, Bleaker Island and North Arm settlements. North Arm, the biggest settlement on my beat had a two room bungalow specially set aside for the itinerant teacher. It's little store room contained all the teaching materials that a teacher would need. My schedule was a week in each place, starting with North Arm, then Bleaker Island, followed by Fitzroy and ending with Teal Inlet for the last week before returning to North Arm. Taking into account school holidays, I would do nine circuits in my year.

The following day was Sunday and that afternoon the three of us occupied the three passenger seats in a Beaver float plane, no wheels. We took off down Stanley Harbour from the float plane jetty and flew anti-clockwise up to the north end of the east island, round the top, across to the west island and, finally on to the southern end of the east island. The plane put down in the sea opposite North Arm settlement and the last passenger, me, alighted, carrying my own bags onto a short wooden pier.

The settlement manager, John, picked me up in a land rover and drove the five minutes up a gentle rise to the teacher's bungalow situated to one side of the settlement green. The manager handed me the key to the front door (no back door and only two windows), showed me the house plumbing, including the tiny, flushing toilet behind a curtain, how the hand-crank telephone worked and, out at the back, where the teacher's peat bog was. There was a small stack of dried peat next to it that looked like it needed replenishing. Before leaving, John invited me to his house, known as the big house, for dinner at 6 pm.

Left alone, I noted that my single bed had been made up and that the whole place had been swept clean and tidy. There was a small cupboard in the bedroom and one rickety chair on which I was about to sit when I noticed a small face peering in through the window. I nipped outside and said hello to a boy and a girl who turned out to be two of my four students in North Arm, a five and nine years old brother and sister respectively.

A few minutes after 6 pm, at sunset, I knocked on the door of the big house and Manager John, as he was known, opened up, welcoming me in with a friendly grin. He offered me a seat in a large sitting room furnished with old, comfortable arm chairs, a central coffee table made of antique, highly polished oak, heavy brocade curtains and a thick-pile carpet. The room was dimly lit with a single light bulb dangling inelegantly from the ceiling. A glowing peat fire in the ornate fire-place spread its warmth like a comfortable blanket. I was offered a drink and soberly asked for fruit juice. John poured me a lime-juice from a Roses cordial bottle.

Moving to the dining room and more of the heavy furnishings, John's smiling, aproned wife brought in a soup, followed by a succulent leg of lamb, boiled potatoes and carrots. John produced a *Pinot Noir* from Chile, very nice. For pudding there was a bowl of jelly topped with hand-beaten cream. My genial hosts enquired of my comparatively lack-lustre life to date, proceeding to fascinate me with lots of stories about their interesting lives.

Among the stories that I was regaled with was that John was a member of the Falkland's Volunteer Defence Force and that he had seen action in 1965 when some student activists from Buenos Aires had hijacked an Argentine Airways DC-4 turbo-prop passenger plane, on an internal flight. They demanded to be flown to the Falkland Islands. The plane did not have enough fuel for the return flight and, in the absence of any decent runway, the pilot had put his plane down on the racecourse. It was winter at the time and the aircraft sank up to its undercarriage in a peat bog. Fortunately no one was hurt.

But word of an 'invasion' was flashed around the Falklands by radio and telephone and, unbidden, many members of the defence force drove land rovers or rode their horses into Port Stanley "...*to have a go at the Argies.*" After the plane had landed the Royal Marines detachment expeditiously took charge of the scene under the direction of the Governor. A window was opened in the aircraft cockpit and a hijacker began to parley with the Royal Marines' platoon commander.

While that was in progress a big crowd coming from the township was gradually assembling, encircling the plane. Mostly just curious, enjoying the spectacle and their grandstand view of the stand-off. But, among their number, members of the defence force were encroaching, a couple of them carrying their own shotguns. Sensing rising tensions the Royal Marines about-turned and began herding the onlookers back, setting up a roped cordon 50 yards out from the stricken plane. But still an elderly lady slipped through the cordon carrying a basket of scones and a thermos of tea for the pilot and the hijackers. At nightfall, some five hours after the crash-landing, the eight hijackers gave themselves up and were taken into custody by the police inspector and his sergeant. The next invasion came in 1982.

On Monday, my first day of teaching, I was up early and walked across to a large, wooden, shed-like building that housed the communal cook house, the bunkhouse (single men's quarters), the settlement store, the dining room and bar, a dance hall and games room – snooker and dominoes – and my classroom. Breakfast was cooked and served up by genial Big Jock, the boss of the cook house, wearing his full length apron, once upon a time white. The menu was porridge, a mutton chop with a fried egg on top, fried tomatoes and a slice of bread on the side, all washed down with seriously strong tea in an enamelled tin mug that had seen better days.

At 9 o'clock I was ready in the school room and first in was a shepherd and his wife ushering along their two children, the girl and the boy whom I had met on the day of my arrival. Moments later a navvy arrived with his wife and two boys. Introductions were made. The navvy invited their new teacher to join him and his wife the following day for smoko (a smoke and a coffee) at their house in the settlement.

Left alone with the children I discussed their education with them and they each showed me their various exercise books, so keen, so eager. I was apprehensive of difficulties in teaching four children, of different ages and at different stages of learning, at the same time. But it turned out to be easy and the girl, Gwenda, the oldest child, was not only helpful but also bright.

Gwenda was nearly 11 years old by the time my year with VSO was ending, time for secondary school for her. Instead of studying at the local secondary school at Goose Green, The Falkland Islands Government also ran a scholarship programme for the two most intelligent children, each year, to go to a good public school in England. So I asked the parents if they would like their daughter to vie for this scholarship? They went away to discuss it and, two days later, informed me that their answer was 'No'. At least part of the reason was their unspoken fear that she would probably never come back home to live.

I always started morning classes at 9 am with five to ten minutes of callisthenics which was efficacious in inculcating a will to work, especially in cold weather. I taught for about 45 minutes before playing games for 15 minutes. At 11am Big Jock or his wife Annie would ring the brass bell outside the cook house door, the signal for the smoko half hour. The navvies and any shepherds in the settlement would down tools, light-up and have a coffee, tea or ma'te. Ma'te is a South American grass drink favoured by gauchos who drink it hot, on the hoof from a gourd, using a bombilla or metal straw. Gauchos are the equivalent of North America's cowboys.

"Sheep dipping at North Arm Settlement"

Every day myself and my students heeded the call to the cook house and Jock would provide a jug of juice and pieces of cake at a table set aside for us. Jock, who ran the whole complex of cook house, bunkhouse and dance hall, was a big fan of country and western music. All day and everyday he played his collection of tapes. After the smoko half-hour it was back to the school room for two hours before lunch, at which time the children went back home, taking some homework with them. And at the end of the week I would set my students three weeks of home work that their parents could help them with. In my free afternoons I prepared lessons, wrote letters home and did the house chores which included cutting fresh peat; back-breaking work! Occasionally, extra hands were needed for help with a job in the settlement eg sheep dipping, I'd go along for that.

Part of the teacher's bungalow inventory was a spade with a 25cm wide head designed to cut a 25cm square block of peat. The theory was that, in three strokes; cutting straight down from the top of the bank, then sideways and lastly horizontally in at the base; one could lift out a solid, sodden, sod, making a sucking noise and weighing about five kilos. When the sod dries out on the ground, over a couple of months, it shrinks to less than half the size and weighs half a kilo. But it burns beautifully.

The deal between VSO and the Falkland's government was that their itinerant teachers were given board, lodging and travel facilities free of charge. So I ate my main meals in the cookhouse at North Arm and, when laundry needed to be done, Annie or Jock took it in. It would be given back, washed and ironed, within a day or two. When I stayed in the houses at other settlements where I was teaching, it was the same deal. Generously I was always treated as one of the family. And I even learned how to butcher a sheep, skin it, take out the liver and lights, incinerate the entrails and hang the carcass. Learning how it was done was fascinating. One even had to check for hydatids disease which was common. It was manifested in white cysts the size of marbles lodged in the gut. The cause was sheep cropping the grass and ingesting the eggs of the hydatid tapeworm left in the faeces of sheep dogs. The dogs picked up the tape worm by eating the uncooked entrails of sheep. Hence the need for incinerating the offal.

In my first couple of weeks 'on the front line' we VSOs rang each other up almost every other day, comparing notes. Using the hand-crank phone was a novelty in itself. My 'phone code was two long, two short and two long rings. Richard and Graham had other combinations. If one of them telephoned me, ringing da-da-dit-dit-da-da, I'd know the call was for me and pick up the 'phone. And quite often one could hear clicking sounds down the line, indicating that others had picked up their phone just to listen in! We quickly learned to be circumspect in our chat! But as the weeks turned into months so the 'phone calls dwindled to one a month, or even less.

At the end of that first week a Beaver float plane picked me up from North Arm and flew me the short hop across the water to Bleaker Island where Sam the shepherd, his wife and their two boys, aged five and seven, lived. The pilots of the Beaver float planes also delivered mail and, on this flight, the pilot had a letter for me from my Mum. It was addressed to "Mr. J C S McDouall, The Falkland Islands."

The shepherd's house, built to the same pattern as for most of the family homes in the Falklands, had a corrugated iron roof, painted red, and sheet metal walls, painted white, fixed to stout wooden planking on the inside, with lots of insulation. The privy was right outside the back door and a 4' high wooden slatted fence, painted white, surrounded the front garden and the house. On one side of the house was a small lean-to, made of wood, housing the petrol-driven electric generator. There was no mains electricity on the island or, for that matter, in the rest of the camp. Outside the fence was a wind-driven water pump over a well sunk vertically into the water table below. Also outside the fence was the peat bog from where Sam, the shepherd, cut his fuel for his peat-burning stoves.

Round the back of the house a wooden gibbet was erected and from which was hanging the carcass of a newly slaughtered sheep. And bolted on to the stout gibbet was a radio aerial some 10 meters tall. There being no telephone line across to Bleaker, Sam used a VHF radio transmitter/receiver. Every settlement manager was an amateur radio ham, able to talk to float-plane pilots on the way, to the doctor in Port Stanley, to the police station and to other managers; a more confidential system than the communal 'phone line. Lastly there was the stable where Sam kept his horses and had a work bench. He didn't have a land rover; more trouble than it was worth in the boggy, tussock-grassed landscape of his island.

Sam's two boys Nick, the older, and Will, were delightful scallywags, full of boundless energy, always laughing. I remember vividly arriving at their home for the first time, and they leading me outside on an exploration tour of their surrounds. There were sheep grazing not far away and Will shouted "*Watch me. This is how to squat a sheep*" and off he ran, chasing one sheep non-stop for five or six minutes before the harried animal sat down on its haunches and the delighted Will called back "*See, I've done it*". They took me over to see the stable and the little wire-netted hen house next to it. Two work horses were inside the stable. And there was one pony which Nick boasted he could ride "*real good*". He lifted a leather halter off a nail in the wall and threw it over the pony's head and neck, securing it in place. Taking the pony out of the stable he suddenly leapt up onto its bare back and urged it on with a kick and a yell. And off they went at a canter round the house.

At dusk it was time to go back inside the house just as Sam was going out to put the generator on. He started it up, sounding like a motor lawn-mower, quite noisy. But when the door was closed one could hardly hear it from inside the house. Dinner was served by Sam's wife Janet; a joint of lamb and, oh, how tasty it was! What the English call lamb is what the Falkland Islanders would call mutton. Janet did all of her cooking on an ancient, blackened, iron range with three ovens of different sizes and a big, solid, flat, iron hob on top. The fuel was, of course, peat and it was kept burning 24 hours a day, damped down and smouldering at night. The range also served as the central hot-water boiler, a 20 gallon tank welded on the back, gravity fed from a roof tank. Sam carved the meat at the dining table and Janet sliced her home-made bread. Roast potatoes and boiled cabbage came from Janet's kitchen-garden patch. I guessed Janet was in her mid-thirties, Sam I think a little older. Janet had the rubicund complexion of Falkland Islanders which I put down to the total absence of air pollution. Indeed the apocryphal story goes that a new surgeon, out from London, at the island's hospital thought he'd discovered a disease called 'pink lung' when operating on a local patient.

Over that week, and subsequent weeks, Sam showed me some of his leather work that he made on his work bench in the stables. Clearly a talented artisan in wood and leather, he spent much of his spare time dressing and preserving cow and horse hides, fashioning it into saddlery; saddles, stirrups, reins, cinches, hobbles and quirts. Ingeniously he also made boleadoras, bandoliers (for shotgun cartridges), hats, sheaths for knives, decorative leather braids including Turks Head buttons, bracelets, hand-bags, gourd covers, etc. He made a nice business selling his merchandise all over the islands. I asked him if I could watch him at work and, one thing leading to another, I was soon making my own 'gear', the generic term for saddlery.

My week on Bleaker Island came to an end all too soon and my next port of call was Fitzroy settlement. I had to take the Beaver float plane back to the mainland for that and the pilot set me down in the sound in front of said settlement. Fitzroy comprised five residential buildings, including the cook house *cum* bunkhouse, and half-a-dozen sheds for storage, garaging a tractor and trailer and two land rovers, another for shearing flocks of sheep and another for packing and stowing bales of wool. Two of three families at Fitzroy had young children, Dave the shepherd had two daughters aged seven and eight, and the navvy had a five year old son. Between them, the families had turned a spare room in the bunk house into a classroom. The furnishing was a single bed raised on blocks of wood and topped with planks. A long bench was the children's seating. The teacher had a chair and a teapoy. A black painted section of one wall was the blackboard.

Ted, the navvy, and his wife Maddie, with their five year-old son Robin, welcomed me into their home, making their spare bedroom available to me for the week. Ted showed me around the settlement and we met the manager who issued his invitation to attend the 'two-nighter' that his settlement was hosting that coming weekend. Most of the bigger settlements each hosted one two-nighter every year to which workers from neighbouring settlements would come along. Subsequently Maddie and Ted described a typical 'two nighter' to me as a week-end of gaucho contests including the strong man, rifle target-shooting, the best at lass'oing, a horse race and, the highlight, the rodeo champion on a brumby.

The Saturday night was given over to Scottish dancing, singing along with country and western music and, of course, drinking. The Circassian Circle was the preferred dance, to Scottish reel music, but with folk origins from north west Europe and Russia. The most popular drink was whisky milk. Johnny Walker Red Label was the principal ingredient, accompanied with a long dash of fresh milk. There was an art to pouring the drink so that it didn't curdle and an art to drinking it, its smooth nature being very moreish! Headaches the following morning if one wasn't careful. The Sunday comprised a large barbecue, a whole roasted sheep and plenty of grog. Some twenty guests coming over from neighbouring settlements joined in the festivities.

The Sunday after, on this occasion, was cold but dry. After breakfast I packed up my meagre possessions, including some school necessities, in the voluminous saddlebags that Dave the shepherd had loaned me, and walked across the green to his house. He was waiting, with his two girls who had been my students over the past week, and led me to the stable where his horse, Nimbus, was chewing hay.

Nimbus had been saddled and Dave had thrown a complete fleece of wool on top of the assembly as the incessant wind was biting cold. I had already been introduced to Nimbus, a ten year old grey, and had been out riding him the last three days for us to get used to each other. The big difference between English style and Gaucho style riding was the split-rein and the method of steering the horse, not by pulling on the bit in the mouth but by pressure of a rein on the neck. Counter-intuitive to the English school of riding. That caught me by surprise, nearly unseating me when Nimbus had turned in the opposite direction to that intended.

It was mid-morning when I rode off with map and compass folded in a leather pouch, looped over the pommel, and a gourd of hot Ma'te in one hand, heading north west to Teal Inlet, my next teaching post, about 30 miles away as the crow flies. For the most part I followed land rover and tractor tracks here and there, knowing that was the way to avoid peat bogs. And there was some fencing, marking boundaries which could be identified on the map. There were the overhead telephone lines too, by which a rider could accurately guess the direction in which a settlement lay. The wild beauty of the Falkland's landscape is the stuff of poetry but, not being a poet, I stuck to simple terms in my mind's eye. That I was all alone, not a living soul from horizon to horizon, was at once as exhilarating as it was daunting. Daunting because if there was a mishap there was no ready means of calling for help. That would depend on the people awaiting a rider's arrival. If he didn't turn up within an hour of his ETA search parties would be called out. We had no long range walkie-talkies.

"Teal Inlet Settlement - water colour painting by Stuart McDouall"

As it was, I made it to Teal Inlet just half-an-hour shy of my ETA. George, the Shepherd, saw me before I was in sight of the house. He was already on horse-back and riding out to meet me. After greetings we rode side-by-side the last 20 minutes to his house, almost a replica to that at Bleaker Island. His was one of four in the little settlement, to the right of the cookhouse in the centre of the green. The weather was getting worse, very windy with a cold wind-chill factor and some light rain coming in.

George stabled the horses, divesting Nimbus of saddle and bags. George's small daughter came running out of the house to help with feeding and watering the horses. The room I was given was sparsely furnished but comfortable. And they gave me a huge towel, more like a horse blanket, which I was able to wrap around myself like a big poncho. I shared the bathroom with my hosts so was careful to keep it clean and tidy. Dinner was the standard fare which I was used to and which I liked. And there was lively conversation throughout.

Next morning I woke up and had difficulty getting started, hips and back aching from the long ride the day before which I was, as yet, unaccustomed to. I was hobbling about, holding my lower back, like an old man. George greeted me with mock concern "M*ornin' Che, saddle sore?*" 'Che' is a Spanish moniker for 'friend'. Breakfast was served and the fare included a boiled gentoo penguin egg. It is about twice as large as a hen egg and the shell has a greenish hue to it. I used a spoon to crack the top open while the family watched intently. And when the solid, clear egg-*white* was revealed they laughed at my puzzlement. Tasting it was another surprise, very fishy but not unpleasant; stringent, like anchovy.

Then it was school time, set up in the drawing room. Smoko was observed at 11 o'clock with a slice of freshly baked cake, straight out of the oven, and builders tea to wash it down. I asked if they had Ma'te? A silly question, they all did. But they were surprised the Englishman liked it. For the rest of the week smoko was ma'te.

On the second day, in the afternoon after school, mother drove her daughter and I over to a penguin colony which they called a rookery. The location of George's house was several miles west of Port Louis, a deserted French settlement close to a gentoo penguin colony situated on low cliffs above the rocky South Atlantic coast. There was a good track from Teal Inlet to Port Louis accessible by land rover. There were hundreds of the comical birds, about a meter tall, coming and going to and fro' the foaming sea around the rocks, leaping out of the water and landing awkwardly. The wind was up and the spray flying. We three spectators sat on some tussock grass 20 meters away, so as not to disturb them, and just watched their antics for half an hour. Spell-binding. And that, I learned, was where George had foraged a few eggs for us the day before.

At the end of the week it was back to base, far too far to ride in a day so the Beaver float plane lifted me off from Teal Inlet and, twenty minutes later, dropped me back at North Arm. In June and into July the weather became increasingly wintery, temperatures dropping to as low as minus 20 C,with wind-chill added, and the lazy winds picking up. Why 'lazy'? The wind doesn't go round you, it goes through you! It wasn't surprising that there were no trees, not even tall shrubs, growing in the hillocky wilderness. The sheep used the tussock grass for shelter, as did the occasional cattle grazing outside settlements. Enterprising settlers had nurtured gorse bushes around their houses but even these were growing at angles of 45% with the prevailing winds.

In the close of May we had a half-term holiday during which myself, Richard and Graham reported back to Mr Draycott. It was then that the latter told me he had arranged for me to undertake a four day expedition with a column of Royal Marines and could I be ready to go the following day? The Marines would supply all my kit and equipment; maps, rucksack, tent, cooking set and provisions. The answer was yes. My rendezvous was 09.00 hrs and I planned a route-march from Port Stanley, south to Bluff Cove, then north to Estancia before striking back east, over Mount Tumbledown and down into Stanley. Fortunately the weather remained fine, brisk and dry, all the way round. I ticked off all the required skills one by one, including lighting a fire and cooking, practicing first aid, map reading, navigation by night, etc. At the end I wrote it all up with photographs, and Mr Draycott signed off on it before sending my report to the D of E office in London.

At the beginning of September, in Spring, North Arm held its two-nighter and visitors came from far and wide, such was its fame or, as I was later to learn, its notoriety. The games were the first item on the agenda and we watched the rodeo. It was just like it is in the movies. Each contestant, wearing leather leggings and a broad-rimmed hat, stood above and facing the exit gate, one foot on either side of the channel planking. The Brumby was put into the channel and, when the horse was standing still, the gate was pulled aside. Simultaneously, the jockey dropped on its bare back as it sprang forward into the corral. There was a serious injury when one rider was thrown before the horse had cleared the exit. The rider hit the gate post with his head, sustaining a bad cut. One of the two doctors on the island was present and he stitched the wound up.

Another incident occurred late at night, around 11 pm, when the festivities were drawing to a close. Gunshots were heard coming from the bunkhouse. One of the residents jumped out of the ground floor window of his room, yelling that the guy next door was blasting holes through the wall. Manager John told me to get on the telephone to the police station in Stanley while he organised the escape of other residents of the bunkhouse. The random shooting stopped shortly afterwards and John was able to get into the shooter's room and seize his gun. The man, a navvy, was blind-drunk and had been "*in the rats*" imagining rats in his room at which he was shooting.

Having reported back to the police station that the emergency had been peacefully resolved, Inspector Peck said he'd come out the following morning. I went to bed. Next morning, at around 8 am, a Beaver float plane dropped off Inspector Peck and his sergeant. Manager John took them to the bunkhouse room where the drunken shooter had been locked in. The Inspector arrested him while the Sgt. stood at-the-ready behind him. The Inspector had a camera and took a few photographs of the scene. He then sat down in the cook house and took statements from Manager John and the navvy who had leapt out of his room window to safety. Lastly, he took possession of the rifle belonging to the arrested man and, at about mid-day, the three of them flew back to Stanley in the float plane.

The very next day the Governor sat as magistrate in the court; a room in the secretariat; and convicted the drunk of affray. He was put on the 'Black List' of drunks for 12 months, ordered to pay the cost of damages and his rifle was confiscated. Being put on the black list meant that the culprit's name was circulated throughout the Islands and it was an offence for anyone to provide or retail alcohol and firearms to the convict. Such an unorthodox sentence, in the same ballpark as corporal punishment, was immediately effective, akin to being outlawed in a place where everyone knows everyone else.

"SS Great Britain in Falkland Islands Harbour"

For the school holidays the itinerant teachers went back to Stanley, living at Mrs. Watt's house. From there we VSOs went out on excursions. One of these was walking round four ancient shipwrecks, the wooden hulks of which were lying on the water's edge around the inner and outer harbours. The most famous of these was the SS Great Britain which was the world's first screw or propeller-driven ship designed and launched by Isambard Kingdom Brunel in 1845. Two of its original four sailing masts remained upright, the for'ard one with a horizontal spar dangling from an iron hoop. Standing on the shore, looking along its iron hull from the stern, I was struck by the beauty and symmetry of its lines. It plied the Bristol – New York route until 1853 when it switched to the more lucrative Southampton – Sydney migrant trade. In 1885, while rounding Cape Horn, it was badly damaged by storms and the captain put it into Port Stanley for repairs.

In the 19th century many sailing ships suffered in the storms of Cape Horn and ship-wrights in the Falkland Islands made a very good living out of repairing them, such a good living that some ship-owners refused the contracts as not being worth the salvage, leaving their vessels to rot in Stanley harbour. The Falkland's became known as a grave yard for ships. And such was the fate of the SS Great Britain. It was anchored in Stanley harbour for three years, serving as a collier, a warehouse and a quarantine berth. In 1889 it was towed to the outer harbour, Port Sparrow, and scuttled on the beach. Seventy years later, in 1969, I was seen scrambling aboard its historical decks. In 1970 engineers lifted the wreck onto a purpose-built pontoon on which it was towed all the way back to Bristol Docks where it had been built.

"Sheep shearers in North Arm Settlement"

In early September, calmer weather, it was sheep-shearing time. North Arm had the biggest shearing shed on the east island, boasting twenty electric-clipper shearing stalls or stands. At this time the Falkland Islands Company, the biggest landowner on the islands, hired gangs of shearers; native shepherds and some on work visas from Chile. They would spend up to a week in each of the large settlements, working on flocks of sheep brought in from miles around. The shearers typically worked for 45 minutes, rested for 15 and then repeated that sequence five times in a day. They all used the Godfrey Bowen method of shearing, perfected in Australia.

The foreman of the gang asked me if I wanted to learn how to shear a sheep? I was up for that and donned a full-length leather apron before being handed a pair of razor-sharp steel hand-clippers. I was put in a vacant stand at the end of the line where I practised controlling a sheep, turning it round between my knees without it escaping. Then the foreman guided me as I started clipping, first under the neck, then down the chest and stomach to the backside, then turning and coming up one flank towards the neck, turning again and clipping down the other flank. Finally the last turn, shearing the fleece off the back. It was difficult to see the blades in the wool and if the sheep wriggled, which it did, it suffered quite a few cuts to the skin, making it wriggle more and drawing blood. That poor sheep had to endure not only the pain of having a dozen cuts but then having them swabbed with iodine to prevent infection. The foreman presented those clippers to me as a grim souvenir.

Towards the end of September, with a week of school holiday left, I booked a cabin on RMS Darwin, going on a cruise right round the Falklands. The ship was picking up all the bales of wool from each of the main settlements and stowing them in its holds. In the six or seven hours at each anchorage I had time to land and see the settlements, particularly those on the west island which I hadn't visited before. One of those was San Carlos where VSO Richard was teaching. I knew people in most of the settlements the Darwin anchored at, if not in person, at least by name over the hand-crank 'phone! The Darwin anchored each night and we experienced some of the clearest nights I had yet seen. Spectacularly, the heavens were myriads of tiny sparkles which one never sees in European skies above ambient light. In amongst that brilliant black velvet cloth were the bigger and brighter stars, glittering in their named constellations. Easy to spot was the Crux, otherwise known as the Southern Cross; four stars in a cross-shaped asterism. Looking upwards from the deck, no sound or movement anywhere, total peace.

The Christmas holidays 1969 began in the first week of December, glorious summer weather, if a bit windy, and one expedition that I undertook was from North Arm down to the southern tip of the east island where there was, and still is, a large nesting place used by black-browed albatross. Their average wing span is an incredible seven feet (over 200 cm). There was a good vantage point some twenty meters away, on a bluff overlooking their runway. It was a stunning sight, watching those huge birds taking off down hill, at the run, and achieving lift-off over the cliff edge some ten meters above sea level. Coming into land was easier for the birds, flaps down and gently settling, into the wind, on the grass.

The Autumn term began in early January, still warm and mostly sunny. Birds had finished nesting and fledglings were learning to fly. Among these were the Upland Goose; the most common bird on the east island. It is eaten as a game bird by the islanders, a change from mutton. In North Arm it was normal to see whole flights of geese feeding on the settlement green or around the out-houses. At Bleaker Island it was the same but there the geese were more wary for the irrepressible boys, Nick and Will, had a set of boleadoras, commonly referred to as bolas, made for them by their Dad.

The boy's bolas was created from one eight foot (2.4 m) long, twisted strip of rawhide and one four foot strip, joined together to make three equal lengths. At the end of each strip a round pebble, wrapped in a piece of thin rawhide, had been sewn on. An adult bolas is bigger. The boys took me 'hunting' and Will and I crouched down-wind of a group of geese while Nick hid in the tussock on the other side of the geese. Then, on the shouted word *Go!* Will and I stood and ran madly at the geese while Nick jumped up, quickly whirling his bolas like helicopter blades above his head and loosing them, whirling them into the path of the flying birds. We didn't snare any but it was tremendous fun.

My last visit to Teal Inlet was tinged with sadness when Nimbus died. I was on my way from Fitzroy to Teal Inlet in the late evening, getting dark and wrapped-up against cold winds, when I felt Nimbus struggling. Dismounting I could see he was suffering as he sank on his haunches. I loosed the cinch and divested him of the saddle and bags, laying the saddle fleece on his neck. I tried to give him water from my bottle but he wasn't having any. Looking at my watch I guessed when the search party would come out from Teal Inlet – I thought within an hour. In that time Nimbus lay on his side and the eye I could see, closed. His chest stilled and he breathed no more. George arrived from Teal Inlet, not on his horse but driving his tractor with headlights on. He had known something must be wrong.

Back at Teal Inlet George telephoned Dave at Fitzroy and, the following morning, he retrieved the carcass on a large wooden sledge towed behind his tractor.

And in April, 1970, as winter approached, my year of VSO was suddenly finished. The three of us did the rounds of good-byes. Police Inspector Peck, who I had already quizzed about joining the Colonial Police, wished me good luck.

Then it was back on board RMS Darwin for the voyage up to Montevideo and our flight back to England. After only a brief respite at home I contacted the Crown Agents in London and so began the application process for joining the Royal Hong Kong Police.

Looking back now, I see VSO as a highlight of my life. And there was a sequel. In September/October, 2017, my wife and I, and my twin brother Philip, flew down to the Falkland Islands. Rooms had been booked in the relatively new hotel in Goose Green and, upon our arrival, we were treated to tea with our husband-and-wife hosts. It was in chatting with them, and me talking of the settlements I had been the VSO teacher at, that the wife suddenly exclaimed *"It's you! I'm Gwenda, one of your pupils at North arm."* What a co-incidence! There and then she got on to her mobile 'phone and soon had made contact with her brother. It wasn't long before him and his wife reached the hotel by roads that hadn't existed until the Argentine war. Listening to them talking about it and learning of their suffering at the hands of the enemy was sobering.

ST JOHN'S CATHEDRAL, HONG KONG

Wars, a fun-fair and a sermon on riots

"St. John's Cathedral, Hong Kong"

The Cathedral church of St John the Evangelist stands in Garden Road, Central, Hong Kong Island, surrounded by tall buildings and just a stone's throw from Government House on the hillside above. At the time of writing (2023) it is 174 years old and has been continuously in the service of God except for the five-year duration of the Japanese occupation of Hong Kong during the Second World War.

In 1846 the Hong Kong government provided the Church of England with what is the only freehold land in the territory, at No.4, Garden Road, in the hub of Central district. The building of the first permanent Christian place of worship began almost immediately and, in 1849, just eight years after the British flag was raised over Hong Kong, the inaugural church service was held in the 'Hong Kong Colonial Chapel'.

Plans for the aggrandizement of this preliminary structure were expedited and, coinciding with the completion of an extension to the cathedral in 1852, the first Bishop of Hong Kong and Macau, the Rt. Rev. George Smith, a Scotsman, took up his appointment. His first task was to consecrate the Gothic-styled building which was henceforth known as St John's Cathedral. Work was done on a 42' extension to the east-facing end of the structure, creating space for a high altar and choir. That work was completed in 1869, in time for the first royal visit to Hong Kong by Prince Alfred, second son of Queen Victoria and styled the Duke of Edinburgh. On 16th November he laid the foundation stone in the east end of the church which is still in place for all to see. At that time the cathedral, with its sixty-five-foot high, battlemented bell tower, was the tallest building in Central posing a visible landmark all around the inner harbour.

Initially the cathedral was largely frequented by the expatriate business community, the British military garrison and senior civil servants. The first governor, Sir John Davis, was a regular worshipper. Of the local population there were few, if any, Christians and not even local dignitaries with government connections attended. This exclusive composition of the congregation continued until the turn of the 20th century. By then Christian missionary societies, both Roman Catholic and Church of England, had established successful schools and their alumni were creating a new western educated Chinese middle class, some entering into the life of the cathedral. And more churches were springing up across the territory.

In 1910 the cathedral was the focal point in Hong Kong's celebrations of the coronation of King George V. There are sepia photographs showing the nave completely swathed in flags and canopies, with punkahs swung from the rafters to cool the summer air.

Between the world wars the Cathedral collaborated with other Anglican churches, extending their outreach, gathering ever larger congregations and assuming a charitable role amongst the poor and needy. In 1932 the fourth bishop to the diocese of Hong Kong and Macau was the Rt Rev. Ronald Owen Hall. He was a decorated WWI veteran who could read and write Chinese and speak Putonghua (Mandarin) and Cantonese. Bishop Hall was an influential and pioneering spirit.

In 1941 he provoked controversy by ordaining a local-born Cantonese lady, Miss Florence Li Tim-oi, as a priest, the first female ordinand in the world-wide Anglican communion. Once peace had been restored at the end of WWII the Archbishop of Canterbury wrote to Bishop Hall formally admonishing him for "...*disturbing the good order of the church in disobeying ecclesiastic regulations*". Bishop Hall was expected to resile his position on female clergy in the face of such criticism. He not only declined to do so but robustly defended his action. However, the Rev. Li, mortified at the furore caused on her account, decided to hand in her licence, fearful of internecine conflict and the possible consequences for her. But within the next few years Bishop Hall's precedent was followed by other Anglican Bishops, firstly in New Zealand and then in other British territories. Unfortunately the post-war governor of Hong Kong, Sir Alexander Grantham (1947-57), was not in amity with Bishop Hall or his social activities, thinking him a communist sympathizer because of his friendship with Chinese Christians on the mainland. A burr under Grantham's saddle, Bishop Hall made himself the conscience of the colonial government, constantly forcing their hand in housing for the poor, medical facilities for the halt and lame, instigating the first welfare laws and more.

On Christmas Day, 1941, during WWII, Hong Kong was beaten into surrendering to the Japanese occupation forces. The usual church services were held that very morning and there wasn't a spare pew left for latecomers. In the ensuing three years the cathedral was still maintained by clergy from non-aligned or neutral countries, particularly Norway, but services were irregular at best and with minimal attendance. But then, in 1944, the Japanese evicted the small coterie of clerics; local and foreign; from the premises and turned the cathedral into a Japanese social club and public meeting hall. All the religious furnishings and fittings were removed or destroyed.

After the enemy capitulation, in 1945, work was begun immediately on the restoration of the cathedral, the main fabric of the building remaining largely intact except for a shell hole through the bell tower. But the innards of the church; all the memorials and monuments, the carved wood reredos in the chapels and the choir, the stained glass windows, the vestibules and the sacristy; had been ransacked by the occupation forces.

One of the first pieces of war memorabilia to be incorporated into the restoration work in St Michael's chapel was the Christian altar piece retrieved from the Stanley POW camp. It had been fashioned from wooden packing cases by POWs in the shape of a decorated Gothic window arch and a small tin tray tacked on the ledge below for candles to be placed on. It is still in use today. Also in St Michael's Chapel are the memorial books to all those who died in the defence of Hong Kong in WWII, a new page being turned every day under the locked glass cases.

Around the architraves of the said chapel hang the disintegrating military colours of regiments long since disbanded. More recently the flags, colours or standards of army, naval, RAF and other disciplined services, including the Royal Hong Kong Police, have been laid up in memory of those who served under them. The RHKP flag, replaced by the post-colonial HKP flag in 1997, was blessed and laid up, in memory of all those officers who had passed under the portals of the cathedral, by the Revd. John Chynchen, Cathedral Chaplain. One eminent member of the congregation, not understanding the traditions of laying up standards or flags in St Michael's chapel, has recently had his secondary schools's pennant hung up in pride of place, supplanting the RHKP flag.

There can be few more poignant occasions in the history of the Anglican cathedral than the funeral service of Governor Sir Edward Youde, GCMG, GCVO, the only one of 28 governors of Hong Kong to die in office. He served from May, 1982, to his death on 5th December, 1986. He died from a heart attack suffered when he was in Beijing for talks following the signing of the Sino-British joint declaration in 1984. Youde, a UK Foreign Office diplomat and notable Sinologist, fluent in Mandarin and written Chinese, was highly respected for his determined advocacy, on behalf of the Hong Kong people, for their civil rights and privileges. Such was the public grief, following news of his passing, that between two and three million (no one ever made a definitive count) residents signed the condolence books, initially in the City Hall, Central, but then in Kowloon and the New Territories where more books of condolence were hastily opened, so great was the demand.

Edward Youde's body was flown to Hong Kong where the British military garrison laid on a state funeral. The cortege, accompanied by soldiers, sailors and airmen marching to the traditional muffled drum beat, passed through Central District, the normally chaotic roads and pavements thronged by silent mourners; a deafening hush all the way to St. John's Cathedral. Then a 17 gun salute was fired across the harbour from HMS Tamar, the crashing roar reverberating right around those ancient shorelines. The great and the good filled the cathedral in solemn array. Afterwards, the Governor's mortal remains were taken to Cape Collinson for cremation and, a week later, Lady Pamela Youde, in her widow's weeds, took the ashes of her late husband back to England where the urn was interred at Canterbury Cathedral.

With the exception of the war years, the cathedral has always hosted an annual 'Michaelmas Fair' in its grounds, an all-day event that musters the congregation-at-large in a common effort to raise money for charity. Some 40 fair stalls were, until recently, constructed in the grounds out of spars of angle-iron, wooden shelving and each capped with a canvas hood. All this heavy equipment was stored throughout the year in the spacious shelter of the bell tower. A few days before the fair the heavy trapdoor in the tower above the west entrance to the cathedral was opened and a large wooden ship's pulley, rigged up under the bells, was used to lower bundles of equipment to waiting hands on the tiled floor below. For over twenty years the good Captain David Wright, wearing his trade-mark bowler hat, masterminded the building and dismantling of the fair, assisted by volunteers from the congregations. Nowadays modern folding gazebo tents have replaced those old stalls.

The Fair has always been a favourite in Hong Kong's social calendar, attracting not just the congregation but the expatriate and local community from across the territory. A variety of stalls includes the ever popular white elephant (a bric-a-brac stall), the books and second-hand clothing, the Punch & Judy show, the Filipino 'Lumpia' stall and the scout's hot dogs, not to mention the 'bar', where old China hands congregate to partake of a libation. Added to that are attractions; school bands and dance troupes, Judy the baggy, red-nosed clown, the stocks where fair-goers throw soaking sponges at the clergy, and the last event, the drawing of the raffle. Top prizes are donated by five-star hotels, Hong's Kong's Airline; Cathay Pacific; with first-class flights to Asian holiday destinations, and sundry others. Once the fun is over building teams get together again, dismantling the fair ground and racing to haul it all up into the bell tower before the service of Vespers.

St John's Cathedral also hosts the popular, English-speaking, 36th Scout Group comprising a Cub Pack and a Scout Troop. And once a year they are the stars in a Scouting Sunday service, parading their flags. Another very busy part of the Cathedral is the counselling service, open to the public at large, for a small fee.

After six months of civil mayhem, in 2019, Hong Kong was practically on its knees; economically mauled with many shops, restaurants and businesses closed down, millions of dollars worth of criminal damage done to the public infrastructure and private property, and the tourist industry all but dead. Socially, families were torn asunder, young idealists pitted against their elders, the forces of law and order stretched to the limits of endurance and politics and governance in tatters.

Against this alarming background, and with the sounds of daily, violent demonstrations still ringing in the ears of the multi-national congregation in the cathedral, the Very Revd. Matthias Der, Dean of St John's Cathedral, ascended the steps to the pulpit and delivered his Christmas Day sermon, first in English at the 9 o'clock service and then in Putonghua at the 11 o'clock Mandarin service. It is worth recording for its sagacity and prescience, revealing the human impact of the riots, and all such brutal upheavals, on society. It was even published verbatim in a normally secular Chinese language newspaper and in a weekly press magazine.

After the opening prayer and greetings the Dean spoke as follows:-

"How many of you look forward to Christmas with joyful anticipation? Please raise your hands...I am with you. Perhaps it is the attractive traditional decorations or the familiar, heartening Christmas carols; may be it is because this season conjures up the warmth of family gatherings, sumptuous food... Somehow Christmas imparts, in the air, a sense of love. It is magical, with a *Romantic* feel to it.

"But this year Christmas comes, more than ever, as a welcome break after half a year of anxiety, frustration and, most of all, fear. We all hope and pray that this Christmas will bring lasting peace and stability to our shores. But the grim reality is that many lives have been filled with hurt, sorrow and shattered dreams. You may well ask *"Is the Christmas message just wishful thinking? Why isn't God stopping the mayhem?*

"If we look more carefully at the Christmas narrative in the Holy Bible we will see that it hardly invokes a *Romantic* view of the Christmas season that we dream of. From the moment that Mary received news of her unexpected pregnancy, it was a frightening time for her. The long, arduous journey from Nazareth to Bethlehem; no first-class treatment, no presidential suite waiting for them; just a mean animal stall to lay their heads. Just imagine the worries, the sense of helplessness, endured by Mary and Joseph. And that wasn't the end of it.

"Mary's time arrives and all she can do is to give birth on the floor in the straw. And still no respite, for then the angels warn Mary and Joseph to flee for their lives, to Egypt, as King Herod orders a massacre of children in an attempt to rid himself of any future rival to his kingdom. A tale of hardship, trouble and fear, coming one after the other, in the year that Christ was born.

"So, perhaps the true Christmas spirit is not the one we often romanticize about. Perhaps it **is** more akin to what God does in our own human experience, more of a story that we encounter everyday, a story often filled, for us, with brokenness, suffering and dread.

"It is within this realm of a suffering world, not just our microcosm, that the angels proclaimed *"Do not be afraid; for see, I bring you good news of great joy to all people; to you is born this day, in the city of David, a saviour, who is the Messiah, the Lord."*

"At Christmas tide God is telling us that the context in which we live may look bleak but that the faithfulness of God's promise is unshaken. Yes, from the day of his birth, He endured poverty, hardship and injustice like so many others in our world. And yet God manifested His transforming love for us through the presence of Jesus Christ. He didn't make a dramatic entrance on our world stage to change all for good and break down inequality. He came as a fragile baby, grew up learning the trade of a carpenter and eventually died as a criminal on a cross. *That* was how God chose to break down the darkness of humanity and to give us hope in eternal life through his resurrection. He chose *not* to come as one of the privileged few but, rather, as a lowly, simple, no-body. In his teachings He wanted us to know that He can be found in the ordinary. His name, Emmanuel, God with us, personifies that truth. He is here. It is His presence, now, that changes the world.

"In our own awful times we are living through dark moments in the history of this territory. Hearts are broken, relationships torn apart, tears have been shed. Prayers have been offered with crying and frustration keenly felt. Many have asked of God again *"Why aren't you doing anything?"*

"The Christmas story tells us that God's working is beyond what we can see or imagine. He is in the most unexpected places and appears in the most unlikely moments. We may entreat from God something out of the ordinary; a miracle; but in the Bible quite often we see God using the most ordinary people and the most ordinary things to reveal His love and presence. He can use a word of encouragement from a stranger to lift our disappointment. He can mend a broken trust through someone who eschews hate and revenge, preferring to give his antagonist the benefit of doubt, forgiveness. One thing we need to hold onto this Christmas Day is the certain knowledge that God *is* with us. Emmanuel! He will never abandon us. He knows our pains, our sorrows and our frustrations, all of which He knew in his own sufferings on earth. He empathises with us. He never gave up and neither should we. At this time we must rekindle our hope in God.

"And so, this Christmas tide, we mustn't forget *why* he came to earth, certainly not for a holiday. His special purpose was to mend relationships, bringing about reconciliation between God and sinful humanity through His teaching, death and glorious resurrection. Out of love He came to earth, in Jesus Christ, to give, to share, to forgive and to reconcile. And by His death He took away our sins that break up and destroy relationships. He *is* the Prince of Peace, bringing peace and wholeness to the world. Through faith we are able to receive these gifts.

"If we believe that God works through the ordinary and in our ordinary lives, we also have to believe that we are those ordinary people that God has called to serve him. In St Paul's letter to the Ephesians, he writes *"Do not grieve the Holy Spirit."* In our city, in our homes, have we grieved the Holy Spirit? Where there is disparity between the rich and the poor, where there is animosity between people, where human dignity is not honoured, we have grieved the Holy Spirit.

"If we believe God is with us, we must accept He is calling us, empowering us and entrusting us with a mission of peace and reconciliation. J. Packer, an Anglican theologian, said *"Jesus Christ came to seek us where we are, in order that He might bring us to where He is."* Christ came to our fallen humanity to raise us to be with Him. It is when we strive for the same kind of love as Christ has; to give, to share, to forgive, to reconcile; especially when that seems so hard to do, that our humanity is raised to where God is.

"Just this last summer I was walking along a street in Central. An elderly man was manoeuvring a cart, stacked with cardboard, down a steep slope. A scene all too familiar in Hong Kong; an elderly man or woman gathering cardboard boxes to make ends meet. Suddenly a young lady went over and offered a helping hand. He seemed shocked and embarrassed by the offer. But then another woman stepped forward to assist this struggling man. He was visibly moved by the concern and kindness shown to him by these two strangers. It was unplanned. Nothing fancy or extraordinary about it. But their compassion surely revealed the love and power of God.

"Look around our city, look around our world! It is for our broken world that God, in Christ, came to us. He came to transform – to bring peace and reconciliation and to restore true humanity so that we can be where God is.

"It was Mother Teresa who once said *"Do ordinary things with extraordinary love"*. That was what God did, through Jesus Christ, at that first Christmas. We can do that too! Merry Christmas. God bless you! Amen."

- End -

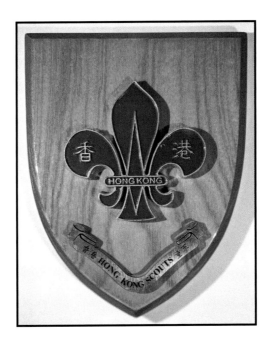

"The Hong Kong Scout Association emblem"

BE PREPARED

The Scout Motto

When my two sons, aged 7 and 9 yrs, were old enough to join the Cub Scouts, I took them along to St. John's Cathedral, our family church, to make an application for them to join. The cathedral has its own Scout Group, the 36th Hong Kong, comprising a cub pack and a scout troop. I received a positive reply from Sheila, the Akela, on one condition. *"As you can see, we already have five Sixes, but we can add one more Six if you agree to come on board as a cub pack leader."* Thus began a career in scouting, having agreed to Akela's terms.

First, a little bit of the history of the world-wide scout movement from its inception in 1907. Beginning at Brownsea Island, just south of Poole, in Dorset, on the south coast of England, it arrived in Hong Kong within three years, 1910.

King Edward VII (1901-1910) was fully aware of a tragedy unfolding among Britain's youth after the human and economic depredations of the Boer War, waged in South Africa between Dutch settlers and the British army, between 1880 and 1902.

Compounding the loss of life in war and the ensuing national debt was the first recorded 'baby boom' in the UK when the population soared from 34 million in 1801 to 41 million by 1900. Social ills and political insouciance rendered welfare and the employment structure of the UK woefully inadequate, government unprepared and unwilling to grasp the nettle.

In this plight King Edward intervened, asking the hero of Mafeking (1900), Lt. General Robert Baden-Powell, CB, to use his acknowledged skills in military scouting for the benefit of Britain's hapless, foot-loose young generation. Heeding the King's wishes in 1904, Robert retired from the army and set about planning and organising a nation-wide scheme that would utilize the energies of British youth, instilling in them social responsibility and personal discipline, most importantly, in the name of God.

Ideas flowed but B-P, as he is affectionately known, could not come up with a suitable hierarchical structure for young people. So, allegedly and probably true, he consulted his older brother Francis 'Frank' who told him about the structure of the Freemasons, of which he was one. Accordingly Baden Powell initiated a system of team building in a meritocracy whereby learned skills would be awarded with badges, accruing to seniority. He designed uniforms and accoutrements along military lines and created Scout Groups, with adult leadership, loosely based on the structure of a masonic lodge. He put together programmes of practical and citizenship training, with tests of achievement in each. And the whole organisation he detailed in his seminal work 'Scouting for Boys' that is still in print.

When the King endorsed the plan, B-P gathered together a group of boys local to Poole and hosted the first scout camp on Brownsea Island. It was successful beyond his wildest dreams, boys queuing up from far and wide to partake in the B-P scout experience. And its fame spread like wild-fire beyond the shores of the UK, reaching Singapore, Malaysia and Japan just two years later, in 1909.

Scouting reached Hong Kong in 1910, experimentally at first in St Jospeh's secondary school on Kennedy Road, on the Island. So successful was the prototype that, in 1913, the scout movement in Hong Kong was put on a formal footing, with government backing. St Joseph's was named the 1st Scout Group and, only a year later, St John's Cathedral was the 36th. Sir Francis May, Governor of Hong Kong, was the first Chief Scout. Successive governors, up to Sir Murray MacLehose, continued that tradition until 1977 when the Hong Kong scout movement was granted independence from the British movement and non-sectarian membership was formally welcomed.

As scouting became more and more popular so came the need for land on which training, camping and wild games could take place. Between 1918 and right up to 1940, parcels of Crown land were leased to the Hong Kong scouts for the proverbial pepper-corn rent. There are more than 20 such sites, dispersed over the territory, mostly of several acres each. And after 1997, these were all granted continued free ownership by the scout movement. The value of all that landed property, nowadays, is in the billions of dollars. They also own residential property and a big hotel, all money spinners. Thus was created the richest scout movement in the world.

My scout leader training took the usual route, over six years, to gaining my Wood Badge, signified by two wooden beads threaded on the end of a leather thong and hung over the uniform scarf, round the neck. Thereafter I took specialized training in pioneering, first aid and life guard; occupational safety and health, etc. Add to that communications and computing in more modern times. In 1991 I took over as Akela for the 36th Cubs and, in 1995 I took on the roll of Group Scout Leader (GSL).

I remember clearly one incident when the scout troop leader, Tim, an expatriate school teacher, sought my permission to take all of his scouts, aged between 10 and 15 years, in uniform, to a big funeral parlour in North Point District, on the Island. They were to pay their respects to a former local Chinese scout leader, with the 36th Hong Kong group, who had died. I gave my assent providing he sought approval from the parents. During evening prayers by Buddhist monks, mourners were allowed to file past the open casket to view the corpse if they wished. Tim decided to lead his troop in single file round the casket. Another scout leader, Graham, who witnessed this, informed me and, the following morning, I telephoned Tim for an explanation. I ended up admonishing him. He had not notified the parents beforehand or taken the public perception into account. Tim should have thought about the possible consequences of his actions.

The young scouts had not been prepared for such an activity and need not have been subjected to it; for all of them the first time they'd seen a dead body. I wondered if there would be any repercussions from parents but I was not told of any. A few days later I received a written resignation from Tim. Whether this exceptional occurrence, this deviation from prescribed scout training, was appropriate or not, I am still in a quandary as to the efficacy of my decision. Tim was a dedicated and talented scout leader, although unorthodox at times. Graham took over as the troop leader and, in 1997, as the GSL of the 36th Hong Kong.

In 1997 I was invited by the Chief Commissioner to take over the role of Dep. Asst. Commissioner of the International Branch and for all English-speaking scout groups in the territory, a total of 17 at the time. My immediate boss, in that role, was retired Commissioner of Police, Eddie Hui. I remember there was a bit of enmity surrounding my promotion in the scouts when Peter, another expatriate scout leader, also a policeman who was senior to me and, at one time, my boss, lobbied the Chief Commissioner for the post. His suit was rejected which I found a bit embarrassing. However he was given an office as head of IT, a newly created post for him, with the same rank as me. We remain friends. In the hierarchy of the Hong Kong scout movement I was the only *Kwei-lo* (white-man) operational scouter. I had a distinct impression of being there as the token expatriate, showing the government and the public at large that Scout HQ were being inclusive in an unspoken climate of Hong Kong-for-the-Chinese after the repatriation.

In my international role I led two delegations of Hong Kong Scouts to two world jamborees, the first in Japan and the second in South Korea. I was also one of the delegates sent to an international symposium on world scouting held in Durban, South Africa. The Chief Commissioner gave me his notes and I wrote his speech for him.

My duties as head of the English-speaking groups were not onerous, largely visiting each group once a year and reading their annual reports. But other duties were delegated by the Chief Commissioner to me and one of those was organising an annual mess night for scout leaders. He himself, a retired senior police officer, designed a mess kit along the same lines as military mess kits, and he wanted all those old colonial traditions included in the entertainment. I was never quite happy with that concept, an imposition of police or military style formal dining which belied the scout model of camp-fire fun and singing. Nevertheless, orders were orders and I organised the first, and several more mess nights, thereafter. If nothing else, they provided an excellent forum for internal communications.

In 1999, coinciding with my police posting to Kwai Tsing District, as the Dep. Dist. Commander (DDC), I set up a scout group, the 1095th of Hong Kong, based in the police station, designed to cater for school drop-outs and youth offenders. One of the responsibilities of the DDC was to run a youth crime scheme whereby a young person, under 16 yrs and arrested for petty crime, could be given a caution, instead of being charged and prosecuted in court. When a CID officer recommended this course of action, known as Superintendent's (SP's) Discretion, it was my decision to approve or disapprove of it. 90% of the time it was approval and I would interview both the *enfant terrible* and his parents. And 90% of the time, I found the miscreant to be the victim of circumstances; mostly poor parenting, the lack of a good education and peer pressure.

I was not the first police officer to set up such a scout group. One with exactly the same motivation behind it was started in Shatin police station just half a year before my 1095th came into being. The District Commander of Shatin was Peter and he didn't publicise his scout group outside his bailiwick so it was a while before we got together and compared notes.

My new scout group came into being in July, 1999, with a formal flag-raising ceremony attended by the chairman and members of the District Fight Crime Committee (DFCC), the district police commander and parents of the 12 boys and girls forming the nucleus of the troop. Eight of that nucleus were, at that time, students of a government band five secondary school and all had been subject of SP's discretion.

The Education Department's banding of schools, from elite 1 to confounded 5, meant that students were selected for the different bands by their levels of academic prowess, behaviour and discipline in school and their degree of social abilities. Far from being effective channelling of learning ability and teaching resources, it served to stigmatize students in the lower bands, probably for the rest of their lives. Fortunately this failed strategy was soon replaced by the two tried and tested levels of grammar and secondary schools.

The scout troop numbered 26 by the end of 1999, including myself as the troop and scout group leader, two rank-and-file policemen from Kwai Tsing District and one civilian, as assistant leaders. In the following year troop meetings were subject to fluctuations; between 10 and 20 regular attendees. The leaders visited absentees at home and discovered that the truants did not like meeting in the police station. I discussed this challenge with the DFCC and they soon came up with a solution, using the school hall and playground of a secondary school in one of the big housing estates. That had the dual benefit of removing any embarrassment at the location of meetings and of providing a nexus for recruitment of boys and girls other than those subject of SP's discretion.

The meetings were held on Saturday afternoon, every week, during term time. They always began with a parade, forming up in patrols of six scouts each, and the flag-raising using a demountable flagpole set up in the centre of the playground. I had managed to obtain a kudu horn on my scouting visit to Durban, South Africa, that had been adapted with a drilled hole in the pointed end, making it playable as a musical instrument. I could only manage two notes on it and I played those at the raising of the flag. It was B-P himself who used a Kudu horn to rally the first scout camp on Brownsea Island.

A full programme of meetings every term was prepared and given to every scout and his/her parents. One meeting a month was a 24 hours adventure in which we would visit one or other of the dedicated scout camp sites around the territory to train in skills such as sailing and canoeing, rope-bridge building, night hike navigation, camp cooking, wide-games of 'cops and robbers' (a glorified hide-and-seek), treasure hunt using map and compass and, of course, having a camp-fire night, complete with sing-songs and roasting marsh-mallows. On each one of these outdoor week-ends we would concentrate on fulfilling the requirements of at least one skills badge. The scouts shirt sleeves began to fill up with badges.

And we did two trips into mainland China, the first to a small impoverished farming town in Yunnan Province, in the south, where one of our local leaders had a contact with a school teacher there. We travelled by bus and took with us at least 50 pairs of plastic shoes donated by a factory, boxes full of a miscellany of clothes ranging from underwear to plastic macs and last, but not least, children's reading books, text books, colouring books, crayons, water-paints and pens.

We arrived on a Friday evening and, on the Saturday morning, all dressed in our scout uniforms, we held a joint flag-raising ceremony in the school playground with the young Pioneers of China (the equivalent of our scouts) in ordinary clothes but with red scarfs knotted at the neck, commemorating the blood shed by martyrs of the 1949 Communist revolution. We raised our green 1095th scout flag and they raised the red flag of China. We all saluted both flags, the three fingers of the right hand for our scouts and, for our hosts, raising of the right hand, palm down, over the top of the crown of the head, signifying the communist state over all. The Scout motto is "Be prepared", The Pioneer's is similar but politicised "To struggle for the cause of communism, be prepared."

Afterwards we did what all scouts do best, a day of games and competitions, ending with a bonfire evening and a sing song. From the looks on their faces I don't think they had ever had so much fun. And certainly they had never seen marshmallows before!

By and large scout training was a successful expedient in moderating anti-social behaviour, anger control and learning the qualities of leadership. But there were occasions when arguments flared and leaders had to step in. There were no punishments meted out. Everything was resolved with consultation and discussion involving the offending parties and their patrol mates. That in its self was a steep learning curve for some of the scouts.

But one incident had much wider repercussions, beyond the scope of the scout troop, when a 15 years old girl scout, Apple, stopped attending our weekly meetings. Having located Apple after school one day, she informed the scout leader, who had tracked her down, that she was pregnant and had not told her parents. I was consulted and a police report was made, resulting in a CID investigation. The father was found to be a classmate at her school, about the same age. The act was consensual and medical tests put the date of conception around Apple's 15th birthday. The boy was charged with unlawful carnal knowledge and the case was dealt with in juvenile court, held in camera (private). Together with Apple's consent, her parent's agreement and a doctor's opinion that clinical abortion was the preferred medical remedy, that course of action took place. All this was kept confidential from the press and the membership of the scout group. Subsequently, on advice from her child psychiatrist, Apple returned to scouting. The last I heard of her was in 2018, that she was married and a scout leader with a group in Kowloon.

In 2005 I retired from the police force but continued my scout headquarters duties and troop activities until my resignation from the scout movement, pending my move from Hong Kong back to the UK, in 2010. The scout group that I started while I was a teacher at the University Graduate's Association secondary school in Aberdeen, Hong Kong Island in 2005-6, was still a going concern in 2010. Also in 2010 I handed over the running of the 1095th scouts to police sergeant Billy, himself a long term scouter since he was at school. At that time there was a regular attendance of between 25 and 30 scouts. In that year, at the annual parade and awards ceremony for Hong Kong Scouts, I was invested with the Scout Distinguished Service Cross.

Presented to Mr J.C.S. McDouall SSP
Deputy Commandant, PTS
from staff of PTS
2 Sep 96 - 7 Nov 98

"The heraldic shield of the Hong Kong Police Training School"

THE PRACTICALITIES OF FENG-SHUI

Anecdotal evidence

The first time that I learned of *feng-shui*, literally interpreted as 'wind-water' or, in common parlance, luck, was during my basic training as an inspector of police. In my squad of trainees we had five local, Hong Kong bred and educated, lads with whom us expatriates spent a lot of our free time talking about anything and everything of Hong Kong, its history, society, religion and politics, etc. And in amongst it all was *feng-shui*, described as an ancient, non-scientific and mythological Chinese tradition of geomancy and fortune-telling.

In the many stories that I have heard involving *feng-shui*, I have learned that the practice of it goes back a few thousand years, with evidence of its use found in old circular grave sites; the alignment of which is in accordance with the forces of nature, ensuring the deceased has a 'view' of air, water and mountain. The design of the grave is commonly like a wide armchair with the space in the middle created for worshippers to burn incense and make food offerings. This particular example of early burial rites comes from the supposition that landscapes and bodies of water have a cosmic current or energy. Such is often illustrated, in the Chinese pantheon, by the notion of dragons ensconced under the ground and in the sea.

The forces of nature are seen in everything, from great to small, affecting surrounding life. The geomancers-of-old invented a compass, based on astrology, which enables the skilled diviner to align it with the existing night sky. By cross referencing that information with the birth particulars of a client, a geomancer is able to ascertain which of the five elements; metal, earth, fire, water and wood; come into play and then to announce his predictions. The *feng-shui* expert was an important man in every community, consulted on where and when to build any structure such as a house or part of it, the most auspicious timing for an event such as a marriage or the naming of a new-born child or the most propitious site for a grave. Everyone wanted "good *fung-shui*".

The most well known example of *feng-shui* practice in Hong Kong are the facts surrounding the placement of two larger-than-life sculptures of lions, crouching in front of the Hong Kong and Shanghai Bank (HSBC) headquarters in Central district. The first HSBC bank built was in Shanghai, China. It was opened in 1920 and its frontage was adorned with two huge, crouching lions, cast in bronze. These quickly became iconic in local culture, representing to the bank's clientele 'safe banking'. Thus it was that this image was chosen as the bank's logo.

In 1935 the HSBC opened an even bigger and grander edifice in Central district, Hong Kong, and transferred their China headquarters from Shanghai to the new building. The directors contracted WW Wagstaff, the same artist who cast the lions for their bank in Shanghai, to cast two more lions in the same mould for the new building in Hong Kong. These duly arrived in time for the official opening ceremony but then the question arose of where to put them?

The obvious place was to have them guarding the front, public entrance of the building. The official address, of what was at the time, the grandest building in Central was, and still is, No. 1, Queens Road, Central, occupying a whole block, with its great front doors opening onto a high embankment across the road and having no good view at all. But the back of the building, on Des Voeux Road, had a pair of equally imposing doors, also open to the public, *and* it had a fantastic view across the open harbour to the hills of Kowloon behind. Thus it was, to no one's surprise, that the geomancer, hired by the bank, ordained that the pair of lions should be settled at the ostensible back of the building where the best *feng-shui* was to be had, with its vista of air, water and mountains. And that is where the lions were placed, effectively reversing the back door into the front entrance of the bank. The lions were still at the Des Voeux road entrance when the second world war came to Hong Kong in 1941.

As the Japanese invasion of Hong Kong rapidly unfolded, the defending troops, including members of the colonial Hong Kong Regiment of volunteers, could only fight a rear-guard action, retreating westward from North Point along the waterfront. The Japanese brought to bear a far superior and well equipped military force which left a trail of destruction in their wake. And one of the HSBC's lions was lacerated by shrapnel in the street fighting. Once the Japanese army had gained control of the territory they confiscated both of those lions and shipped them to Osaka for their bronze to be used in the production of munitions and armaments.

After the capitulation of Japan in 1946 the HSBC went in search of its lions and were fortunate in finding them still intact in Osaka. They brought them back to Hong Kong and reinstated them in their original positions.

On 26th June, 1981, the old HSBC headquarters closed its doors for the last time, the hoardings went up and the demolition crews went in. Over the succeeding two years the new building replaced the old with a unique design by the famous British architect, Norman Robert Foster. I am told that his architectural drawings were vetted by a local Chinese geomancer. True or false I don't know but it would have been a logical step to take. A stitch in time saves nine.

When the completed structure was unveiled to public view it was given the nick-name 'The Oil Rig' for, with all its entrails, as it were, on the outside of the building (a Norman Foster trade-mark), the resemblance was uncanny. A popular hypothesis for the oil-rig design was that, with no obstruction between the building and Victoria harbour, the structure could be launched and towed away, off shore. Given the 1997 handover and subsequent unrest in the city, that interpretation was not lost on its clientele.

At the grand opening of the bank the lions were fixed in their positions, as allocated by the hired geomancer, at the popular Des Voeux Road side of the building. And passers-by still rub the paws and noses of the lions for good luck.

"Hong Kong Police officers parading in front of the newly aligned flag poles"

A much more mundane example of *feng-shui* in action, but different in its usage, occurred at the Hong Kong Police training school (PTS) in Aberdeen. A local instructor at the school recounted to us trainees from the UK a spate of bad incidents that had occurred in 1967-8 at police training school, a couple of years before our arrival in November, 1970. There had been several deaths of students within a single year. These were a suicide, an accidental death on the firing range, a death from heart attack during a training run and a death from a fall during on an overnight exercise on a rocky hill-side in the New Territories. Superstition was rife, both amongst the trainees but also among the public reading those press reports. Morale was badly affected and the commandant of the training school petitioned the police director of management services to allow the hire of a well known Chinese geomancer with a view to allaying these egregious superstitions. The request was approved and the cost was crowd-funded among all the staff at PTS.

The result of the geomancer's deliberations was that one of the three flagpoles, erected to one side of the parade ground, was in the wrong place; that it was, in *fung-shui* terminolgy, interrupting energy lines and, mythologically, irritating the dragon under the earth. To rectify the imbalance caused by shifting one pole, all three flag poles had to be re-sited so as to preserve their symmetry. The geomancer made his measurements and marked the exact spot where each flagpole was to be stepped. A government contractor did the work and that completed, the commandant ordered a Bai-Kwan-Dai ceremony; worshipping of the god Kwan-Dai; to be held in the trainee's canteen after a Saturday-morning parade. Did it work? Apparently so as no similar spate of such serious misfortune has occurred since then.

Kwan-Dai was a Chinese army general who lived in 160 AD, and who was known as a model of rectitude and military virtue. Upon his death he was deified and, in modern times, his severe, red-faced countenance and brave effigy, set up in a wooden altar, with candles and incense, is revered in every police station in Hong Kong. A Bai-Kwan-Dai, literally 'prayer to Kwan-Dai', is the usual practice when a thanks-giving or a plea for courage and wisdom is required; worshipping him with incantations and the burning of incense. Afterwards there will usually be the cutting of a roast pig and, finally, a feast of roast meats, lasagne, vegetables, sandwiches and spring roles, etc.

Finally, there is a third example of the practicalities of *feng-shui* that directly involved me.

My last posting in the police force, before my retirement, was as deputy district commander of Kwai Tsing police district. The district commander (DC) was a local chief superintendent who had strong beliefs in *feng-shui*. Indeed he was, himself, an amateur practitioner, possessing equipment (the special compass) and books on the subject.

On my first day in office the DC came in and, sitting down opposite me, he asked if I believed in *feng-shui*? My off-the-cuff reply was that I had a healthy respect for it. He proceeded to obtain details of my birth; place, date and time; which he made a note of and with which he was able to divine my signs of the zodiac and the dominant elements that I was born under. We chatted a while longer and he told me about the *feng-shui* of Kwai Tsing police district; not very good, two suicides in the station in the last two years. And, he noted, the address of our district station, No. 999, Kwai Tsing Road, implied that our station was permanently on an emergency footing; in other words attracting emergencies all the time. He went away to make his calculations.

The following morning he came back into my office and, consulting his hand-written notes, he gave me a set of instructions, with their symbolism explained, as to how my office furnishings were to be arranged. Since I was his officer in charge of the station; its administration, the welfare and training of the 700 officers and civilian staff on the nominal roles, and all the equipment on our manifest; his objective was to ensure that the peace and stabilty of the whole district might not be compromised by any deficiency in my *feng-shui.*

Accordingly my instructions were as follows. First the most auspicious positioning of my office furniture. With a felt-tip pen in his hand he bent down and carefully measured and marked on the floor the exact placing of my desk in the office. From being directly opposite the door, on the far wall, my desk had to be moved across to one side and not in straight alignment with the open door or the adjacent wall. My secure metal filing cabinet had to be moved away from the wall safe (which could not be moved) and placed in the far corner from my desk. A bit inconvenient but of no great consequence. In the other corner, behind the door, I was to set up a water feature by which he meant a small fountain in a decorative setting. And lastly, on the window sill opposite the door, two small porcelain riderless horses must be placed, one at each end of the sill. These can be purchased cheaply in any bric-a-brac store in the old town nearby. All this to harmonize me with the *fung-shui* of the station and the district-at-large.

Anyone reading this, and not being versed in the Chinese tradition of *feng-shui*, can be forgiven for thinking that I was the victim of an elaborate joke. But it was no joking matter to the majority of the local officers serving in the station. And being cognisant of that fact I duly conformed to the dictates of the DC. And my last 18 months in the force, before my retirement, were indeed peaceful, orderly and angst free.

POLICE OFFICER'S MESS

Kwun Tong Police Station, Kowloon.

In May, 1971, Probationary Inspector (PI) Course 62 passed out of the Police Training School at Aberdeen, Hong Kong, and 15 young men, newly qualified one-pip (military star) police inspectors, were despatched to postings all over Hong Kong. Some 300 newly made police constables (PCs) also graduated that day.

After the parade each inspector picked up his kit, walked round to the car parks behind the drill shed and found the heavy general purpose (HGP) lorry, in police livery, that had been sent from the police station he/she was being posted to. Myself and sixteen constables were duly driven off to Kwun Tong police station in east Kowloon.

On arrival our driver parked our HGP in front of the main entrance to the Station. At the top of a short flight of steps stood a smartly suited Chinese gentleman, arms akimbo, looking down at us as we disembarked from the vehicle. Assuming he was a ranking officer I snapped to attention with a salute. He sauntered down the steps, holding a hand out to greet me, saying *"You don't have to salute me, Sir. I'm the Sgt. Major here."* I was soon to find out that the Sgt. Major, nick-named S*hapei Gau*, literally 'sand-skin dog' which is an ugly, wrinkled, bad-tempered animal, was the most influential man in the whole district of Kwun Tong. Bar none. In uniform he wore a broad, crimson-red sash, knotted at the end with tassels, a symbol of power wielded by only 34 officers in the Royal Hong Kong Police.

But I digress.

While the new constables were shown to their barracks. I was welcomed into the officer's mess, a two storey, white-washed building situated on one side of the police station compound. The ground floor was occupied by the lounge bar, the dining room, the kitchen, the laundry and quarters for the amah and the cook.

One officer gave me the keys to my room on the first floor which was an air-conditioned bed-sit with a toilet and shower shared with my next door neighbour. He turned out to be a local senior inspector named Benny Ng.

Over the next few days I made the acquaintance of my mess mates. Benny was on full-time secondment to Hong Kong University as a law degree student. He was also the elected chairman of the officer's mess.

There were Dave and Ted, who were both ex-Royal Navy and inseparable friends. The former was a big man, slow and solid, while the latter was more wiry of physique. Then there was Harry, of eastern European ethnicity, Robert, a Canadian recruit, Wesley, known simply as Wes, a former constable from the northern counties of England with a dour sense of humour, and Mark, a rather tall, lanky, upper crust Englishman, of independent means, from the southern counties.

Other members of the mess were the officer cadre of Kwun Tong police station, including the Auxiliary police force. There were also several honorary members; civilians working in Kwun Tong area. One of those was a captain in the Macau Ferry Company, who 'flew' hydrofoils plying between Hong Kong and Macau and two more were engineers who were contractors building the extension to the Kai Tak airport runway. The mess was a highly entertaining place.

The district superintendent (DS) was Ian Hyde, an English colonial policeman who had previously served in Malaya and, during the insurgency, won the George Medal for gallantry. He was a genial man and a good leader. The sub-divisional inspector (SDI) of the station was a local officer of chief inspector rank. The chief inspector in charge of district criminal investigation (CID) was an old colonial Irishman, Paddy O'Byrne. He loved his whisky and a good yarn in the mess. Speaking very softly and shuffling his tall, lean and hunched frame round the corridors of power, he earned the nickname 'Gray Ghost'. He and his wife Joan very generously used to invite the single members of the mess to his spacious government quarters in Ede road, west Kowloon, for Christmas lunch. One of the local detective inspectors, flamboyant Rufus, was a regular mess member. He used to wear fashionable flared trousers under which he would strap on his ankle holster with a snub-nosed .38 revolver secured in it. One of the three auxiliary police officers was Arjun, a middle-aged Sikh from the Punjab. By profession he was a teacher at a local secondary school. He usually worked a couple of shifts at the weekends and supported the bar afterwards.

Occasionally there were impromptu parties where, for example, a birthday might be celebrated. Members would gather in the bar and sing a boisterous 'Happy Birthday' song. One such night in 1972 the aforementioned Mark retired to his room early so Dave and Ted went outside, climbed onto the first floor ledge under Mark's bedroom window and created a lot of noise, waking up their fellow officer who was not best pleased. Ted tried to clamber down quickly but lost his footing and, tumbling backwards, mercifully landed on top of the DS's landrover. If the vehicle hadn't been there it could have been far worse. As it was he put a bit of a dent in the roof and broke a leg. Quite a lot of explaining to do the next morning! There were many more shenanigans that went on in officer's messes, some quite unworthy of the best traditions. The merry-making was a good way to let off steam though, after the high pressure work that most front-line officers had to contend with.

Wes owned a second hand junk-heap of a car which he would drive down to Tsim Sha Tsui, taking one or two other members of the mess with him, for an evening out on the town. On the way back home, quite late one night, and in passing the street sleeper's shelter run by the Government Welfare Department in Kowloon City, someone in the car had the bright idea of purloining the sign board above the entrance, bearing the legend 'Street Sleeper's Shelter' in English and Chinese. Wes parked his car in front of the door and the sign board was duly 'borrowed'. Back at Kwun Tong police station Wes and his slightly inebriated passengers erected the sign above the DS's office door. The next morning there was a hiatus but the DS saw the funny side of it, merely ordering the residents of the mess to return the board to its rightful owners with suitable apologies.

Then there was young Richard; Dick to his pals; who was resident in Wong Tai Sin police officers' mess but attached to Kwun Tong Division. One morning he was instructed by the assistant divisional commander to visit the three banks in the town centre and carry out an arms and ammunition licence check. In those days nearly every bank hired a guard, armed with a shotgun, who would stand outside or just inside the entrance of the bank as a deterrent to would-be robbers. Police inspectors did the checking and also confirmed that the guard had done his training, was named in the licence and his gun was in working order. A mainland Chinese bank was one of the three and, after Dick had checked the validity of their arms licence, he turned his attention to the Pakistani guard on duty and looked over his weapon, a Remington shotgun. When asked if there was a cartridge in the breech the guard smiled as he swivelled his head, which Dick took to be a 'No'. He pumped the shotgun and BANG, a six-inch hole appeared in the white plastered ceiling above him. All hell broke loose in the bank hall, tellers pressing their alarm buttons and the manager dialling 999 as fast as he could. Needless to say Dick was carpeted for that error and, in his case, it was a matter of "Not him again". He had a reputation for being accident prone.

Dave was posted to Traffic Branch and, after obtaining his police vehicle and motorbike driving licences and completing a traffic course, he was given Kwun Tong district as his traffic zone. As a single officer he lived in the officer's mess and was often seen parking his traffic bike, complete with blue flashing lights and squawking radio, outside the mess and coming in for breakfast, lunch or dinner. He always wore his long white traffic sleeves and, down the lower reaches of them, he often used a pen to note the registration plate numbers of offending vehicles that he intended to summons when he returned to the office.

A stickler for the minutiae of traffic law; the 'construction and use' rules and regulations; Dave liked nothing better than detecting the most detailed little infringements that he spotted in vehicles. Traffic was his joy. He ate, slept and drank it as the saying goes. On the back of his traffic police helmet he had stuck the sign 'Think Tank'. In his panniers he always carried traffic regs together with a tape measure and even a pair of calibrating pincers. Sure enough, one day, a triumphant Dave came into the mess boasting that he had been able to inform the surprised owner of a new Rolls Royce that he had measured two infringements, the aerial was too high at full extension and the car body exceeding the regulated length of a private car by a full two inches.

In the early hours one morning, around the time of Chinese New Year, February, '73, a fire broke out in a large conglomeration of make-shift wooden and tin huts erected by squatters on a barren hillside in the Diamond Hill area [bounded by Choi Hung Road and the northern side of San Po Kong factory area] of Kowloon. It was home to perhaps to a thousand or more souls.

Efforts to quench the fire with buckets of water failed and, given the density and close proximity of highly inflammable structures, the fire began to spread rapidly. The emergency services were soon converging on the scene, blue lights and sirens on, and inspector Barry Griffin, on duty at the time, rode to the scene on his traffic bike. Dave, coming from Kwun Tong, was on his way too. It was traffic's job to keep the roads clear for fire and ambulance service access and to allocate traffic officers to road intersections and re-direct traffic. Being among the first policemen on site they were also in a position to assist with the orderly evacuation of the, by now, blazing squatter village.

Once the situation was under control and the emergency services were clearing up, Dave and Barry mounted-up to leave. There were still lots of fire hoses snaking across the road from fire-hydrants, some still in use for damping down hot spots. Not all of the hoses were covered with protective ramps and it was over one of these that Dave bumped his motorbike, his rear wheel skidding along it. The friction broke the heavy canvas hose and a jet of water, at 200 psi, blasted the bike and Dave, into the air and off the road. The fire crews saw the accident and shut off the broken and wildly thrashing hose, extremely dangerous in that situation. Dave, in the urgency of the moment, grabbed the exhaust pipe of his bike to pull it clear, burning his fingers in doing so. And a single decker public bus, passing by and, fortunately with only a few gawking passengers on board, got a soaking when the windows were hit and broken by the powerful jet of water. More excitement than those early morning passengers were bargaining for!

There was a sequel to the event when, a few days later, Dave was complaining that the radio on his bike was out of order. He took his bike to the traffic operational base at Mongkok, Kowloon, where there was a radio work shop. The technician dismantled the box and found a sludgy green mess of copper wiring inside. Barry Griffin, looking on, realised that it must have been the soaking it got from Dave's burst fire hose. It had been attached to a salt-water hydrant. In those days fresh water supplies to Hong Kong were not reliable and a system of sea-water supply to fire hydrants all over the territory was available to the fire services for emergency use. Yellow-painted fire hydrants delivered salt water while the red delivered fresh water.

Another of Dave's exploits was brought to light by a correspondent to the editor of the South China Morning Post daily newspaper. He wrote a letter complaining of the behaviour of an expatriate police inspector whom he labelled 'The Leaping Lizard'. He accused this officer of hiding behind street furniture, in 30 mph areas, with his hand-held speed camera, catching out unwary motorists. Then he'd leap out, stop the vehicle and issue a summons to the offending driver. The laugh, of course, was the thought of our bulky, unfit, friend trying to hide his hulk behind a thin light pole before adroitly leaping into the road.

There was a benevolent side to Dave. Once he was asked to contribute to a local charity and he came up with the idea of shaving his mop of hair off, getting his mess mates to bet him that he wouldn't go bald. He did and made a substantial donation to that charity.

Previously mentioned was the propensity for some officers, frequenting messes attached to police formations, to get into their cups, more than was good for them. Dave was a frequent bar fly and eventually his formation commander reported on him, recommending that he was no longer fit for service in the police force. He was given counselling and a lot of advice from his friends and fellow officers and he'd go 'dry' for a week or two, but then relapse. Finally he was given a medical discharge from Government service and, on the eve of his departure back to his home town in the UK, a small, congenial and saddened farewell party was held for him in the police headquarters mess.

After my first three years in the police force, living in Kwun Tong officers mess, I went back to the UK on home leave. Upon my return I was billeted in the Wong Tai Sin district officers mess, still in east Kowloon. Mess life was along much the same lines as in Kwun Tong, just a bunch of different characters. One of the local inspectors who always came to breakfast in the mess was Jesus Lee. I remember his table manners were appalling. On more than one occasion I witnessed him eating a fried egg, sunny side up.

He used to bend his head down so that he could suck up the yoke straight into his mouth, the white skirt of the egg flapping about on the side. Yuk!

Then there was a rather frightening occasion when a local detective constable stormed into the officers mess to confront a local inspector in the dining room. There was a shouting match in which the incensed constable accused that officer of cuckolding him. During the exchange the wronged officer threatened to shoot the culprit whereupon the SDI, an Australian by the name of Ivan Cutler, quietly stood up and forcefully bundled the irate detective out of the mess and over to the police station. Later I was told that the accusation was founded on fact. The accused was transferred out of the district.

On the plus side, because of the proximity of Wong Tai Sin police station to Kai Tak airport, we sometimes hosted aircraft crew to drinks in the mess. These were popular occasions when single officers from other messes descended on ours in order to meet air hostesses. On 6th July, 1998, the mess hosted a farewell reception to Kai Tak airport which was shut down that night. The bar was packed to the gunnels with pilots and stewards while we watched on television the runway lights being switched off after the last flight had taken off. A historical and, for some, an emotional moment.

Also in 1998 or thereabouts, the then commissioner of police, TSANG Yam-pui, concerned that there was a drinking culture among some of his senior officers decided that it was time to curb it before it got out of hand. Accordingly a headquarters order was promulgated, the gist of which was to close all officer's messes during normal working hours, except for meal times, and to ban the drinking of alcoholic beverages, throughout the force, whilst on duty. Most officers, in practice, already complied with this new edict but, nevertheless, it had a stultifying effect, spelling the end of the traditional, old colonial officer's mess.

The positive side of that order was, of course, sobriety, greater manpower efficiency and adherence to duty hours without exception. But with those welcome changes came some disadvantages; a decrease in personal, social communications in police stations and districts. Partially lost was the off-duty forum in which discussion, debate and just idle chat used to take place. It also became noticeable that officers, working shifts, had much less interaction with their counterparts from one day to the next, losing some of that information-sharing that can be so important. And handicapped was the camaraderie necessary in disciplined organisations, such as engenders good morale. But, as time marches on, substituted arrangements have come about, addressing those inexpediences.

Looking back on those pre-handover (1997) days, many officers, now retired, consider that the district officer's mess was not merely a colonial institution without any more substance than a haven from work but one that had a genuine part to play in the welfare and social cohesion of a police district.

"The 6' tall granite statue of the 'Lady of Justice' that stands high up above the portals to what was the Supreme Court of Hong Kong until 1997."

POLICE OFFICERS AS COURT PROSECUTORS

A review.

From the time that the judiciary was set up in Hong Kong in a traditional British-law setting; identical systems and procedures in place; it was the police who prosecuted their own cases in the magistracies ie minor crime cases that attracted penalties of up to a maximum sentence of three years imprisonment. After WW II and the reorganisation of the judiciary, police inspectors and above, usually the officer in charge of a case, prosecuted in the magistracies only. For the most part this system worked but there were disadvantages such as the case officer being sleep-deprived or sick when required to be in court ready to present a case. Some case officers were not so adept at stepping back, taking a fair and holistic view of the evidence they had put together. Neither were they all sufficiently experienced in trial procedures to effectively marshal and examine their witnesses, answer and make objections in court, etc. Such a haphazard system of case officers, mostly CID inspectors, prosecuting their own case investigations, had more disadvantages than advantages. Whereas a dedicated cadre of police officers, prosecuting all police cases in magistracies, certainly had more advantages than disadvantages.

And so it was decided sometime in the 1960s that a permanent cadre of police officers, as prosecutors, would be formed. A full-time posting to the courts would normally be for two years or more. And that was the system until 1986 when the Hong Kong Government Legal Department were sufficiently resourced to take over all prosecutions in the courts. This twenty-odd years of the establishment of a permanent cadre of police prosecutors played a small but significant part in Hong Kong's justifiably meritorious reputation in upholding the rule of law.

From a police perspective, it was a big time-saver too, there being no need, in most cases of a minor nature, to forward case papers to crown counsel for their approval, answering their queries and then accompanying them to court. Secondly, police officers are all trained in criminal law and police practice and procedure. They are in a position to answer most queries a magistrate or a defence lawyer may have relating to arrest, interrogation, handling of exhibits, taking statements, etc. It was this latter consideration that magistrates appreciated. When asked for their views on keeping a permanent cadre of police prosecutors, the majority agreed that the system was an efficient and valuable asset to magistracy court hearings.

But bigger guns in Hong Kong's Law Society and the Bar Association objected, hinting darkly at a police state; cover-ups and associated injustices; and the fact that police officers neither have sufficient legal training nor the high ethical and moral standards of lawyers. They conveniently didn't mention their real concern that the police cadre of prosecutors was doing trained lawyers out of business. And when the cadre was disbanded in November, 1986, there were many wags laughing at the assertion of 'high ethical and moral standards' among lawyers.

But I digress.

In early July, 1972, as a one-pip (or star) probationary inspector of police, working in uniform branch in Kwun Tong police station, Kowloon, I was asked if I would like a posting to court as a prosecutor. I needed no second bidding, a nine-to-five job, away from shift work and a new work experience. Usually it was detective inspectors, who had done their time in the field, so to speak, who were selected as prosecutors but perhaps the bottom of that barrel had been scraped when I was posted to court.

New prosecutors were given a one-day induction course held at detective training school. Andy Quinn, a widely experienced detective chief inspector, was the instructor and there were three lectures, the first from the course instructor, the next from a legal department barrister and the last from a sitting magistrate.

The crown counsel lecturing us explained that, not being qualified lawyers, we were neither expected nor allowed to argue points of law. The magistrate would step in on our behalf if needed. Court procedures were explained in depth. He further put emphasis on being alert to malpractice; the possibility of witnesses having been suborned, a situation that came to light particularly in gang-related crimes. In such instances the prosecutor would be allowed to declare to the court 'hostile witness' and, if granted by the court, to seek an adjournment pending investigation. Otherwise one had to continue, being allowed to cross-examine one's own calumnious witness by putting leading questions. Generally all that did was to discredit him or her and, if one did not have good corroborating evidence, the case was lost. I dealt with a hostile witness on two occasions, losing both cases and referring them back to their case officers.

The other legal chicanery that the sitting magistrate mentioned to us was defendants being advised by solicitors' clerks to claim, in court, that they had been assaulted by police. Indeed, claims of assault were numerous and all the prosecutor could do was to glean as much detail as possible from police witnesses as to their correct and lawful handling of the investigation. The training school instructor told one particular anecdote in this regard.

The story line was that a suspect, under interrogation, had been roughed up; dangled by a strap round his ankles, upside down, from a second floor office window at the back of a police station. The suspect had managed to score marks with his fingernails in the grimy, outside wall, in front of his face. Subsequently, facing a charge in court, the defendant described his treatment at the hands of his police investigators. The court adjourned to test the veracity of that allegation and, on seeing the marks, the allegation was proved. The officer in charge was himself charged.

At the close of the course, the new prosecutors were given their postings. I was transferred to Kwun Tong magistracy, in east Kowloon, which was not a big or particularly busy court.

My first day in court began at 08.00 hrs when I was welcomed by the OC court, the police officer in charge, a chief inspector on his last posting before retirement. Also at the same time the cell block doors were opened for the police vans to disgorge their prisoners into the cells. I was escorted round the offices, meeting the two sitting magistrates first and then, on a quick tour of the building, visiting the cells and the general office. Next I was given a copy of standing orders relating to the management of public disorder in the court, handling the press, dealing with the medical and victualling needs of prisoners, the safety of witnesses, monitoring the coming and going of lawyers and, lastly, where the best places for lunch were in the vicinity, that last *not* being in orders.

One of the two sitting magistrates, John Griffiths, a retired government lawyer who saw service in India before the partition, liked to take lunch with his prosecutor, taking it in turns to pay. Neither party talked shop and John Griffiths had a vast fund of interesting stories to tell. The other magistrate, an Australian named Barnes, preferred his own company, usually sandwiches in his chambers.

I started work in No. 1 court, before John Griffiths, where all the fresh-case pleas were taken in the morning, often spilling over into the afternoon. His opposite number, in No. 2 court, was Inspector Wong Bat-loong, known to one and all as One-bad-lung, an affectionate sobriquet given him by his contemporaries. He prosecuted the cases where 'not guilty' pleas had been taken and for which the giving of evidence could last for a whole day or two, occasionally longer.

The plea court was a scene of organised chaos every morning. Crowds of often ragged and harassed illegal hawkers, who had been charged and given bail to attend court in the morning, jostled in the queue to plead guilty, pay their HK$30 fine and get back to work. There were those in court for minor traffic offences eg operating an illegal taxi service (*pak pai*), street gambling (*chee fa* - a form of lucky-draw), street obstruction by on-street car repair shops, simple (sec. 8) possession of illicit drugs and the more-than-occasional charge of fighting in a public place.

Two of the public housing estates in Kwun Tong, built in the first rush of forced immigration from mainland China in the 1950s, were resided in, predominantly, by natives of Chiu Chau province in south-east China. This ethnic group, noted for its intemperateness, caused more than its fair share of public disturbances. Police were often called to neighbourly rows, frequently escalating to violence, between the occupants of these basic one-room, ill-ventilated flats with insanitary common facilities and all in vastly over-crowded, resettlement blocks.

In the 1960's, through the '80s, opium and then heroin addiction was rife in the numerous squatter hut villages that hugged hill-sides throughout the territory. It was the same in government resettlement estates that were being built to absorb the squatter population, the public toilets on the upper floors being used to purvey heroin and inject it. Every police division had at least one special duty squad whose primary focus was the interdiction of illicit drugs and illegal gambling, mostly targetting squatter areas and the resettlement housing blocks.

Every day there were queues of defendants taking plea in court. Many of these were drug addicts who were impoverished and the worst afflicted, physically and mentally. Impecunious, unable to afford bail, addicts would be held in custody over night and put in the court-house cells pending their case being called. Most would plead guilty to simple possession and the magistrate invariably issued an order for the defendant to attend a drug addiction treatment centre. Occasionally ambulances had to be called by the police to take addicts who were ill to hospital. On one occasion an addict, due to appear in the plea court, quietly passed away in his court cell. I was tasked with taking statements and preparing a coroner's file known as a 'Cor 9' or Coroner's form No. 9.

As each plea case was called by the clerk of the court, the prosecutor stood to read the charge against the defendant. His or her plea was taken and, if 'guilty', the prosecutor read the brief facts, listing the evidence against the defendant. The Magistrate then asked the prosecutor for that person's criminal record, if any. These were sometimes pages long, full of misdemeanours and minor infringements of the law for the most part. Some of the older hands, with criminal records going back to the 1950s, even had canings recorded; four strokes for this or six strokes for that. I learned from one old lag about a caning he had had as a younger man "Weren't you deterred from a life of crime?" I asked. The reply was positive...but only for a year!

As a historical note, caning was struck (no pun intended) from the penalty clauses of Hong Kong statute law in 1968. Hong Kong usually followed UK law closely in such matters and, when the UK abolished corporal and capital punishment in 1965, Hong Kong followed suit. Caning used to take place either in prisons or, more often, in the cell blocks of the courts. When the abolition legislation was passed, caning was described as "a barbaric punishment" in that the convict, wearing only his underwear from the waist down, was bent over a gym horse with hands and feet strapped to the wooden legs. A protective canvas pad was placed over the base of his spine and then a prisons officer would use a 6' long cane to strike the backside with the prescribed number of strokes. Either a police or a prisons' inspector presided over the delivery of the punishment.

When 'One-bad-lung' was posted out of Kwun Tong magistracy I took over as No. 2 court prosecutor, a job that I was not particularly relishing. Magistrate Barnes had a reputation for being unduly hard on the police, stemming from the time, as the story goes, that he was locked up, overnight, in police cells in Tsim Sha Tsui police station. He had been arrested for being drunk and disorderly when he was a young soldier in the Australian armed forces on tour in Hong Kong shortly after the war.

I found, as Barnes' prosecutor, there was no question as to his scrupulous application of the letter of the law. Indeed I learned a lot from him. In one prosecution, where all the facts fulfilling the charge had been elicited from the primary witness, Barnes announced "No case to answer". It was a few seconds before I realised my omission in not having the prisoner in the dock formally identified by the witness. Even though it was blatantly obvious who the witness had been talking about; the man in the dock; he had not been pointed out by the witness to the magistrate.

There were two occasions when Barnes was unnecessarily critical of police witnesses and the outcome of 'Not Guilty' was reached unfairly. In those cases the prosecution papers and the magistrate's comments were referred to legal department, through the officer in charge of the magistracy, for a decision as to appeal or not. One of those was upheld. After a year in Kwun Tong court I was posted to the Police tactical unit (PTU) as a two-pip (confirmed) Inspector.

I completed an eight month tour of duty in the PTU and was then posted back to court as a prosecutor, this time in South Kowloon magistracy, the biggest and grandest court house in Kowloon and the New Territories. There were six sitting magistrates and I became the prosecutor to New Zealander P.G. O'Day, the principal magistrate. His initials always made people laugh. The term 'PG' was that used for 'plead guilty'. The OC court was Chief Inspector Graham Livesy, a florid, genial Englishman with a Geordie accent. Every morning he would hold a pre-court-opening meeting, in his office, with his six prosecutors seated in his office. And every morning the room boy would poke his head round the office door and Graham would drawl "*Senile budgy please.*" When I first heard this I had no idea what he was talking about until the room boy reappeared with a small glass bottle of *Sin-lai* (milk) and the newspaper (*Bo-ji*).

The six court rooms each had their case speciality. There was the 'serious case' court where committal proceedings; the preliminary hearings to test the evidence for cases destined for trial by jury; were held. Committal proceedings were normally prosecuted by legal department lawyers, known as crown counsel, sitting with the case officer concerned. As an aside, crown counsel were nick-named 'clown counsel' from the time that a Chinese officer, speaking less than fluent English, did the proverbial; mixing up his 'r's and his 'l's. There was one court dedicated to traffic cases and another purely for first-plea cases. The other three were for PNG (plead not guilty) cases. O'Day had one of these and I enjoyed some six months in his court prosecuting a wide range of casework, in approximately half of which the defendants were represented by a lawyer.

In one of these cases a lawyer for the defence, a young barrister named Martin Lee Chu-ming, in his initial presentation of the defence case, referred to me as "*My learned friend*", a title normally reserved for professional lawyers. Then he appeared to remember that I was not a lawyer and corrected himself. But then, realising another *faux pax*, smiled at me asking "*Can I still call you my friend?*" By this time the whole court was grinning. After that we got to know each other quite well. Martin Lee went on to become one of Hong Kong's leading barristers; one of the city's most respected legal minds. After 1997, he moved on, achieving fame, or notoriety, depending on whose side you were on, as an influential politician in the democrat camp. In the late '80s, ahead of the 1997 handover from British to Chinese rule, Martin Lee was one of the 23 Hong Kong citizens invited to join the drafting committee for Hong Kong's new constitution; the basic law. However, he was quite outspoken and, at the behest of the Chinese delegation, was expelled from that committee.

In May, '74, the start of the typhoon season, court was in session when the police OC Court quietly entered, approached me and, without a word, slipped a piece of folded paper on top of the case file in front of me, and left the court room. The defence solicitor was on his feet; had been for a while at the time; so I picked it up, opened it and saw the single digit '8' written on it. I waited just long enough for the barrister to take his next breath and then sprang to my feet. "*Your worship, please excuse me for the interruption. Typhoon signal No. 8 has been hoisted. I request that you adjourn this court as soon as possible.*" Magistrate O'Day sat back in his red-leather covered high chair, topped at the back with a small gold crown, put his pen down and, addressing no one in particular, said "*Granted. And I hope there is less wind outside than there has been inside.*" I had to suppress a giggle.

I remember one incident, more serious, that occurred in another court, when a young, recalcitrant man, charged with an offence against the societies ordinance – triad membership or possession of triad writings – had vociferously alleged being beaten up by his police interrogators. The weight of evidence went against him, however, and he was convicted as charged, with the magistrate giving him a severe warning about his dissembling and disrespectful behaviour in court. The youth answered back that someone in his solicitor's office told him to say that. The magistrate asked the defendant's solicitor, who was sitting next to the barrister hired for the defence, if that was true? The solicitor stood and denied all knowledge of it. "*Nevertheless*" said the magistrate, "*it is a serious allegation and should be reported to the Law Society.*"

After just three months I was asked to fill-in for a prosecutor vacancy that had occurred in North Kowloon magistracy. I took over as a traffic court prosecutor. The work was not as varied as the general crime cases that I prosecuted in South Kowloon magistracy but it was still interesting and, at times, complicated. A colleague of mine, the then senior inspector Ian Stenton of traffic branch, gave me a copy of Wilson's Traffic Law which proved a God-send to me, given my ignorance on the subject. And, once again, I found myself sitting before the bench, beside Martin Lee Chu-ming. He had been hired on a permanent retainer to KMB (the Kowloon Motor Bus Company) who were upset with what the company perceived to be heavy-handed police enforcement action being taken against them. Every moving traffic offence in the book, every infringement of the construction and use regulations, was being thrown at their buses and drivers. Quite a few of the cases were indefensible; absolute offences; and Martin would, rather lamely, be reduced to pleading for leniency.

And there was one memorable PNG traffic case, not in my court, in which an elderly, slightly doddery barrister, Mr Leung, was appearing for the defence. The police prosecutor later regaled a group of his colleagues as to how, when it was Leung's turn to present the defence case, he had dozed off; head bowed, gently snoring, in his age-stained, tatty barrister's gown and his equally tatty wig perched slightly askew on his balding head. The magistrate had called politely, "*Mr Leung...?*" Pregnant pause. Then Leung looked up, struggled to his feet, and his baggy trousers fell round his knees. One presumes he'd been inadvertently fiddling with the trouser clasp or neglected to properly fasten it.

My last assignment, before going away on my first vacation leave, was to the Kowloon Coroner's Court in Sham Shui Po district. This was a former residential brick-built bungalow building with Chinese-styled roof tiles. There was only the one court, plus an office, a lawyer's room, a tiny canteen and a large, comfortable waiting room, the whole surrounded by lawns, azalea bushes and aspidistras growing here and there and a white-painted flag pole from which the Union Jack fluttered on high. The type of work was unique, only dealing with cases where deaths had occurred in other than normal circumstances; where either the cause of death was in question or where death had been occasioned through violence or criminal activity, by suicide or by accident.

The Coroner was a barrister fresh out of the UK, magistrate Michael Newell. He was a young, slightly chubby, mussy-haired man with pudgy, baby-faced features. He was highly intelligent; a classics scholar; after which he took a law degree and was then called to the Bar in London. Working as his prosecutor it was my duty to acquaint him with the details of each case; going through the police 'cor 9' (coroner's investigation file) forms with him every morning. In about 60% of the cases there was no legal representation and a court hearing was not required. But in cases that were 'in the public interest', where culpability might have to be decided, there were hearings. These were, for example, where deaths had happened in police or prison custody, in traffic accidents, house fires, drownings in public swimming pools, etc, and lawyers, experts in various fields, forensic scientists and the pathologist were generally in attendance. Newell had a prodigious memory, able to call up facts and figures, details of law and relevant case studies. His comprehension of scientific and medical evidence was good. His ability to sort the wheat from the chaff and martial the evidence did speed up proceedings a great deal.

A case of multiple deaths that came through the Kowloon coroner's court while I was there concerned fatalities occasioned by Typhoon Rose, a natural disaster that hit Hong Kong on 16th June, 1972. In the deluge from the typhoon four major landslips occurred in densely built-up areas of Hong Kong Island and Kowloon. The worst and most tragic of these was in east Kowloon at Sau Mau Ping. A new government housing estate had been built on a hilltop overlooking the district of Kwun Tong and a sprawling squatter-hut area on the hillside. Storm drainage built round the estate channelled flood water down through the hillside to the valley below. Subsequent expert examination revealed that the diameter and strength of the water-escape pipes was not fit for purpose. They had broken under pressure and the water, added to the already sodden ground, caused a mudslip that engulfed the squatter area below and poured across the road into another housing estate. The final death toll among the inhabitants of the squatter huts alone was 71.

As an aside, at the time of Typhoon Rose, I was a patrol sub-unit commander in Kwun Tong district. I was off duty, asleep in my quarter, when the alarm was raised at four in the morning. Every one in the officers' mess turned out for duty, heading just up the road, in heavy rain, to the site of the landslide. Ambulances and fire engines were arriving. Emergency flood lighting was being installed and a police command post had been set up by the sub-divisional inspector, Jock Atkinson, in the back of a police lorry, from where he was organising a police cordon and search-and-rescue parties. I was detailed, together with another inspector, to be an incident recorder. Bodies recovered from the debris were being laid on the roadside pending collection and transport to the mortuary.

The coroner's court hearing into the 71 deaths aforementioned was held two years later. Experts from the government Buildings Ordinance Office, Architectural Services Department and the Hospital Authority (A&E and Pathology) as well as witnesses from the fire services and the police force were present. Family members of the victims were in attendance too, and they had solicitors keeping a watching-brief on proceedings. That would have been with a view to mounting a class action for compensation on behalf of the relatives of victims. As the evidence was unfolding, and photographs were being passed round the participating witnesses in the hearing, the relatives of the deceased became increasingly distraught so women police officers were called in to accompany them. There were some 20 witnesses called to the stand and I was most interested in the fact that the seven or eight witnesses giving evidence of what happened at the scene all differed in detail when under examination by the lawyers. One senior fireman was emphatic in his recollection until he was shown photographs that disproved his point. An example of how fallible the memory can be. The hearing lasted three days after which the jury returned a verdict of unlawful killing and the coroner referred the case to the police and the judiciary for investigation and prosecution respectively.

All of the coroner's cases were particularly sombre by nature but of all my prosecution experiences I found the coroner's court to be the most interesting. Just on two years since joining the police force cadre of prosecutors, a new posting to Triad Society Bureau in CID HQ came up. And when the powers-that-be decided to abolish the police court prosecutor cadre I believed that was a mistake.

- End -

THE TRIADS

A criminal fraternity

In January,1976, I was a newly-made senior inspector and posted to Triad Society Bureau (TSB) in CID Headquarters on Hong Kong Island. I took over an operational investigation team. In charge of the bureau was Detective Chief Superintendent Teddy U. Under him was his deputy, a senior superintendent, then two superintendents, one of whom was in charge of the operations teams. The bureau occupied two whole floors in the CID HQ tower block. My ops team comprised a detective sergeant (D/Sgt) Toby Lau and four detective constables.

History.

As the name of the bureau indicates, its charter was to investigate and prosecute the illegal activities of triad societies and their membership in Hong Kong. In the local Cantonese dialect the popular pseudonym for TSB was *Faan-Haak-Jo*, literally Anti-Darkness-Group. My induction into TSB was a day of meetings and receiving briefings. I was given some essential reading matter on which to bone-up, principally a book titled 'Triad Societies in Hong Kong' by Police Sub-Inspector W.P. Morgan. Picking up this book, I was suitably impressed and intrigued to read an acknowledgement in the book's fly-leaf to a paternal uncle of mine, J.C. McDouall, the government's Hon' Secretary for Chinese Affairs in 1960. It states that the early history, part 1 of the book, was "...*largely his work.*" To understand the part played by triads, throughout the history of Hong Kong, it is necessary to recount, here, the salient features of their existence.

The first English settlers quickly established law and order and in 1843, just three years after the raising of the Union Jack over Hong Kong, the first ordinance against unlawful societies was promulgated. And it was the English law draftsman who coined the term 'triad' to describe the ancient symbol used to identify the society's adherents; the Chinese character 'Hung' centred in a triangle. It symbolises the union of heaven, earth and man, hence another pseudonym for the triads; the Heaven and Earth Society. The Chinese character 'Hung' is derived from the regnal name of the first emperor of the Ming dynasty, Hung Wu, who reigned from 1368 to 1397. That same Chinese character is used in the romanised word 'Hung Mun' which is the proper Chinese name for 'Triad Society'.

A Triad society leader in full ceremonial robes.

"A Triad official in ceremonial robes using the secret hand sign of his rank"

The Manchu invasion of China in 1644 supplanted the Ming with the Qing (Ch'ing) dynasty and it is roughly from that time that the formation of the triads began, first among Buddhist and Taoist monks; the educated class; using their temples as bases for recruiting like-minded patriots operating to the mantra of *"overthrow the Qing, restore the Ming"*. A Manchu prince was proclaimed the first emperor of the foreign Manchu Dynasty with the regnal title 'Shun Chih'. The Ming general, Wu San-kuei, withdrawing his army guarding the Great Wall, threw his lot in with the conquering Manchus and served Emperor Shun Chih by implacably hunting down Ming loyalists.

A succession of pretenders; self-styled Ming emperors; attempted to regain the imperial throne, relying on support from influential Buddhist and Taoist monasteries, but to no avail. Vanquished. Thus the patriotic movement was forced underground, forming highly secretive cliques, with identifying signs and passwords, operating mainly from temples up and down the length and breadth of China. They employed guerrilla tactics in their patriotic pursuit. It was in the province of Fukien that the original Shao Lin Temple of triad legend was said to have existed, opposite Formosa (Taiwan), which was noted for its strong Ming sympathies. The subsequent fame of this temple is entirely mythical, based on many imagined stories of daring-do by its monks, all martial arts devotees, and, thereafter, exaggerated by many film stars and their movies, Bruce Lee being just one of them.

Triads have lived and operated in Hong Kong since the first year of the existence of the colony.

Thus it was that Ordinance No. 1 of 1845 "...*for the suppression of the Triad and other secret societies*" came into being. In 1843 there were perhaps a thousand indigenous inhabitants in Hong Kong Island. By 1845 the island was already the main storage centre for the difficult but profitable China trade; tea, porcelain and opium. Military and naval depots had been established and the resident population was 15,000 strong and growing rapidly.

In October 1845 a report appeared in the local newspaper concerning what may have been the first arrest of triad members in the colony. It mentions a police raid '...*upon a secret Association of Triad which had exercised evil influence over the Chinese...a body of Police captured 17 members of the society, who made desperate efforts to get away.*' Such was the threat of triads to social stability that, in January, 1846, the penalty for membership was increased from one to three years imprisonment plus branding on the left cheek and deportation from the colony. Apparently, however, these draconian measures did not have the desired effect. The police force, officered largely by British ex-soldiers and sailors, was inefficient in those days and triads based in Hong Kong were increasing their influence throughout the territory and across a vast swathe of southern China.

Around 1857 the Taiping rebellion, the last great putsch against the Qing in the north of China, was on the back foot, and the monks were fleeing and/or returning to their monastic lives. But the remaining secularised triads, who had grown used to their parasitic lifestyle, discarded their flimsy mantle of respectability. No longer the loyalist, religious and altruistic movement that gave succour to the poor and subjugated Chinese people, working for their emancipation. They adopted their now familiar morally corrupt, parasitic persona and rapacious, criminal activities.

By 1886 the triads had grown so powerful that it is estimated they controlled the entire labour market in Hong Kong and southern China. They had long since split into factions, largely along 'village' or dialect lines; Hakka, Cantonese, Hoklo, Chiu Chau, etc. Two of the earlier triad societies, the San Yee On and the Fuk Yee Hing, were still extant in the 1980s. They had their roots in the Man On Society founded in Hong Kong in 1886 by natives of Chiu Chau, Hoklo and Hakka from the southern provinces of China.

In 1895 the republican party, under Dr. Sun Yat-sen, raised a revolt in the Canton area, spearheaded by triads. The Chinese government quickly and ruthlessly crushed it. Thousands of republicans and triad supporters fled, many into British Hong Kong, including Dr Sun Yat-sen. The colonial authorities, knowing of his triad connections, immediately issued an order of banishment against him and he left, making his way to London. Not being welcome there either, he travelled back east to Japan and, from there, again sought settlement in Hong Kong. J.H. Stewart Lockhart, colonial secretary, answered his application with an emphatic 'No', couched in the following diplomatic terms:-

Colonial Secretary's Office,
Hong Kong.
4th October, 1897.

Sir,

In reply to your letter, undated, I am directed to inform you that this government has no intention of allowing the British Colony of Hong Kong to be used as an asylum for persons engaged in plots and dangerous conspiracies against a friendly neighbouring empire, and that in view of the part taken by you in such transactions, which you euphemistically term in your letter, 'Emancipating your miserable countrymen from the cruel Tartar yoke', you will be arrested if you land in this colony under an order of banishment against you in 1896.

I have &c
Sd. J.H. Stewart Lockhart.
Colonial Secretary

Lockhart appears to have penned this missive in some dudgeon at what he saw as the brazen temerity of Dr. Sun.

Operating from Japan, with forays into South China, Dr. Sun Yat-sen's republican party suffered little from the Hong Kong rebuff and his emissaries actively whipped up support among triads in Hong Kong. This directly resulted in the formation of the first home-grown Hong Kong triad society, the Chung Wo Tong. Its purpose was to co-ordinate support from all local triads. After Sun Yat-sen established the Republic of China in 1911, sweeping away the Qing dynasty, the Chung Wo Tong turned its attention to the local scene and, from it, emerged the Wo group of societies which wielded the most power and influence in the territory well into the 1950s. There were smaller triad groups expanding as well:- the Tung, the Chuen, the Shing, the Yee On and the Luen.

Without a shred of patriotic motivation left, the Wo group were totally self-centered in their pursuit of riches by any means. They exerted corrupt influence at all levels of society, were aggressive in territorial expropriation and ruled with an iron fist. Inevitably splits and internecine warfare erupted. At this point there was a meeting of minds in which spheres of influence were decided amongst the top seven groups in order to prevent their fratricidal demise. By 1912 the resident population of Hong Kong had reached 600,000. Population concentrations were on the water front of the island and in Yaumati, Mong kok and Sham Shui Po in Kowloon. Each had different ethnic characteristics, including dialect, and were under the 'protection' of triad groups with similar ethnicities. W.P. Morgan continues, as paraphrased, below:-

"Each of these groups consisted of a headquarters branch and a number of sub-branches operating in their respective areas. They were far better organised and disciplined than the later societies of the mid '60s onwards when traditional structures and discipline were disintegrating. Group leaders were men of authority who maintained active control of subordinates. This was beneficial to themselves and senior officials, facilitating the collection of revenues from members and their clients.

"Quarrels between sub-branches were referred to the group leaders for arbitration. Major disputes at group level were dealt with at the very top with the result that serious in-fighting was rare prior to 1941. On the one hand, Triad societies operated freely while, on the other, they displayed no outward manifestation of their presence in public. This paradox is explained by their habit of operating under the guise of trade guilds, benevolence associations and sports clubs. These facades gave them an aura of respectability and enabled them to operate from fixed addresses as their offices. This last expedient was later denied them when those cover organisations were outlawed.

"In the '40s the Fuk Yee Hing triad existed as the legally registered society *'Fuk Yee Industrial and Commercial General Association'* with at least 12 branch offices, all above board, for its predominantly native Hoklo membership in all districts of Hong Kong, Kowloon and the islands. This same strategy was used by the other main triad societies. There was a beneficial side to them, for those living in the sphere of their influence, but this gradually disappeared as greed and perfidy resulted in encroachment on each other's territory which, in turn, necessitated increased recruitment and the need for greater bonding through the taking of triad oaths.

"An unfortunate knock-on effect of this mistrust was that bona-fide labour organisations felt threatened and, in turn, began forming their own resistance movements. A typical example of this type of society is the Tung group, originally formed by workers in the government hospitals, clinics, welfare and sanitary sectors of Western District. As they gained traction their protective activities spread to Central and Eastern districts. Workers in sanitation, who were eventually corralled into the Urban Services Department, formed what was, in all but name, a triad society, with their own oaths and secret signs. Another of these was the Luen group of societies which began with metal workers but which rapidly spread through the ranks of blacksmiths, tinsmiths, foundry and dockyard workers, accruing some 20 branches and dominating Eastern and Yaumati districts.

"The war years, '41 to '45, saw a three-way ideological split between the principal triad societies; one camp working against the Japanese aggressors for the Nationalist (Kuo Min Tang or KMT) cause, another camp actively supporting a Japanese invasion of the territory (fifth columnists) and the third camp sitting on the fence, waiting to see which way the dice rolled. The pro-Japanese camp concerned the Hong Kong government the most because its membership was known to have infiltrated nearly every government department, including the military establishment.

"On day one of the Japanese land attack, pro-KMT triads were out on the streets, wearing identifying armbands and summarily dealing with any pro-Japanese supporters they found. And the Japanese were equally well organised having secretly recruited triads, on the promise of wealth and power, in the months preceding their attack. Once the Japanese government was established in Hong Kong, their triad collaborators shared in the open organisation of prostitution, narcotics and gambling. The Japanese occupation forces, however, did not trust the triads and whenever a leader became too rich and/or powerful, there was a culling.

"After the Japanese surrender in 1945 there was an immediate aftermath of triad reprisals, hegemony and wresting control of the burgeoning black market. Personnel of the former British administration, including its law enforcement agencies, had been crippled by wartime death, injury and rife absenteeism. The military maintained physical law and order as best they could, at the same time dealing with re-provisioning, infra-structure repairs and public rehabilitation.

"It was a couple of years before a fully functional civil government was on its feet. In the meantime shortages in the fabric of basic living standards, currency difficulties and medical and health deficiencies created a flourishing illicit market. Looting and violent crime was rife and the triads were engaging in serious crime and all the vices, as well as blackmailing former Japanese collaborators. And the old vice of opium smoking, outlawed in 1946, suddenly gave rise to a lucrative triad-controlled trade in opium and the protection of opium divans.

"As life normalized in the late '40s and early '50s entrenched triad control of the labour market proliferated through the coolie cadre on the docks and public wharves, the growing recent immigrant hawker population, public and commercial transport workers, construction site labourers and even labouring sections within government departments. Policing was inadequate in the aftermath of war; understaffed, poorly trained and ill-equipped. In the docks and jetties of Western district, control of labour units and the lucrative trade in pilfered goods off the ships and in warehouses, was keenly fought over, with blood shed, by the Wo Shing Tong, Wo Yung Yee and Wo Hop To factions of the Wo group of triads.

"Even with assistance from the military the police force was unable to stem the spiralling crime rate in the '50s, exacerbated by an influx of refugees from China after the communist victory over the KMT in 1949, many of whom had triad affiliations. There was no spare time to launch enquiries into triad organisations who were responsible for the inundation of serious crime reports. There were instances when it was in a triad's interests to tip off the police about other triad's illegal activities. Triads allowed themselves to be recruited by police detectives as paid informers and they co-operated with bent [corrupt] police officers controlling the staging of raids on opium divans and illegal gambling establishments.

"Among the '50s flood of Chinese refugees were members of Shanghai's Green and Red Pang Triad Societies with the more numerous Green Pang adroitly establishing themselves in Eastern district where many northerners had flocked to live. They threatened and cheated wealthy fellow refugees, using the money to set up vice establishments, bigger and better than ever seen before, and to supplant the local Hong Kong triads who could not compete or deal with them because of language barriers and different triad-cant. The Green Pang grew in stature and confidence, their gangsters committing spectacular armed robberies while highly skilled pick-pockets roamed the streets.

"The police, equally handicapped by the language barrier, expedited recruitment of native Shanghainese into the force. In 1952 their investigation successes resulted in the arrest and deportation of the leader of the Green Pang, Li Chi-fat. With that came the inexorable decline of the Green Pang and the gradual assimilation of their members into other triad societies, particularly the 14 Association who were based in Canton and who had been part of the flood of post-war refugees."

The introduction to an intelligence brief on the 14K triad by the police Criminal Intelligence Bureau (CIB) dated January, 1979, takes up the story.

"The original nucleus of the secretive 14 Association was Lt. General Kot Siu-wong of the KMT and his followers. He arrived in Hong Kong in '49 and wasted no time in establishing his base. His recruitment activities came to the notice of the authorities who had him arrested and deported. In Canton he continued with his Nationalist campaign and so great were the numbers flocking to his banner that many knew little more about the organisation they had joined save that their headquarters was at No. 14, Po Wah Street.

"Kot Siu-wong's co-conspirator was a Mr. Shum Kwai-cho who settled in a far-flung corner of east Kowloon, Rennie's Mill Village, escaping the attention of the police. By 1952 membership of the 14 Association was estimated at 20,000 across the colony. That same year they instigated a bloody confrontation with the Yuet Tung triad society who controlled the sprawling squatter-hut settlement of Shek Kip Mei, Kowloon. The victorious 14 Association took control of west Kowloon's most lucrative criminal rackets and, advertising their ascendency, changed their name, with the addition of 'K' for carat gold, to the 14K, a fully fledged triad society proscribed by law."

Modern times

We now fast-forward to the 1970s where we still have some triad hierarchical cohesion among the factions of the major players; the Wo Shing Wo and Wo On Lok of the Wo group, the Fuk Yee Hing, 14K and the San Yee On. But, at this time, there were also increasing numbers of gangs simply borrowing triad nomenclature to instil fear in their victims. In 1970 TSB intelligence was able to name 195 illegal societies, more than half operating under the guise of triads. And some were muscling in on the territory of the established triads, causing friction. To this extent triad culture was endemic in all levels of Hong Kong society. There was no genuine patriotic aim or lawful means of making a living among them although some still attempted to legitimise their existence under cover of legally registered associations, societies, sports clubs and business fronts. The TSB were becoming more successful in garnering information from informers, resulting in a bank of detailed knowledge; a whose-who in triad and pseudo-triad circles.

The Bun Festival

One such intelligence gathering foray conducted by the TSB was the annual Pak Tai Festival or, as it is more popularly known, the Bun Festival, held on Cheung Chau Island, a couple of miles south of Hong Kong Island. In May, '76, I took a team, with two other teams led by more experienced, local senior inspectors, to Cheung Chau Island in the early morning. There were already crowds of tourists, local and expatriate, milling around the narrow streets; just two or three feet wide; in the old fishing village. In the square in front of the temple to Pak Tai, the most important deity for the island, three 60' tall towers, built with bamboo scaffolding poles and wrapped round with sheets of paper, had been erected, rocket-shaped. They were covered on the outside with thousands of white buns, each decorated with a red paint spot on top, glued to the paper.

The festival has its origin in the 18th century when the fishing village was ravaged by a deadly pestilence. The villagers prayed to Pak Tai, the deity for calm waters and healthy lives, and the survivors passed down the tradition of parading the image of Pak Tai round the village, warding off evil spirits. Lion dances accompany the procession with much clanging of cymbals and banging of drums. Martial arts groups on the island have, for years, played a major part in these ceremonials and many of the players are known triads. One can always tell the triad lions by their colour, not the usual red and gold but black with white trimming. And such is the spectacle that many senior triad members attend. A few of our detectives operate undercover, using hidden cameras to record and identify these men.

To cut a long story short, we come to the late afternoon climax of the festival. Teams of bare chested, mostly tattooed, swarthy young men, wearing plimsolls, baggy black trousers tucked into socks and red headbands stand opposite each tower. A local dignitary gives the signal and, amid wild shouting and cheers, the teams, ten or twelve strong, dash into the bases of the bun towers, clawing their way up the dark interiors to the top. And just seconds later a fist can be seen, then another, and another, punched through the paper top, bursting out and grabbing the prized buns.

In 1978 disaster struck. The bun tower scramble ended in the toppling of one of the three towers, occasioned by the weight of numbers in it and a weakened structure. It fell across the crowd of spectators and over 100 people were injured, some so seriously that they were airlifted to hospitals on Hong Kong Island. Among them were two uniformed policemen. Fortunately there were no fatalities. Since then only one person has been allowed to be 'in the race' for each tower.

Triad settlement talks

In April, 1978, information of top-level meetings between factions of the 14K was received. Of about 36 such factions five were organising the meetings. The spur for this summit was the opening of the Royal Hong Kong Jockey Club's new Shatin racecourse and the opportunity for illegal bookmaking there. Such a large scale criminal enterprise would require unifying different factions of the 14K with a view to maximising profit and minimising exposure to police enforcement. A secondary aim was to prevent further disintegration of the 14K into a conglomeration of rudderless gangs.

To this end 14K triad officials decided, in October, '78, to form a central committee headed by Mr Kot Chi-hung, son and successor to General Kot Siu-wong. Five faction leaders, alongside Mr Kot and his Treasurer plus three more officials, were duly elected and one of those faction leaders, Mr Leung Chi-sang, a solicitor's clerk by day, offered the premises of his martial arts school in Mong Kok district, Kowloon, as the headquarters. The senior partner of the solicitors' firm registered a new name for it, the Hung Fat gymnasium, incorporating the 'Hung' character as in 'Triad'.

Needless to say, the parcelling out of power by just five of the 36 factions of the 14K proved disagreeable to the majority of side-lined entities who then organised their own summit, electing a committee in direct opposition to the first. And the duplicitous Mr Kot Chi-hung was also *their* elected chairman. Strife ensued and, in the time honoured strategy of *divide and conquer*, the police succeeded in pitting one against the other, thus eliminating triad controlled illegal bookmaking at the new Shatin racecourse.

More settlement talks

Throughout '96 and '97 CID TSB conducted an intelligence-led operation on the Yee On triad and its several factions. It culminated in November '97 in a large scale offensive, mobilizing all six operations teams plus back-up from police emergency (999) units. It is particularly memorable in that it exemplified the public respect and absolute awe in which that branch of CID was generally held.

Intelligence operatives had obtained information of a major 'settlement' meeting of Yee On triad factions, to be disguised as a birthday celebration for one of the officials, and to be held in the nightclub of Tsim Sha Tsui district's infamous Chung King Mansion on Nathan Road. This provided the perfect platform from which the police could conduct a raid. The said building is a 30 storey apartment block built in the late '30s. Over the years tenants had turned it into a maze of small, often illegal businesses, in many cases tampering with and modifying the internal structure and breaching fire regulations. The ground floor was a shopping arcade and the basement was one huge nightclub *cum* ballroom with dozens of exits and entrances. The building still exists but in 2010 it was practically gutted from the inside out and re-built. The basement nightclub disappeared, replaced with a supermarket.

Knowing that there was a possibility of confrontation and violence among the different triad factions in such a large gathering, the decision was made by the hierarchy of TSB to raid the establishment at the start of the 'party', disrupt the proceedings and forestall any violence. A few hours before the event all the teams quietly and unobtrusively entered the building so as to nullify the possibility of detection by lookouts posted outside in the streets when the party began. The estimated attendance was in the region of 360 'guests' seated at 30 round tables. It was decided to mount the raid after the first course of the banquet had been served, with all teams entering the ballroom simultaneously from every entrance/exit. It was then that my experienced D/Sgt, Toby Lau, jumped atop one of the tables, scattering bowls and plates, and silenced everyone with his shouted announcement that '**_Faan Haak Jo_** are here'. Silence. He ordered everyone to squat down on the floor with their hands on their heads; this as the raiding teams quickly spread round the tables ensuring compliance. There was no resistance whatsoever. The police 999 car crews were not needed.

There were quite a few women and children present who were released. Every suspect was searched *in situ* and their identities checked. And while that was in progress many of the suspects surreptitiously discarded incriminating evidence including some weapons, illicit drugs, triad-related documents, name lists and so forth. Everything was collected and seized as exhibits and taken back to CID Headquarters together with 64 arrested persons. Several of those arrested were checked as being wanted by police for other crimes and all were interrogated about their illegal activities. That process lasted through to the early morning. All were arraigned before a magistrate the same day. There were some very tired detectives wending their way home after a busy 36 hours. Subsequent trials resulted in prison sentences for the main players and the dissolution of the power-base of the Yee On triad. Into that vacuum stepped the hegemonic Sun Yee On triad, consolidating their empire in Tsim Sha Tsui, Kowloon.

Triad control in the film industry (1)

In the same year, 1977, the TSB set up an under-cover operation to infiltrate the San Yee On triad society [not affiliated with the Yee On triad] whose influence was rapidly radiating through the Kowloon peninsula.

The San Yee On was formed by Mr. Heung Chin, formerly an officer in the spy section of the KMT and who, in 1949, fled not to Taiwan but to Hong Kong instead. He gathered a number of former KMT personnel around him and took advantage of the comparatively lawless situation that existed in the east of Kowloon at the time. He prospered financially and, by 1960, had four wives and 13 acknowledged children. It was in 1960 that Mr Heung was arrested, convicted of unlawful society offences and deported from Hong Kong. He went to live in Taiwan. The first three of his wives remained in Hong Kong with their children.

Like father, like son, as the saying goes, three of his sons, Messrs Heung Wah-yim, Heung Wah-shing and Heung Wah-keung became leaders in the San Yee On triad. Wah-yim, the eldest, by his father's first wife, inherited his father's 'business interests' and status as head of the San Yee On. Wah-shing, son of the second wife, and Wah-keung, son of the third wife, had no inheritance. Wah-keung, a sickly child who was bullied at school, lived in Kowloon City, with his mother, in straightened circumstances. In 1970 Wah-keung, aged 20, travelled to Taiwan with his older brother Wah-shing, to meet their father and seek financial support from him. Their mission was unsuccessful but, while in Taiwan, Wah-keung landed a job with a film agent, helping him make in-roads into the martial arts film industry recently popularised by actor Bruce Lee.

After Wah-keung returned to Hong Kong he and Wah-shing spent the next five years or so pouring their energies into the film industry, using triad coercion in furtherance of their nefarious activities. In 1973 Bruce Lee died of an accidental overdose of barbiturates at the age of 33 in the bed of a popular and well endowed film actress, Betty Ting-pei. He left a widow with two small children. There was considerable public hostility towards Betty and it was Wah-keung, already friends with her through the film industry, who took her under his wing. In '76 Wah-keung married her but the marriage was short-lived when Betty embraced Buddhism.

Having accumulated funds, Wah-keung turned his hand to being a film director. Simultaneously he and Wah-shing were recruiting the best actors in town to their own stables, 'protecting' them from the clutches of other film companies. His first two movies were box-office flops and his capital was all but wiped out. However, in '78, Wah-keung made a scoop, recruiting the legendary beauty Chan Ming-ying, the most popular model in Taiwan and with a following in Hong Kong. He married her and she helped him stay afloat with her fashion clothing business while he and Wah-shing recouped their losses through crime, building up their triad influence in the San Yee On at the same time. Wah-keung's wife turned actress and their third movie proved a success. He set up his own film company, Wing Shing. In '82 Wah-keung made a second scoop, recruiting the rising star Miss Cheung Man. She went on to marry Wah-shing.

In 1992 Wah-keung tried to poach a famous kung fu actor, Jet Lee, from Golden Harvest films, offering him personal protection and better working conditions in his own film company. Jet Lee's agent handled settlement talks between the two companies and Wah-keung lost out. The very next day, said agent was killed in a drive-by shooting. Jet Lee's brother-in-law took over negotiations which, again, didn't go well. A week later he died in a car crash. Jet Lee fled to Singapore.

The same year one of Hong Kong's most famous pop singers, Anita Mui, insulted a 14K triad boss, Wong Long-wai. Wong very publicly slapped her face. The story goes that Anita then put in a 'phone call to Wah-keung. Within a week Wong Long-wai was the victim of a vicious triad attack; the muscles and sinews of his shoulders and legs severed with a beef knife; carried out by an infamous San Yee On fighter known as The Tiger of Wanchai. In 1993 The Tiger, himself, was the victim of a 14K triad assassination. These incidents are mentioned as being examples of the extreme measures resorted to by triad societies in protecting their interests, animate and inanimate.

Triad control in the film industry (2)

A newspaper article in the Hong Kong Standard, dated 17-JUN-1981, recounts the trial, in Tsuen Wan District Court, in the New Territories, of 17 defendants, all in the film industry and all members of the Sun Yee On triad society. They were charged with and convicted of (1) conspiracy to kidnap a kung-fu film star, Wong Yu. (2) conspiracy to commit criminal intimidation, (3) being office bearers of the San Yee On triad and (4) unlawful assembly; taking part in a triad ceremonial.

The investigation began with the infiltration of three undercover police officers into the San Yee On in November, 1977. On 9th May, '78 they, together with four civilian recruits, were put through an initiation ceremony. Two office bearers of the San Yee On assisted the initiates as their guarantors, one of them taking a leading role in the ceremonial. One of the undercover officers later testified in court that:-

"...he and the new members first knelt down and then Chan Kai [a senior triad office bearer] made them read out some poems. After this Chan patted their shoulders with a knife indicating how traitors to the society would die. Chan then used a pin to prick the middle finger of each of the new members until they were bleeding, then telling them to lick their own fingers clean of blood. Next, Chan produced three 'ghost' papers and wrote Chinese characters on each of them. Placing them on the floor he asked the new members to step on them. Chan explained that these papers represented the three rocks 'Tin', 'Hoi' and 'Pau' and that whenever a person wanted to join the 'Hung Mun' he has to pass those three rocks.

"After treading across the 'ghost' papers the initiates knelt down again while Chan, holding a strip of red paper, moved it around their heads. Putting it down he took a hen's egg, drew some figures on it and placed it on the floor in front of them. He then asked them to all hold onto the handle of the knife, telling them to chop the egg in pieces together. He explained that this demonstrates how traitors are treated.

"Chan picked up a sheet of red paper which had some figures on it. He then proceeded to write the new members' names on the paper, below the figures. Having done so he gave each of them a number to remember, telling them that these are peculiar to the San Yee On. And that marked the end of the ceremony.

As an aside, the ceremony described above is a farcical parody of the original; bearing little resemblance to the theatrical and more meaningful ceremony of the '50s described by W.P. Morgan in his book on triad societies.

The trial evidence continued:-

"On 4th October, '78, two of the undercover policemen were part of an ambush set at a construction site in Tsim Sha Tsui to which 'Tai Huen Chai' [Big Circle Gang from mainland China] members had been lured by false pretences. They didn't show up.

"On June 18th, '79, two of the undercover officers were ordered to a restaurant in Caernarvon Road, Tsim Sha Tsui. Outside they were met by another two members of the San Yee On who went into an adjacent tailor's shop. They were soon followed by three more members, one of whom signalled the undercover officers to follow them in. There the witness recognised Heung Wah-shing with another senior member. Moments later they all processed out and down the road to Mr. Lo Wei's film company.

"On arrival Lo Wei himself opened the door to them. Once inside he, Wah-shing and two other senior members of the San Yee On went into a separate office. Later one of them came out and telephoned a restaurant, asking for Mr Chan Cheung by name. He was not to be found.

"Afterwards the undercover policemen, with two other members, were told to find David Chan Cheung at Finland Court, his home, and tell him to leave Tsim Sha Tsui, with the message that if he was ever seen there again they [the triads] wouldn't be so kind to him.

The four were also instructed that, if they found the actor Wong Yu with David Chan they were to assault him, threatening him not to interfere. One of the four asked a senior member why they had to assault Wong Yu and the reply was that he had invited another Kung Fu actor, Shing Lung, to dinner, telling him not to work for Lo Wei's film co. The four located David Chan but Wong Yu was not there. Under dire threat, David Chan agreed to quit Tsim Sha Tsui.

"Upon reporting back to Lo Wei's film studio, Wah-shing and his entourage, including the two undercover policemen, left for the New World Night Club, situated in a huge hotel, shopping mall and entertainment complex on the Tsim Sha Tsui waterfront. This was Wah-shing's territory. Sometime later a senior member told the four to come with him to the Fu Yiu restaurant where they would find and abduct the actor Wong Yu. This place was also a haunt of Heung Wah-keung and it was Wah-shing who told his team that, if they saw him there, they were to ignore him."

From these accounts it is clear that the principal triad societies were, in reality, large scale, organised crime syndicates, operating right through to the end of the '70s and into the '80s. But it was the fact that all semblance of traditional triad activity had long since been discarded that led, on 15th March, 1978, to a police headquarters policy decision to disband the TSB and integrate its charter with the newly formed Organised Crime and Triad Bureau. I was posted to the Criminal Intelligence Bureau (CIB) thereafter and one of my first assignments was to research and draft the CIB intelligence brief on the 14K Triad. This was published in January, '79; the document I referred to earlier in this piece.

ICAC initiate corruption investigations into the police force.

At the beginning of this chapter Chief Superintendent Teddy U and D/Sgt Toby Lau are mentioned. The latter was a dedicated, hard-working and skilled detective, demonstrating initiative. He was a triad expert, was thorough in his work and reliable. So when he was arrested in early 1978, one of 119 officers taken in one purge by the Independent Commission Against Corruption (ICAC), I, being his immediate senior officer, was surprised.

It turned out that the evidence against him was the name 'KS Lau' in a note book found in the possession of a Yaumati fruit market vendor, dating back several years. Allegedly, it listed bribes to Urban Services Department workers, Customs and Excise staff and policemen. Toby Lau was neither identified in a subsequent ID parade nor fingered in dozens of witness statements obtained by ICAC. He told me of his innocence of the charge.

A few days after the ICAC raids and arrests, a thoroughly demoralised and angry crowd of rank and file members of the police force, about 500 of them, descended on police headquarters, in Wanchai, demanding to see their commissioner, Brian Slevin. He refused to come out and face his officers. Instead he slipped out of a back gate in the PHQ compound [since then known as traitor's gate], going to see HE the Governor. About 300 of the junior police officers, feeling thwarted in their endeavour, made an unplanned march, which could and should have been forestalled by Slevin in person, heading for Government House. Detective inspectors, including myself, were hurriedly detailed to marshal the protestors *en route* as best as we could but, on the way, in passing the ICAC HQ, some forty or fifty of the marchers broke away to attack the offices of ICAC. There was much shouting and one expatriate ICAC officer suffered minor injuries but, otherwise, there was little damage; one broken glass door and the large flower pot that went through it.

As a result of Slevin's meeting with HE the Governor it was agreed in Exco (the government executive council) that there had to be an amnesty for junior police officers and that their comparatively low pay and conditions of service should be revised upwards. Toby Lau, alongside most of the other 118 ICAC arrestees, was eventually released without charge. But a policy decision was made, in view of the public mood, that they would all be ordered to resign; what we now call constructive dismissal. As for Toby Lau I found him a clerical job with a reputable solicitors' firm whose partners I knew well from my days as a court prosecutor. Myself and Toby remain friends to this day.

The traditional Chinese 'bone-setter' practitioner.

The work load as an operational team leader in TSB, and then in CIB, was demanding, long hours, often at week-ends and on public holidays. These demands required physical fitness. I was a bit of an athlete, a member of the Police Athletics Club, and one summer I took part in a series of cross-country orienteering races. In these events two runners teamed up and, equipped with map and compass, ran to a list of map references, collecting a coloured tab at each target hit. During one of these races I suffered the misfortune of breaking a couple of metatarsals in my left foot. Charging down a dusty, scrub-covered slope I trod, full force, on a knot of gnarled root which did immediate and painful damage. Taken to hospital the doctor took an x-ray and then wrapped my leg, up to the knee, in plaster-of-Paris. In mid-summer, hot and humid, this plaster boot was most uncomfortable. A few days later Teddy U, my boss in TSB, noting my discomfort, asked if I would trust Chinese *dit-da* medicine? *"If so"* said he, *"I know just the man to mend your foot without all this western medicine stuff"*, looking disdainfully at my heavy plaster-cast boot.

Chinese d*it-da* medicine practice goes back since time immemorial, principally based on herbal remedies with the addition of many dried bits and pieces of animals, insects and reptiles. In the Northern Sung dynasty (960-1127 AD) the term used for a practitioner's clinic was *jing-gwat-foh* meaning 'bone-setting-office', hence a common pseudonym 'bone-setter' for those early medics.

Dit-da, a Cantonese expression, is the shortened form of *dit-da-seung-foh* meaning, literally, 'falling-down-injury-office', a term descriptive of its purpose.

Having accepted Teddy U's suggestion, the latter took me, in his official car, on a drive into the back streets of Western district on Hong Kong Island, the oldest part of town. The driver parked outside a 60 or 70 year old stone-built, four storey tenement block. The large wooden name board, above the wide-folding and slatted front doors at street level, was painted black with the name of the *dit-da* shop in large gold lettering. Teddy U, evidently well known there, introduced the patient to the 'Master' Chiu Shing-lam, a stocky, muscular Shanghainese in his late 50s, with a full head of black hair, rugged facial features and a kind smile. Teddy U didn't mention anything about his being a triad and I didn't ask, though I surmised that his membership could be taken for granted. I was shown a seat; a carved teak-wood bench well polished by the backsides of many patients; and given a porcelain cup of Chinese black tea.

The *dit-da* clinic comprised a 30-foot square single room on the ground floor. The once cream-painted walls were uniformly stained brown, rising to black at ceiling height, especially above the large, tall and elaborately carved, wooden altar to *Kwan-Dai*, the red faced, stern, military general, armed with a halberd, who lived in the Eastern Han Dynasty (5-220 AD). The old war lord is reveared by policemen and triads alike for his loyalty, forbearance and courage. Incense burns before him all day, hence the smoke blackened ceiling.

There were two alcoves on one side of the room, each with faded green chintz curtains screening the teak-wood divans upon which patients were ministered to. Around the walls were shelf upon shelf of glass bottles, large and small, filled with concoctions. There were black antique wooden chests comprising dozens of small drawers filled with herbs and associated embrocations. On shelves were brass weighing scales, pestle and mortar, etc. Gaps in the wall-shelving sported a few Chinese pennants, testifying to the expertise of Master Chiu, and several dusty, framed, black and white photographs, mostly of martial arts groups all clad in traditional black garb and one or two ancient portrait pictures of the ancestral type. I recognised a younger Chiu Shing-lam occupying pride-of-place in a couple of the sepia photos. He was evidently a prominent martial arts expert in his time. I wasn't surprised as it was common for exponents of the martial arts to apprentice themselves to a 'bone setter' so that, at the end of their sporting days, they had a good, well-paid profession to take themselves into retirement. And in one corner stood the only concession to modernity, a black and white TV.

Waiting some 15 minutes for my turn for attention, while others were being seen to, I remembered watching a middle-aged man limping out of one of the two 'operating theatres', his torso completely bandaged, looking like a live Egyptian mummy.

At last the master pulled up a short wooden stool on which he sat, in front of me, and started cutting away the plaster boot with a heavy pair of tailor's scissors, exposing whitened, damp-looking skin underneath. Taking my injured foot in his lap he kneaded it, feeling the toe bones with his tensile fingers. I was expecting pain but there was none. After a few minutes the master explained, in simple Cantonese, for he had no English, that two bones were broken – a fact that he had not been previously appraised of - and that he proposed a healing regime of a herbal poultice covering the affected area. I would have to return to his clinic everyday for week for the medication to be renewed.

I watched as he prepared the poultice on a table, similar to a tea-poy, next to him. Having spread a sheet of polythene on it, then a single layer of cottonwool material over that, the master opened the lid of a large metal cooking vessel and ladled out a dollop of a steaming grey-green mix of muddy consistency. He wrapped that in the cotton sheeting, picked up the polythene sheet by its corners and folded it round my injured foot. Then came the bandaging to hold it all in place. The whole session lasted about ten minutes.

I dutifully attended his clinic every day, as appointed and, on the last day, Chiu Shing-lam felt around my toes once more, smiled and said that the bones were healing very well but advised no sports just yet. Another week passed and it was time for my first appointment, since the plaster cast had been put on, to see the doctor at the government (western medicine) hospital. He took one look at his patient, as he walked in to his surgery, with no plaster cast on, and said *"I know where you got your cure."*

- End -

THE MV SKYLUCK

A cargo of Vietnamese refugees

The MV Skyluck, a 3,500-ton Panamanian-registered dry-cargo freighter, 'loaded' with 2,651 refugees from Vietnam, stole into Hong Kong's (HK) Victoria Harbour around mid-night on the 7th February, 1979, under cover of darkness, with navigation lights extinguished. But the radar, in the Marine department's harbour control room, did pick it up and they passed a message to Marine Police headquarters. So began a huge undertaking by the HK Government to manage all those war refugees, and to investigate and prosecute the perpetrators of that criminal enterprise.

By way of background, that vessel began life in 1951 in the ship-building yards of Leith, Scotland. It was built for the Union Steam Ship Company of New Zealand (NZ) who named it the Waimate (pronounced Why-matty) after a township in Canterbury, in NZ's south island. It operated around NZ, to and fro' Australia and other ports in SE Asia. In 1972 she was sold to Eastern Shipping Lines of Manila and renamed Eastern Planet. In 1977 she was sold to a Panamanian ships charter company and from them, in December 1978, the ship, now named Skyluck, was chartered by a group of HK businessmen.

The end of the long-running US-Vietnam war came on 30th April, 1975, when Saigon, the capital city of South Vietnam, fell to the communist forces of North Vietnam. This resulted in the rapid exodus of the local ruling classes, the elite of society and business leaders, with President Thieu of South Vietnam leading their flight. Subsequently the Socialist Republic of Vietnam, amalgamating the south with the north, was formed with General Ho Chi-minh as its first president.

For the vast majority of South Vietnamese citizens, however, a long period of uncertainty as to a sustainable, peaceful future, living alongside their northern cousins, began. Initially it was just a trickle of refugees, particularly those with former ties to police, military or other government organisations, setting sail on fishing boats, pleasure vessels and coastal shipping for non-aligned countries. But, by the end of 1976, the new regime began to sanction the former southerners, mostly ethnic Chinese, causing them economic hardship, food shortages, social stigmatization and business repression. A stream of refugees ensued. Then, in 1977, dichotomous strategies, creating political and societal economic zones and setting up forced re-education camps for southerners in northern Vietnam, turned the refugee stream into a flood.

From 1977, through to the mid-90s, an estimated two million people fled Vietnam. And there is evidence, from US and British government sources, that that flight of largely economic refugees, who were dubbed 'capitalist roaders' and 'anti-communist activists' by the new socialist regime, was covertly encouraged and actively assisted. There was big money in it for those involved in the refugee trade. Throughout 1979 the average price that an adult paid for his passage out of Vietnam was 12 taels of 24k gold. Lesser fees, on a sliding scale, were paid for children, the elderly and invalids. One tael weighs 38 grammes or 1.27 troy ounces. In '79 the going rate was US$240 per ounce. Thus 12 taels of 24k gold was worth about US$10,000

It was in that humanitarian crisis that the Skyluck criminal conspiracy was hatched. And it was by no means the only one that ended in HK. From as early as 1978 well over 100 vessels, ranging from coastal trawlers to ocean-going cargo ships, entered HK waters, carrying refugees from Vietnam. In December, '78, the biggest influx of refugees, thus far, arrived in a Taiwan-owned freighter, the MV Huey Fung, which put into HK harbour with a total of 2,700 Vietnamese refugees on board. They were allowed to land on humanitarian grounds and the police Criminal Intelligence Bureau (CIB) investigated the circumstances of this illegal immigration. Three months later in came the MV Skyluck.

At about 02.00 hrs on the morning of 8th February my home 'phone rang, a call from the police regional command and control centre, HK Island, advising me, as the CIB reserve duty officer, of the arrival of the Skyluck. Within an hour I was in the offices of CIB, and other operational team leaders, rubbing the sleep from their eyes, were coming in. By 04.00 hrs, the briefing room was full and 'Operation Skyluck' was underway, all hands on deck so-to-speak. The chief superintendent of CIB, John Clements, officially designated me as the officer in charge of the case (OC case). The Marine police officer who was first on board the Skyluck, Chief Inspector John Turner, described the scene of the captain and his Bosun found tied up on the bridge with five armed refugees standing guard. It had all the appearances of being a staged act. The marine police boarding party secured the bridge and released the 'hostages'. The captain was directed to drop anchor off the western shore of Green Island, at the west end of Victoria Harbour. Marine department moored a huge pontoon to one side of the vessel from which all official activity relating to the MV Skyluck would be conducted.

At 09.00 hrs the same day the government's chief secretary convened an emergency meeting of heads of departments whose charters included law and order and refugee management. In the wake of the Huey Fung refugee ship, the government machinery was now well oiled. Their most urgent decision was what to do with the refugees. It was decided, first, to assess the possibility of turning the ship round and sending it on its way to Taiwan (The captain was Taiwanese) or, failing that, to keep them on board for the time being at a safe anchorage in HK waters. An assessment of the legal and political ramifications, never mind the insistence of all the refugees on board, quickly determined that forcing the vessel out of HK waters to Taiwan was not feasible. That same evening the ship, with its landing pontoon, was moved to an anchorage in the sheltered West Lamma Channel, between Lamma Island and Cheung Chau Island. The refugees were told they were being kept on board for mandatory quarantine purposes.

The first task of the police investigation teams was to establish order on the ship, to separate and question the captain and his crew, identify leaders and influential refugees on board and find any sick, injured or otherwise incapacitated individuals needing medical treatment. That was easier said than done. The refugees were holed up in every nook and cranny on the ship with the majority being herded into the vessel's three main cargo holds.

In the first day police investigators established the numbers of refugees on board, identified the refugee leaders and accompanied two medical teams checking casualties (the sick and etc). Body lice and malnourishment was the scourge of most refugees; for about a month their diet had comprised sugared rice cakes and water. The 13-member crew were taken away to police headquarters on HK Island for investigation. Among the casualties was one ethnic Chinese refugee with a suppurating wound in a leg. In hospital the doctors found and removed an oblong (4 X 6 cm) wedge of 24K gold, about two taels in weight, amateurishly stitched under the skin of the man's right calf muscle.

Meanwhile the HK Marine department were checking on the route recently sailed by the MV Skyluck. They found that the vessel had sailed from Singapore on 12-JAN-1979 with a cargo of plywood filling about 1/3 of the ship's hold capacity. The ship was destined for Taiwan, via Hong Kong but, as was ascertained from the ship's crew, the captain diverted his ship to Vietnam, anchoring off the Mekong Delta for two days, around the 19th to 21st January. And at that anchorage the bosun directed two seamen to change the name of the ship, painted on the bows and at the stern, from Skyluck to Kylu by the simple expedient of blocking out the letters 'S' and 'CK' so as to avoid detection. In subsequent investigations the Government forensic chemists took paint chippings from the name and were able to prove, by the white and black layers of paint on top of each other, this ruse.

Having loaded approximately 3,200 refugees the captain set sail for southern Philippines where, on or around the 24th of January, he lay his ship off the island of Palawan over night. In that time evidence in statements taken by the police from some crew members and several of the refugees revealed that some 600 refugees were voluntarily off-loaded and shipped ashore in small boats. The remainder insisted on being taken to Hong Kong. At the same time witness evidence emerged of a small boarding party coming out from Palawan island to meet the captain. In a later statement made by the captain, and partly corroborated by the radio officer, that boarding party left, carrying gold bullion with them, with the last boat load of refugees. The dog-leg from Vietnam to the Philippines, plus some stormy weather, resulted in a journey time of 27 days from Vietnam to Hong Kong.

Interestingly, concerning the investigation into the earlier refugee ship, the Huey Fung, at least part of those refugee's gold was found on board; 4,000 troy ounces worth in the region of US$1 million at the time. News of that discovery was in all the Hong Kong papers and it is a reasonable assumption that the Skyluck conspirators learned a lesson there, to take their gold bullion off the Skyluck before it reached Hong Kong.

"The MV Skyluck at anchor off Lamma Island "

In those first few days, after the Skyluck had entered HK, flotillas of pleasure boats carrying journalists and inquisitive HK citizens flocked to the scene, taking photos and even shouting questions and greetings from one to another. And when two young men jumped overboard from the Skyluck to board one of the small boats, the police picked them up and then threw a 100m cordon round the ship, enforced by police dories patrolling 24/7.

"The decks crowded with refugees demanding to be landed "

Very soon the refugees, capitalizing on all the press interest in them, painted slogans on the top-sides of the hull and on the white super-structure ranging from '*SOS*' to '*Have a pity on us. Let us land please. We are lonely. Come to see us daily*'.

Three weeks went by and, in CID headquarters, police investigations were going fast apace, statements having been taken from all of the crew; Chinese officers and Indonesian deckhands; and from the putative leaders of the refugees. It was during these sessions that I banned the Indonesians from smoking their obnoxious-smelling brand of cigarettes in the offices of CIB. Complaints were being received from other CID units, based in police headquarters, of the smell being spread through the communal air-conditioning system in the building. Their fag packets were confiscated but I did replace them with packets of western-style cigarettes – out of my own pocket.

By now my team knew the identities of persons behind the conspiracy to smuggle a ship-load of refugees from Vietnam to a safe haven. There were six men involved, three of them Hong Kong businessmen who had financed the whole operation from their company, including the chairman of the board. We knew where the company office was and where the director's homes were in the territory. Those three company directors were out of HK at the time of the Skyluck's arrival in Victoria Harbour, as were two of their three agents. Inquisitive journalists were told that the 'master-minds' had not been identified. But those five were quietly put on the HK Immigration department's highly confidential watch and stop list. Six weeks after the event, when they believed the police had *not* identified them, our suspects were stopped and arrested at the airport, re-entering the territory.

Under interrogation the three ring-leaders said nothing, as advised by their solicitors. And it was the same with their three agents. All six applied for bail but this was refused by the magistrate upon evidence of their involvement and that they had the means to flee the territory and justice. They hadn't bargained on the possibility of being held in custody for months. They were held in separate cells, not given any opportunity to communicate with each other and visits by relatives and lawyers were closely monitored. Thus it was that detectives visiting them every other day were able to befriend them and, bit by bit, glean information from them.

Initially they imparted sanitized versions of events; carefully exonerating themselves of complicity; in their dealings with the new regime of Vietnam. These statements, taken under caution, contained damning evidence of high-level corruption and illicit collusion on the part of Vietnamese police and military authorities with shipping owners and agents in the transportation of refugees. Again and again the detectives, using information garnered from members of the ship's crew and other evidence from the refugees, were able to trip up the key conspirators, resulting in a drip-feed of the truth.

The captain, the 1st mate and the chief engineer made similar statements, also under caution, having been coached by the three shipping agents and, even when faced with evidence to the contrary, stuck doggedly to their story. The youngest officer in the crew was the ship's radio officer, barely out of his teens. I remember him as a slim, bespectacled and soft-spoken individual. During his interrogation and statement-taking it was evident he was not a glib liar and, although he initially held fast to his captain's line-to-take he was soon tripped up when faced with incontrovertible evidence to the contrary. When asked if he would be prepared to be a crown witness, with his personal safety assured, he made the switch to cooperate with us.

Weeks before the Skyluck anchored in Vietnam waters senior officers in the Vietnamese police and military had been in contact with the agents hired by the principal conspirators, making arrangements. Literally thousands of refugees and their families, mostly ethnic Chinese, were being rounded up; some volunteering and others press-ganged; and herded northward to coastal towns. The military and the civilian police provided make-shift accommodation; tents and corrugated iron billets; for the masses.

Those destined for embarkation aboard the Skyluck were holed up in Ben'Tre coastal port. All the volunteers had paid the militia an average of 12 taels of gold per adult for their passage at the start of their journey and the smaller number of the press-ganged had been relieved of their valuables at the same time. We learned from a later statement of the Captain that the likely agreement struck between the organisers was half of the profits, in gold, to the authorities and half to the organisers of the voyage.

Upon the arrival of the Skyluck off Ben' Tre the refugees were readied to be ferried out to the ship on small craft. And before they set off all were searched by the low level marshals and militia for any more money and valuables they might have on them. And the searching was rigorous, every bit of luggage and its contents were taken apart at the seams and some refugees, male and female, were subjected to orifice searching. It was prior to that exercise that our injured refugee, the one with the gold wedge sewn into his leg, underwent his clandestine operation.

In the closing days of May '79 I carried a suitcase full of statements, photographs, registration documents and my own 26-page encapsulation of the case against the perpetrators of the Skyluck refugee incursion into HK to the chambers of Crown Counsel. One senior counsel and a junior were handed the case by the deputy public prosecutor. Throughout the months of June and July more avenues of investigation and searches for pieces of evidence, as directed by the crown prosecutors, were carried out.

By this time the Skyluck's hapless human cargo had been on board for nearly four months and police intelligence suggested that the refugee leadership were planning desperate measures to make landfall. In high level government consultations it was agreed that the Marine department's chief engineer, Bob Vart, would be taken on board by a police escort, under my direction, to surreptitiously disable the engines. Entering the engine room Bob Vart spent about five minutes looking over the huge engines. Then, with spanner and hacksaw, he took out a tiny 12" length of thin copper pipe, the essential fuel injection line, impossible for anyone to replicate on board without sophisticated equipment and without which the engines could not work. Leaving the ship, apparently empty handed, the restless refugees suspected nothing amiss.

"The wreck of the Skyluck on the rocky shore of Lamma Island"

Just a week later, in the heat of summer, the refugees, still incarcerated on board the ship, took matters into their own hands and cut the mooring chains one windy night, allowing the vessel to drift onto the rocky shore where it foundered. An emergency operation, pre-planned by police and Marine department officers, swung into action, safely disembarking everyone on board and re-housing them in a dozen different locations around the territory. The refugees were not held under lock and key. They were allowed some freedom of movement and to travel within the confines of Hong Kong.

The chief engineer of the Skyluck, an ethnic Chinese from Indonesia, struck up a relationship, during the voyage to HK, with a female refugee from Vietnam. They lived together in his cabin and came to shore together. Their prospects of a future together, in marital bliss, must have looked particularly bleak to them; he thinking he was going to prison; so they seized the opportunity for a day trip on a ferry to Lantau Island. On the return trip, in the darkened evening, the two, in a lover's tryst in the open and secluded aft-deck, tied their wrists together with a thin, nylon rope and jumped overboard. Not having returned to camp by the 21.00 hrs curfew their absence was reported. The following afternoon a local HK trawler informed Marine Department that the bodies of a man and a woman had been caught in their nets. The police were notified and, suspecting the worst, I went to the Marine department pier in Western district to inspect the catch. I was able to identify the body of the chief by sight and, in searching their clothing, found their HK refugee temporary registration documents as well.

In early August the government's legal department had finalized their review of the police evidence and advised on charging the three company directors, the three agents and the Captain of the Skyluck with a combination of offences committed under the immigration and the crimes ordinances. On Monday, 3rd September, 1979, the six prisoners were arraigned before Judge Daniels in the district court of Tsuen

Wan. Word of the court appearance had quickly spread among the press and courtroom No. 1 was packed with journalists.

The trial lasted seven weeks. The trail of witnesses for the crown was extensive. The lawyers for the defence were at pains to find fault with each and every one of them, drawing out proceedings. Once, during that time, the judge ordered a day-long adjournment for the court to visit the wreck of the Skyluck, at that time still beached on the shores of Lamma Island. After the morning visit, touring the wreck, lunch was arranged in a seafood restaurant on Lamma Island and some 20 of us; court staff and interpreters, counsel and solicitors on both sides, police case officers and the government ship's surveyor; had a very pleasant afternoon of it, beer and wine flowing, at government expense.

Finally the denouement of the trial approached with counsel for the prosecution and defence presenting their concluding submissions. That was a Friday morning and Judge Daniels adjourned for the weekend, calling on again at 10.00 hrs the following Monday, 22nd of October. His summation of the evidence was unexpectedly short and to the point. Starting with a castigation of the three principal prisoners as being thoroughly "evil" in their machinations, "unscrupulous" as to the execution of their criminal enterprise and "avaricious" in their pursuit of riches, he went on to lambast the agents and the Captain for their complicit roles in the crime. But, turning to the evidence, he had one devastating conclusion to make and that was the lack of proof that the conspiracy, with which they were all charged, had not been proven to have taken place in HK.

The prosecution had evidence, with dates, that the agents and the company directors had all been in Hong Kong, at divers times together, in the six months preceding the Skyluck's entry into HK waters. There was evidence a-plenty of a conspiracy being hatched between the defendants and the Vietnamese authorities but there was *no* incontrovertible evidence to prove that the conspiracy had been hatched in Hong Kong territory. Case dismissed.

How did that judgement sit with me and the rest of my colleagues in CIB? Of course disappointment that justice had not been served by the letter of the law, on a technicality. But also relief that it was over and that the conspirators had all suffered eight months of imprisonment, embarrassment for them and their families at the hands of the press and that they had, almost certainly, not profited from their crimes. Their cohorts will have helped themselves to their ill-gotten gains in their enforced absence.

A few years later, in 1985-6, I had a chance encounter with a man running with the Kowloon Hash House Harriers, a social athlete's club, meeting every Monday evening after work. The two hares had booked a village restaurant, somewhere out in the north Kowloon hills, for the *apres-run* eating and drinking session. I found myself sitting next to a fellow hasher, Bob Higgins *aka* "Wee Hig". He was a fairly tall, stoutly built New Zealander in his 40s, an electrical engineer by trade and employed by the Dairy Farm, a well known HK supermarket chain, responsible for their refrigeration units at their warehouses. In exchanging stories of our respective careers, I happened to mention the MV Skyluck and its origins as the Waimate (I mispronounced it as the Why-mate) belonging to a New Zealand shipping company. Wee Hig looked at me incredulously, asking *"You mean the Waimate?"*. And then he recounted how he had been apprenticed as ship's engineer, some 20 years previously, on board that very same ship. Some coincidence.

In November, 1979, the wreck of the Skyluck was towed to Tseung Kwan O or, in English, Junk Bay, in East Kowloon, where there was a ship-salvage and breaking business. Before they began taking the vessel apart I made one last visit to the ship. Clambering on board with screw driver and pliers to hand, I found the ships cramped radio cabin and prized the ship's clock off the wall. I then made my way up to the officers' mess and prized that ship's clock off the polished wood-panelled wall as well. Two souvenirs of my case investigation that had taken up just about every minute of nine months from February to October, 1979. Both of those clocks are still working and hang side by side on a wall in my home, one showing Hong Kong time and the other GMT.

Another souvenir of the case was my own set of the prosecution papers which I had privately bound as a large and heavy hard-cover book. In 2005, when doing my final packing, leaving my government quarter upon retirement, I decided to donate it to the police force library, a little piece of Hong Kong's history. Much later, in 2018, I re-visited the force library with a view to 'borrowing' my Skyluck case book for research purposes, only to be told that it had been badly flood-damaged and disposed of. The air-conditioning systems room in CID HQ, situated in the basement next to the library books and documents store, had, over time, been leaking, causing extensive flooding, damaging the contents of the lower storage racks. It seems that the then librarian made no attempt to salvage any of it. I then enquired with the Legal department and they replied that they had disposed of their prosecution papers back in 1989, ten years after the event. I was irritated. Such a mishap represents an irretrievable loss of a piece of Hong Kong's history and the facts surrounding it, now supplanted with reports of dubious veracity, as I have lately discovered.

Without the case book all I had was my personal diary which, on consulting it, jogged memories and enabled me to put together some semblance of the case investigation. I also turned to the internet for any nuggets of information I might have forgotten. To my surprise I found quite a few entries about the Skyluck and its Vietnamese refugee cargo. Most of them concentrated on the lives of those refugees, before and after their flight from Vietnam. Comparatively few dealt with the human trafficking element and the voyage of the Skyluck. In reading the latter accounts I was dismayed at the amount of incorrect reporting; contributors positing guesswork as facts and some just making up events. I even found misinformation in a book, published in 2020 and compiled/edited by the Royal Hong Kong Police Association, '***Stories from the Royal Hong Kong Police*** - *fifty accounts from officers of Hong Kong's colonial-era police force*'. A former senior marine police officer, author of the chapter titled 'Huey Fong and Skyluck refugees', included many inaccurate statements about both ships. In his report on the Skyluck the following quote is just one example:-

"A few weeks later, on 28th February[1], 1979, a second large freighter, named *Skyluck*, carrying over 2,400[2] refugees, attempted to enter the Western harbour after darkness…."

"One task remained – where was the gold? We had reliable intelligence that payment in gold intended for the traffickers was to be delivered in Hong Kong[3] or Taiwan. Already gold to the value of HK$1.5 m had been recovered from crew members and refugees[4], and after several hours searching the ship's engine room by a CID team led by Det. Superintendent[5] John Clements and Det. Chief Inspector Lional Lam[6], the extraordinary sight of a gold-encased propeller shaft[7] was revealed! The gold was valued at $5m. Total value of gold recovered, $6.5m[8]. Case closed. Time to celebrate[9]!"

[1] The date of the ship's entry into Hong Kong waters was the 7th of February, not the 28th February.

[2] The refugee count was 2,651.

[3] There was no such intelligence. Statement evidence was later adduced of a likely transfer of gold at Palawan Island, The Philippines.

[4] No gold was recovered from the crew [or taken] from refugees*.

[5] Det. Chief Supt. John Clemence was head of CIB and he did not lead a search team on the ship.

[6] Sen. Supt. Lional Lam was not in CIB and he had no role in this case. However there was a Det. Chief Inspector Gregory Lam in CIB who was involved in this case.

[7] There was no gold-encased propeller shaft. However, also in 1979, there was a much smaller refugee-smuggling vessel, *not* linked with the Skyluck case, that was found to have had some gold sheeting wrapped around its propeller shaft.

[8] Total value of gold found on the Skyluck was 2 taels hidden under the skin of a refugee's leg. And that refugee kept his gold,* It being his property.

[9] A somewhat fatuous statement. The case was *not* closed; it was only just beginning; and gold was certainly *not* the priority outcome of the case investigation. There were no celebrations.

In his defence there were many boat-loads of refugees from Vietnam in 1979 and this marine police officer will have seen most of them. I can't blame him for his confusion.

THE CHATER COLLECTION MYSTERY

An unofficial investigation

"Government House, Hong Kong"

This tale of wonder and mystery, surrounding the life-time legacy of Sir Catchik Paul Chater, a gentleman entrepreneur who lived in Hong Kong in the late 19th and early 20th Century, is succinctly captured in a 'case investigation' conducted by a former Assistant Commissioner of the Royal Hong Kong Police, Angus Stevenson Hamilton, QPM, etc.

As a younger superintendent of police, Angus was seconded as Aide-de-Camp (ADC) to the Governor of Hong Kong, Sir Murray Maclehose, GBE, KCMG,KCVO, between 1978 and 1982. His office was in Government House on Upper Albert Road. Already a seasoned detective when he took up the office of ADC, Angus took a personal interest in rumours, being aired *sotto voce* by government officials, as to the disappearance of a large part of Sir Paul's valuable collection of Chinese art and artefacts during Word War II.

Angus began his enquiries by eliciting the background and known facts relating to the accumulation, housing and eventual disappearance of this fortune in paintings and sketches, engravings and furnishings, porcelain, pottery and jade, all cultural artefacts and antiques worth a fortune. Apparently no official valuation of the full collection was ever completed.

Life of Sir Paul Catchick Chater

Catchick was one of a family of 13 children born in Calcutta to his Armenian parents Mr. Chater and his wife Miriam. Catchick's father was a colonial government servant in British India.

Orphaned at the age of seven, Catchick was taken into care and, exhibiting academic potential, won a scholarship to a Calcutta College. In 1864, as a youth of 18, he moved to Hong Kong to live with the family of his sister Anna and her Armenian husband. He adopted the Christian name Paul.

"Sir Paul Catchik Chater"

Paul Catchick Chater started work as an assistant clerk in the Hong Kong branch of the Bank of Hindustan, China and Japan. A while later, with a grounding in finance and a chance liaison with the well-established Sassoon family, he set up his own business as an exchange broker, the beginnings of an incredible success story. He went on to build a business empire, expanding into the food industry, dockyards and warehousing, land reclamation and building development, *and* setting up the world's first electric power station and urban grid in the Central and Western districts of Hong Kong island. At the age of 50 Paul Chater was one of the wealthiest citizens in the colony, a philanthropist, a grand officer in English Freemasonry and a highly respected citizen of Hong Kong. He was appointed to the Governor's executive council and, in 1902, he was knighted by King Edward VII at Buckingham Palace.

Among his many interests, Sir Paul was a connoisseur of the arts and an antiquarian of distinction. Most of the valuable original paintings that Sir Paul bought were landscape scenes of Southern China trading ports in the 18th and 19th centuries. In 1901 he began the construction of a fine family home at No. 1, Conduit Road, in the mid-levels; half way up the Peak, with a view over Victoria Harbour. He named his grand edifice Marble Hall and it was here that he housed his famous collection.

Sir Paul died in 1926, bequeathing Marble Hall and its contents to Hong Kong. His wife lived on in the house until her own death in 1935 when the property passed into the ownership of the Hong Kong Government. The collection was the subject of a book by author James Orange at which time the collection stood at 430 items, excluding the rare porcelain.

Preserving the collection.

Sir Cecil Clementi, the Governor of Hong Kong in 1935, inspected the property and its magnificent collection, personally directing that the items be disbursed around the Colony for the people of Hong Kong to admire. Recipients included Hong Kong university, the City Hall museum, government secretariat and some of the collection being left in Marble Hall which was renamed Admiralty House, becoming the official residence of Hong Kong's commander-in-chief of the naval and military garrison. More valuable items were displayed in the Governor's residence, Government House (GH), on Upper Albert Road, Central district.

Due to the vagaries of south China weather; the colony's hot and humid summers, typhoons and the winter monsoons; and air-conditioning not being widely available in the early 20th century, many of the more perishable pieces; paintings and silks, books and scrolls, carved wooden furnishings and furniture; required regular maintenance plus varying degrees of restoration work. In 1935 a Hungarian artist by the name of Von Kobza Nagy was contracted to carry out this work, aided by his Chinese assistant, Sinn Chi Lam.

Preparations for the invasion of Hong Kong.

The speed with which the Japanese army swept down through south China in 1941 caught everyone by surprise, not least the Hong Kong government. Scrambling to prepare for the expected invasion, hectic work began on defence lines, gun emplacements, munitions dumps, air-raid shelters in urban areas and store depots for essential supplies, all hastily designed and erected. It turned out to be a case of too little, too late.

These preparations also included the construction of a system of underground tunnels running from GH to Lower Albert Road, opposite the secretariat, a distance of a few hundred meters. An access shaft from the basement of GH was sunk about 15 meters deep, leading to a dual tunnel system comprising a small generator room, a bomb shelter, first-aid area and stores and admin' rooms. There were also two ventilation shafts. It is apparent that, in the dire circumstances of the time, the plans for the tunnels did not take into account the possibility that the foundations of GH, which were already creaking with age, might be further compromised. Simultaneously tunnels branching out from under Flag Staff House, the residence of the Commander of British Forces (CBF) situated in the Victoria Barracks complex, were also being dug less than half a mile away from GH.

When Angus was appointed ADC in 1978, he became responsible to the governor for the efficient administration of the official residence and rendering operational assistance in all official matters relating to Government House. In other words he had the run of the house and grounds. As such he was in a position to access the war-time tunnels beneath GH and carry out some exploration and research of his own. He found them of safe construction; reinforced concrete throughout; clean and dry and uncluttered with debris such as one might have expected after five years of war and a lack of maintenance. Besides Angus, only the government's Public Works department (PWD), responsible for the safety and maintenance of the fabric of GH, were allowed into the tunnels.

One of the first things Angus checked on was the rumour that the tunnels under GH and Flag Staff House were designed as escape routes for the Governor and the CBF in times of emergency. One GH tunnel was said to exit in some hidden spot at the lower end of Ice House Street. Angus found no evidence of this. If it had ever existed it was certainly well blocked up now. What Angus did find were relatively spacious tunnels and rooms, one of which had evidently housed a generator for electricity. Two other rooms, roughly 10' square, may have been used as stores and/or as a bomb shelter.

It was a different story with the tunnels under Flag Staff House. These did not appear to have been much disturbed since they were last used in 1941. In 1979, when Angus first saw them, there was a skeleton of a cat in one corner. Round the walls could be seen some loose telephone lines. In the centre of the room was a large, square pane of glass, supported upright in a wooden frame, with some words, lines and arrows, drawn with wax crayon, still visible on it. It was fairly obvious that these writings related to battle. On one side of the glass was a table, with a tattered map of Hong Kong on it, and a few chairs facing the glass. On the other side was a small table but no chairs. From the layout it appeared that signals staff wrote up information, as it came in by telegraph, on the sheet of glass in mirror (reverse) script, which the chiefs of staff could read from their side of the glass.

Sir Mark Young, GCMG, Governor of Hong Kong from 10-SEP to 25 DEC-1941 and again, after the war, from 01-MAY-1946 until his retirement in 1947.

Sir Mark succeeded Sir Geoffrey Northcote as governor and must have been made aware of the threat of war in the Far East and also the possibility of it engulfing Hong Kong. In consultation with the British War Office, through the then commander-in-chief of British Forces in the colony, Major General Maltby, he set about putting Hong Kong on a war-footing, organising his troops and throwing up such defences as his limited resources allowed. But it was only a few months later that reports of a 50,000 strong Japanese army, massed in Canton, was ready to invade Hong Kong. On 7th December it was Maltby who informed the governor that the enemy were at the border.

Preserving the Chater Collection at the outbreak of hostilities.

As luck would have it a copy of a closed file, dating back to 1945 and belonging to the PWD, was found in the government secretariat in the 1970s. An examination of its enclosures revealed useful information about GH. the former Admiralty House, Flag Staff House, the City Hall and other government buildings in and around Central district. And among its pages, like silver threads gleaming in a black cloth, Angus found clues as to the existence of the Chater collection.

The City Hall had a number of items from the Chater collection on display in the years before the war. From the contents of the PWD file aforementioned an allusion to the secreting of those items in a basement room under Western Market was found. It was also ascertained that the bulk of the Chater porcelain collection, on display in the City Hall, had been moved in boxes to Government Stores in North Point, under the care of Government Supplies Department. *And* it was discovered that a number of paintings, undergoing restoration work in North Point Stores, shortly before the invasion of Hong Kong, were packed into tin cases or trunks and deposited in a government furniture store in Arsenal Street, Wanchai. A record was found that precious paintings and silks displayed in Admiralty House were presumed destroyed, either by enemy bombing or a fire that raged in the house shortly after the enemy occupation had begun.

Apart from the revelations in the PWD file there was information gleaned from memories of former civil servants, tapped into years after the end of the war. According to Mr. John Deakin, the custodian on the staff of GH in 1941, Sir Mark Young directed that steps be taken for the safe-keeping of the GH Chater collection, plus some family silver and other valuables of his own and that of Captain Batty-Smith, his ADC. Angus resorted to the architectural plans of GH, looking for the locations of possible strong rooms or places in the basement that could have been made into secure hiding places. But there was nothing and all furnishings and fittings in store rooms of one sort or another had been dismantled and removed, seemingly long ago.

However, the mystery deepened when it was learned that, just two days prior to the land invasion, Captain Batty-Smith had asked the Hungarian artist, Von Kobza Nagy and a Mr. Harmon of PWD, to arrange for the safe repository of particularly precious items from the Chater collection in the house and grounds of GH.

This came to light in 1943, when the editor of the China Mail newspaper visited the terminally ill Von Kobza Nagy, a friend of his, in hospital and the latter told him of his secret. Nagy knew that the Japanese were about to rebuild part of GH under the expert guidance of a former PWD buildings engineer, an internee of the POW camp at Stanley. The foundations needed to be made safe after the air-raid shelter had been built among them. Nagy continued *"I'm afraid they will find the secret chamber where we hid the best of the Chater collection."* And to another friend of his, an Austrian, he described how the paintings had been taken out of their frames, rolled up, sealed in metal containers and hastily buried in the gardens of GH. There is no corroboration of Nagy's statements as the other two persons, who were privy to the secret, died in the war years.

One of Nagy's assistants was a Mr. Fung Ming who had been made aware by his boss of plans to secure the safe keeping of pictures from the Chater collection. Fung visited Nagy when he was dying in hospital and the latter swore Fung to secrecy about the matter. But all Fung seemed to know was that pictures had been hidden in the tunnels under GH.

The Japanese remodelling of Government House.

His Excellency the Governor, Sir Mark, was obliged to surrender the colony to the victorious invaders on Christmas Day, 1941, just 106 days after his appointment as the governor. Two months after the capitulation Lt. General Resuke Isogai arrived to take over the administration of the territory as its new potentate. Isogai chose not to live in GH it being traditional Japanese practice to always separate work from home. In any case, he had been advised that the foundations of GH had been compromised, resulting in structural impairment.

But, in the interests of Japanese prestige, it was Isogai who ordered repairs to the foundations and for an architect to create a fusion of Japanese and Western style architecture in the remodelling of GH. A civil engineer from Japan, named Seichi Fujimura, was contracted to lead the project, presumably assisted by the PWD buildings engineer who was, at the time, a POW in Stanley. Whilst the foundations and the state rooms on the ground floor only needed repairs and refurbishment, the upper storeys were dilapidated and partly damaged to the extent of needing to be re-built. Japanese styled fixtures and furnishings, cornicing and roofing were effected and a new and dominant feature, a Shinto tower in traditional form, was built, rising above the rest of the house. Shintoism was and remains the imperial religion of Japan.

The building works were contracted out to a Japanese firm who then sub-contracted work to local construction firms. And one of those was a partnership of Mr Sinn Chi-lam and others; Sinn having been the assistant to Nagy before the war.

Peace and subsequent events.

In August, 1945, when the battle of the Pacific had been fought and won by the allies, Rear Admiral Cecil Harcourt and his fleet sailed into Hong Kong's Victoria Harbour and, on 16th September, 1945, formally accepted the Japanese surrender from Vice Admiral Fujita and Major General Okada. After securing the territory the British navy's next task was to release the POWs from the camps in Kowloon and on the Island. Among their number were Messrs Gimson, the former colonial secretary, and John Deakin, the former custodian of GH. Gimson ordered Deakin to make GH habitable for Admiral Harcourt and his staff to occupy.

David MacDougall, who had managed to escape from Hong Kong at the outbreak of war, returned and took over as head of the secretariat with Claude Burgess as his deputy. The latter, having heard various rumours and stories of the missing Chater collection, whilst he was a POW, and having talked to Deakin about it, planned a project to recover it. Burgess had also known Von Kobza Nagy before the war and was convinced that the latter would have tried his very best to preserve the collection for posterity, either by himself or with the cooperation of others.

When Burgess came across the information about part of the collection being buried in the garden of GH he informed David MacDougall who convinced Admiral Harcourt, the then resident, to allow exploratory digs to be made by PWD staff and the GH gardeners. In the ensuing three months much fruitless digging was done, turning the admiral's flower beds and lawns into what looked like a cratered battle field. An irritated Harcourt summonsed Burgess to his office and told him to call off the search and take his men with him. After Sir Mark Young's resumption of his gubernatorial duties, having recuperated from the privations of a POW camp, the latter, when asked, could shed no further light on the fate of the Chater collection formerly displayed in GH.

After both McDougall and Burgess had retired in 1947 a fresh perspective, in the person of a senior administrative officer, Austin Coates, was brought to bear on the vexed question of what had happened to the Chater collection. He found out from staff who had served in government stores before, during and after the war years that, in Summer, 1942, Japanese soldiers, under the command of senior officers, had loaded all the boxes of porcelain; an inventory of 987 pieces; and taken them down to the naval dockyard by lorry. Coates also located John Deakin, still living in Hong Kong, and found out from him that, when he was refurbishing GH for the use of Admiral Harcourt, he had seen that the underground storerooms had been demolished, with new ones built. That was part and parcel of Seichi Fujimura's work, renewing the foundations of GH. There was no sign of the Chater collection.

The controller of Government Stores, both before and immediately after the enemy occupation was W.J. Anderson. Coates found that it was Anderson who, in 1946, was tasked by MacDougall to investigate and report on the whereabouts of the Chater collection. In his report, which landed on Coates's desk, was information gleaned from former staff at the secretariat and at the university of Hong Kong, telling how Japanese military, in taking possession of works of art and other valuable items, had been advised by them of the antique value of those pieces that belonged to the Chater collection, hoping against hope that their information would secure their survival. A Japanese art expert, Ogura, was tasked to collect those items. He disappeared from Hong Kong before the end of the war. Initially soldiers had been placed on guard duty in those buildings but when they were withdrawn, after the most precious pieces had been taken away, all the rest had been stolen in a looting spree by locals.

Anderson had also interviewed a Mr. J. Braga, of Portuguese descent, from Macau, who stated that his father had been loaned a number of photographs of former Hong Kong governors and that two paintings had recently turned up in a Macanese antique shop. Although they may have been part of the Chater collection they were found to be of little value.

Coates initiated enquiries, through official channels, with the US General Douglas MacArthur, supreme commander of allied forces in Japan. He named three of Lt. General Resuki Isogai's senior staff in Hong Kong, during the war years, and three more officers of the Japanese twenty third Army HQ in the occupation forces. Circumstantial evidence linked all of them to the Chater collection. And at Coates's request, the art expert, Ogura, was traced. Under questioning, he admitted he had an interest in the Chater collection, having read the catalogue put together by James Orange all those years ago. But he denied all knowledge of the collection beyond a few pieces that he had seen hanging on a wall in the HKU library. His statement is at variance with intelligence from three separate sources that he was the principal agent in the disposal of a large part of the art collection. MacArthur's staff got no further with him.

Recent events and research.

GH underwent three major refurbishments between the end of the war and 1980. First, Sir Alexander Grantham, in 1947, had air conditioning installed throughout the main building and, at the same time, had the interior decoration restored to a more western appearance. Second, in 1962, while Sir David Trench was in residence, mostly minor decoration work and up-grading the air-conditioning system was carried out. Third, and latest, the most comprehensive works were undertaken under the governorship of Sir Murray MacLehose. He, his family and all the GH staff were temporarily housed in Flag Staff House. All the roofing woodwork was renewed and some tiles were replaced. The old air-conditioning plant was modernised as were the kitchens and last, but not least, the electrical and plumbing works, throughout, were all renewed. Even the gardens were extensively re-designed and planted. *"And in all that time,"* says Angus, *"the only buried treasure found was an unopened bottle of brandy"*. But it wasn't from want of trying! Angus used the opportunity to tackle the basement, foundations and tunnel systems in both GH and Flag Staff House, having the works contractor at GH drill exploratory holes in four apparently solid granite blocks that were part of the foundations from the beginning. There were four remodelled store rooms in the basement and Angus had those walls tested as potentially hiding treasure behind them. Again negative.

Sometime after the refurbishment had been completed Angus was informed that British Forces HQ had ordered 'bug cleansing' electronic sweeps to be carried out on all officially sensitive areas in GH. A team from the UK Ministry of Defence was tasked with this function. When Angus conferred with the officer in charge of the operation he mentioned his project of locating at least part of the missing Chater collection to him. The 'bug cleansing' did include making structural cavity searches, a procedure that required the approval of the CBF. Angus obtained that through the ADC to Major General Sir Roy Redgrave, CBF. Two days were duly allocated for the team to work in the basement and foundations area of GH but their equipment's limit of penetration in concrete was two feet and so it was, that despite a comprehensive set of cavity searches being executed, a blank was drawn.

Angus is sure that he is the last of a line of treasure seekers since the end of the war, certainly the first *and* last to have made such a thorough and comprehensive search of the house and grounds at GH. His conclusions, partly based on the work of Austin Coates and Claude Burgess, are as follows:-

There is evidence that

- the hierarchy of the Japanese occupation forces were complicit in appropriating the porcelain collection and, most likely other looted items, storing it at the naval dockyards before shipping it out of Hong Kong in 1942, presumably to Japan.

- In the summer of 1942 the dry cargo vessel, MV Lisbon Maru, sailing under the Japanese flag, was chartered to convey 2,000 POWs from Hong Kong to Japan in appalling living conditions. As it passed through the Taiwan straits a US submarine, hunting enemy shipping, sank it with a torpedo. The US Navy had no knowledge of the ship's human cargo. The other cargo it could feasibly have been carrying was at least part of the Chater collection; the porcelain; as there is no evidence that it was ever landed in Japan.

- Less valuable items of the Chater collection did begin to surface after the war, in shops and in sales in Hong Kong and Macau.

- Only one painting found in Japan has been identified as part of the Chater collection. There may be others that have not been identified. Most likely that one painting and others were Ogura's contribution to the thievery.

- Von Kobza Nagy mentioned items being hidden in a secret chamber in GH basement and pieces being buried in the gardens. If that was true then it is highly likely that they were uncovered during Seichi Fujimura's rebuilding of the foundations and upper floors of Government House in 1942-43. A locked door of a basement storeroom would have posed no obstacle to the contractors. Likewise the tunnels under GH certainly would not have escaped the attention of Seichi Fujimura.

- The evidence found in the PWD file, pertaining to GH, is that officials had two to three weeks before the invasion in which to secrete items from thieves. They even had time to make sealed metal tubes for storing painting canvases in. *"And"*, remarks Angus, *"how is it that the governor, Sir Mark Young, resident in GH at the time, apparently had not an inkling of any of these specific plans to save the Chater collection?"*

- Are there any more leads left? Angus mentions a note in the PWD file which seems to imply that some of the more precious items were stored in a purpose-built strongroom or vault, perhaps concealed in an air raid shelter, in the house or grounds of the then Colonial Secretary's home on the Peak. The present chief secretary has an official house, built in the 1920s, on Barker Road, the Peak, too. Is it the same one? No one seems to know if a search has ever been carried out at that house.

- Finally, another little mystery. There is circumstantial evidence that British regimental silver was hurriedly wrapped up in oilskins and buried in a deep hole dug in the grounds of Flag Staff House. In the days before and during the invasion, the Commander of British Forces was still in residence. Angus has had a good look around but not with his spade, mindful, perhaps, of the furore over the digging-up of the governor's lawns in 1947.

Amanuensis: J C S McDouall.

End

"The Colt .38 Police Revolver"

ATROCITY AND DELIVERANCE

Murder

At 01.14 hrs in the morning of 17th March, 2006, in Hong Kong's Tsim Sha Tsui (TST) police division, Kowloon, an off-duty police constable, Tsui Po-ko, attacked two uniformed police constables who were on beat patrol. In the ensuing gun-fight Tsui was shot dead but not before he had killed constable Tsang Kwok-hang and seriously wounded constable Sin Ka-keung, using a stolen and rusty police-issue .38 calibre revolver.

Earlier, at around 23.00 hrs on the 16th instant, constable Sin (pronounced "seen"), at the age of 30 and with 12 years of service in the force, had reported for night duty ('C' shift from mid-night to 08.00 hrs) at TST police station. In the barracks assigned to his patrol unit he changed into his washed and pressed police uniform, buckling on his webbing belt with water bottle, torch and short baton in their respective pouches. He then joined the queue outside the station armoury to sign-out his equipment; a revolver and 12 rounds, a canister of pepper spray, handcuffs and a beat-radio. After that he took a seat in the briefing room with his colleagues. Shortly after 23.30 hrs. his station sergeant called for hush and began the shift briefing. There was nothing particularly special in the briefing. Sin was assigned 33-year-old constable Tsang Kwok-hang as his patrol partner and they were given their beat number.

Tsang, three years older and with three more years of service than Sin, was a newcomer to TST Division. Sin, therefore, was told to plan their beat patrol routing. Once out on the streets, Sin talked Tsang through the locality they were in, pointing out matters of policing interest, the night life going on around them and relating incidents that he had previously encountered.

At around 01.00 hrs. Sin led the way down a fairly well-lit pedestrian underpass near the YMCA. Initially he thought it was deserted until he spotted a man standing against a corner and whose presence there appeared to him to be suspicious. Sin and Tsang decided to stop and question him. As per their training Tsang dropped a couple of paces behind Sin, ready to cover his approach. From just a couple of feet away, Sin asked their suspect to identify himself. In Hong Kong it is law that every citizen must have a government identity card and should carry it when away from home. Sin watched the man put his left hand into the bag hanging from his shoulder, assuming that he was going to fish out his ID card. He watched him grip something and then, in a sudden motion, the man drew a gun and, aiming directly at Sin's face, almost at point-blank range, fired.

The sequence of events from that point on is unclear. There was no CCTV coverage of the pedestrian underpass and Sin is the only living witness as to how the drama unfolded; who fired, when and at whom?

Sin's recollection after that first shot is, understandably, confused, vague. However, a reasonable reconstruction has it that, having shot Sin, the assailant immediately turned his gun on Tsang and fired again, hitting him twice, in the neck and a leg. In that second Sin, sufficiently recovered from the initial shock, managed to grasp the man's gun-hand. An immediate and violent struggle ensued with a shot fired, hitting Sin in his left foot. Sin disengaged, taking out his own revolver as he did so. On seeing this, the assailant tried to wrestle Sin's gun off him and two bullets were fired from it, harmlessly hitting the floor and wall of the underpass. At that moment Tsang, mortally wounded, was able to return fire, shooting their assailant dead with five rounds in quick succession. Sin reached for his beat radio and pressed the alarm button, the last thing he did before losing consciousness.

In the aftermath police emergency crews quickly secured the location, administered first aid and assisted the ambulance men in getting the injured to hospital. Tsang died of his wounds and Sin spent the next 71 days in hospital, undergoing several operations that saved his life. The first bullet had entered his head beside his nose and exited through his right ear causing extensive injuries to his ear, his right eye and his teeth. The nerves were so badly damaged that surgeons thought his face would be permanently paralysed but, in the end, they healed his injured face virtually intact. The wound in his left foot was amenable to remedial surgery, beginning the healing process, but, up to the present time, Sin still feels the pain. Tsang, posthumously, and Sin were both awarded the Hong Kong administration's Gold Award for Bravery in the line of Duty.

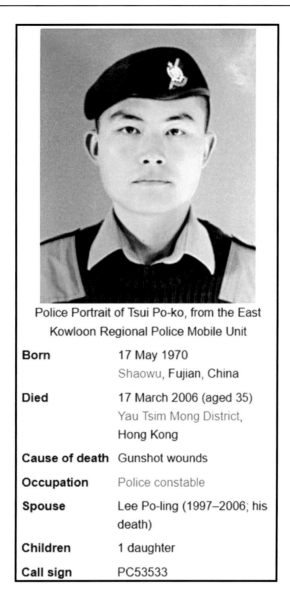

Police Portrait of Tsui Po-ko, from the East
Kowloon Regional Police Mobile Unit

Born	17 May 1970
	Shaowu, Fujian, China
Died	17 March 2006 (aged 35)
	Yau Tsim Mong District,
	Hong Kong
Cause of death	Gunshot wounds
Occupation	Police constable
Spouse	Lee Po-ling (1997–2006; his
	death)
Children	1 daughter
Call sign	PC53533

"TSUI's antecedents"

The newspapers, TV and radio channels were full of the atrocity and as the police investigation, led by the police Organised Crime and Triad Bureau, continued, snippets were released to the press, most significantly, that the assailant, identified as one Tsui Po-ko, was a serving police officer who, off duty at the time, had used a stolen police-issue colt .38 revolver in attacking constables Sin and Tsang.

Three weeks later, on 7th April, a senior police officer was required to appear before the Legislative Council Security Panel. He erroneously stated "*...were constable Tsui Po-ko still alive, there is sufficient evidence to charge him with three fatal shootings*". He was referring to (1) the killing of a constable and the theft of his police revolver on 14-MAR-2001, (2) a bank robbery and the killing of a civilian security guard in January, 2002 and, (3) the shoot-out on 17-MAR-2006. Nothing was said about a possible motive for those violent crimes. Rumours began to circulate as to what might lie behind these killings and other seemingly associated crimes.

Some of these rumours were wild, way off the mark, and there was nothing forthcoming from the police to scotch them. So journalist Niall Fraser did some patient research work and, in a feature article, published in the *Sunday Post* (HK) in February, 2007, linked a chain of events that began on 14-MAR-2001, with the murder of a uniformed constable and the theft of his police revolver, in a pre-meditated ambush, continuing all the way to the shoot-out on 17-MAR-2006. Enmeshed in the story were allegations of bribery and corruption, illegal soccer gambling in police stations and internal police feuding,

In the case of the first murder, when the revolver in question was stolen, a complaint of 'public disturbance' had been made by a man using an untraceable mobile 'phone just after mid-day on 14-MAR-2001, to the police station in Lei Muk Shu division, New Territories. In response, an instruction was passed to 24-year-old, and soon to be married, constable Leung Shing-yan, on beat patrol at the time, to attend at the given address in a nearby housing estate and investigate. On arrival he sent his last radio message at 12.25 hrs that no one was at the given address. Moments later he was ambushed and beaten to the ground. His gun was snatched from him and used by the culprit to shoot him dead; two bullets to the head and three in his back. Taking his victim's gun and his speed loader with six rounds in it, the assassin disappeared. The police have never adduced anything more than circumstantial evidence that the assassin was Tsui Po-ko; certainly insufficient evidence to prosecute and convict him of murder..

The next time the gun in question surfaced was in January, 2002, at the scene of a bank robbery in a small branch of the Hang Seng Bank in a housing estate. A hooded, lone criminal, brandishing the revolver, forced his way into the teller's space and pocketed HK$500,000.00 in cash. As he was making his get-away the security guard, Mr. Zafar Iqbal Khan, blocked his way whereupon the robber shot him dead in his tracks, jumped over the body and disappeared on foot. From the forensic examination of the spent bullets it was proved that they were fired from the aforementioned stolen police revolver. But again the police did not adduce anything more than circumstantial evidence; that it was Tsui Po-ko who pulled the trigger on this occasion. Exhaustive police enquiries turned up no conclusive evidence implicating Tsui in this homicide.

While Tsui was apparently not short of money at the time, it should be noted that, in 2002, the take-home monthly salary of a constable, at entry point, was approximately HK$20,000.00 and, at the top end of the pay scale, HK$30,000.00. This haul of half-a-million bucks amounted to two year's salary.

And then came the third and final shooting on 17-MAR-2006.

By way of background information, from the year 2000 the Police Internal Investigations Bureau were tackling an outbreak of illegal soccer gambling being perpetrated in police stations across Hong Kong. Rumours of bribery and corruption surrounding it were rife. Triad involvement from outside was suspected. In 2005 alone, three police officers died in shootings under questionable circumstances. A fourth committed suicide while facing allegations of bribery. No evidence of police criminality was unearthed with the first three police officers aforementioned. However the rumour-mill kept on churning. A persistent rumour as to the reasons behind the TST shoot-out on 17th March, was that Tsui Po-ko was waiting in the pedestrian underpass, keeping a rendezvous with fellow policemen and/or triad gang members involved in illegal gambling and the handling of indebted police officers.

Six months later, in September 2006, constable Wong Siu-pang was shot in the thigh by a fellow officer during a scuffle. This arose out of an incident where Wong, who had been to hospital for treatment of mental issues, was returning home by taxi. He evaded payment by fleeing on foot but was caught by two patrolling constables with whom he fought. On the face of it, no connection with any other illegality. He was recovering well from his wound when, less than a month later, he died suddenly, while out exercising. The rumours continued unabated.

Nearly a year after the TST shoot-out the formal inquest was held into the deaths of constables Tsang Kwok-hang and Tsui Po-ko. And, as well as those two deaths, the Coroner, Michael Chan Pik-kiu, was asked to adjudicate on events surrounding the two killings of March, 2001, and January, 2002, where the same firearm had been used. 37 days of hearings were held, one of the longest inquests ever and, said Michael Chan, the most complex that he had presided over. Evidence was heard from uniformed police officers attending the scenes of crime, the investigating detectives, the Government pathologist, Dr. Pang Chi-ming, hospital doctors and dozens of experts ranging from firearms technicians to psychologists.

Tsui Po-ko was born in mainland China. In 1978 his parents brought him, aged eight, with his baby brother, to Hong Kong. He was a high-achieving student at school and was accepted into the police force in 1991. In his basic training at police training school in Aberdeen, he came top of his intake and was awarded the coveted silver whistle. No mean feat. He was also a top-scoring marksman and ambidextrous in that skill. In his initial first three years in the force his annual reports depicted a dedicated and diligent policeman. In the 13 years to the date of his death he was always well reported on. The evidence aired about constable Tsui Po-ko's career in the force revealed that, far from being the 'Devil Cop' that the press had branded him as, he was actually a model policeman. So much so that he was featured in the Hong Kong Police news paper 'Off Beat', back in 2000. He was charicatured as the perfect family man; wife and young daughter; an avid sportsman; para-gliding; completing the 100K Oxfam charity Trail-walker and having an interest in the martial arts. He and his wife achieved minor celebrity status when they entered a popular TV knock-out quiz competition for couples and won a HK$60,000.00 prize.

But, contrariwise, police evidence was led that, on 13 occasions, Tsui had not been recommended for promotion on grounds of 'character defect'; a bit stubborn and having inadequate communication skills apparently. A psychiatrist in the witness box, who had never seen Tsui, let alone examined him, opined that such career set-backs could alter a person's mental equilibrium. An unfair insinuation for the ears of the jury in the circumstances.

There were also rumours, cited in the press, of a darker side to his persona; heavy gambling, especially on soccer, and visits to Shenzen, across the border, to karaoke bars, massage parlours and prostitutes. There being no direct evidence available, however, none of this was mentioned at the inquest. But there was circumstantial evidence of something amiss found by police investigators; assets worth HK$2,977,513 disbursed in seven personal and 12 investment accounts in his name but using a friend's contact address and not his own. His wife knew nothing about these. In addition he had purchased a property on Lantao Island costing around HK$2 million and settling the ten year mortgage in less than half that time. These assets were many times over both Tsui's and his social-worker wife's personal emoluments, combined.

At the conclusion of the inquest, after the coroner's summation, the five person jury returned a finding that the deceased, Tsui Po-ko, was responsible for the gun-fight killing on 17-MAR-2006. They also concluded that Tsui was the only and likely suspect in the killing of constable Leung and the theft of his revolver in March, 2001, and the killing of Zafar Iqbal Khan with the same gun in January, 2002. The Jury returned a verdict of the 'lawful killing' of Tsui Po-ko by constable Tsang Kwok-hang.

The very next day the press had a field-day with lawyers complaining that the verdict of the inquest was out of order, the coroner misdirecting the jury. By law, the purpose of a coroner's inquest is to determine when, where and how a person or persons died, and their identities. The one thing an inquest does *not* do is apportion the blame or guilt for deaths. That is the prerogative of the criminal courts alone. However, since police investigations had not found any other suspect, the finding was allowed to stand, alongside Tsui's assumed but untried guilt for the first two murders, as well as his unequivocal guilt for the third.

It was noted, too, that legal aid for a watching brief on behalf of Madam Cheung Wai-mei, Tsui Po-ko's mother, at the inquest hearing, was denied because she was adjudged to be over the threshold of financial entitlement. But the fact is she had no access to her son's wealth and could not afford a lawyer. It was only at the last moment that the legal aid office relented and a solicitor and barrister were briefed, too late to properly prepare.

Meanwhile Sin Ka-Keung continued his recuperation from his gun-shot wounds; on sick leave for 18 months before he was sufficiently recovered to return to duty. But even then there were challenges he had to meet. There were continuing and unwelcome 'phone calls, from journalists and other strangers, to his parent's home where he lived. He needed his own place and received scant help from the powers that be. Eventually a police quarter, adjacent to a police station, was found for him. He needed transport to help him get to regular medical appointments and PHQ readily authorized police transport for his use. For the most part this arrangement worked well but, at busy police station level, it was sometimes grudging.

Back in the station barrack room there was sarcasm. Sin was said to be exaggerating his trauma and there were unkind jokes about his foot injuries; 50% off for a foot massage; and criticism of him not preventing the death of his beat patrol partner. Depression set in. He wasn't sleeping well; plagued by nightmares. He had a few solid friendships amongst his peer group in the Force but others regarded him as being self-centred and attention-seeking. His temper deteriorated and he started drowning his sorrows in alcohol. His police psychologist eventually referred him to a psychiatrist under whose care a diagnosis of post traumatic stress disorder (PTSD) was made for Sin. That was a full two years after the incident. He did not take sick leave but went back to work on indoor duties. However, despondency had set in and he began thinking of resigning until his senior officers counselled him that he was much better off in government service than he would be, on his own, in the private sector.

It seems fairly clear, now, that within a short space of time after the calamitous events of 17th March, 2006, Sin was already suffering from PTSD, a condition first recognised in the late 70s, after the Vietnam War; symptoms being flashbacks, loss of concentration, sleeplessness, high anxiety and aggression.

Modern treatment for PTSD is based on bringing to the surface the fear and shock that was first experienced, either in group therapy sessions or simply through a patient, understanding listener.

In 2008 Sin had an impromptu meeting with the police regional commander (RC) of The New Territories in Hong Kong. The RC, an assistant commissioner of police, lent him a sympathetic ear. This meeting quickly led to a long-term policeman-to-policeman relationship; one of mutual cognizance, without any bias, that had eluded Sin all this time. It was the start of a complete turn around for him, more than all the experts he had consulted over the years had achieved. For the first time he regained a positive outlook on his life, being able to discuss it at length with a senior officer. He was able to rationalize the paranoia that had been stalking his every step. And, having found genuine and lasting concern for his predicament, Sin was even inspired to further his basic education but, first, the symptoms of his PTSD needed treatment. He volunteered to be an in-patient in a psychiatric hospital where his dosage of psychotropic substances could be closely monitored. And part of that cure was Sin's first experience in an asylum public ward, a sobering eye-opener for him.

Sin's *'significant other'*, as he took to calling the senior police officer who had, in reality, become his *alter ego*, was further promoted to the top echelon of the force, yet continued to maintain the trusting relationship between them. In 2012 Sin's alter ego encouraged him to embark on a public speaking programme, sharing his experiences, both within the force training environment and outside, building up his self confidence as he went. But it was a shaky start, his first 'performance' bringing back the still vivid, traumatic experience; forcing him to face his near nemesis again and leaving him emotional. He retreated to his flat, a last-resort comfort zone, and thoughts of suicide. He resorted to the bottle again. In his desperation he telephoned the Samaritan's hotline in the sleepless middle of the night.

Sin's psychiatrist wanted to commit him to the psychiatric hospital on a temporary basis. Initially Sin refused but, after negotiations, he saw the sense of it and acquiesced.

The treatment was successful and a month later he was out again, his alcohol dependency cured as well. But it still wasn't the end of his difficulties. Now the normal vicissitudes of life bedevilled him, one of his brothers getting the family into debt through his irresponsible behaviour. Sin used his savings to clear the debt. In this time he had moral support from his best friend, Simon, who, unbeknownst to him, had terminal cancer and succumbed not long afterwards. Then Sin's father became seriously ill with heart failure. Once again Sin's demons, plus a certain amount of self-pity one suspects, landed him, for the third time, back on the psychiatric ward.

Having regained some mental stability and confidence Sin again got in touch with his *'significant other'* who had recently retired from the Force in 2013. Sin had collected documentation from his first 71 days in hospital and made contemporaneous notes as well. Now Sin's *'significant other'* encouraged him to collate this information and, together with his memories, compile a proper journal. He did so and, in 50,000 words, covered the 71 days in hospital, after his shooting, and his subsequent fight with PTSD. Ming Pao Publishing Co. turned it into a slim book in Chinese with a print-run of 1,500 copies. It was a sell-out in just two months. And then people started getting in touch with him. First a headmaster of a school asking him to give a talk to his sixth-form pupils. Word got around and there were more invitations to talk to this school or that society. The hidden hand of Sin's *alter ego* was at work. Sin's own police force asked him to run sessions on some training courses and in-service promotion/command courses. These were an unqualified success and Sin began to feel that, finally, after a life-changing hiatus of nine years, he was normal again.

And, at last, he decided to take up the challenge of university studies. He joined an undergraduate programme 'Crime investigation' provided by Teeside University, UK, through a tertiary learning institute in Hong Kong. He attended classes and engaged in self-study. He graduated with a 1st class BSc (Hons) and was elected student of the year.

Finally, deliverance.

Sin Ka-keung has been promoted to Sergeant and is still a working police officer at the time of publication.

Compiled by Stuart McDouall in 2021.

All of the names and personal information cited in this chapter have been in the public domain since 2007.

"The heraldic shield of the Hong Kong Police Narcotics Bureau"

17th November, 2021.

DRUG MONEY LAUNDERING

The Hong Kong connection

What is money laundering? The term 'money laundering' is derived from Al Capone's (1899-1947) practice of 'washing' his ill-gotten gains by dividing the cash up through a chain of laundromats that he owned in Chicago, USA, thus distancing the money from crime and, incidentally, reducing his tax bill. The theory of money laundering is simple. Placement which leads to layering which leads to integration.

Placement occurs when the proceeds of crime are placed into the public financial system via bank accounts, paying off legitimate debts, buying assets such as property and even casino chips. *Layering* happens when dirty money is mixed with legitimate funds, moving the proceeds of crime through multiple accounts, in multiple jurisdictions and using multiple banking instruments. *Integration* is the untainted or laundered assets integrated into above-board financial systems, ready for use by the originating criminals.

But the mechanics of money laundering are *not* so simple.

First, a little bit of background. In 1989 leaders at the G-7 summit in Paris agreed, in a ministerial meeting, to set up a Financial Action Task Force (FATF) in order to tackle an alarming, global rise in drug money laundering. The French hosted it in Paris. The FATF defined money laundering as "*...the process of legitimising assets obtained through illegal activity.*" They went on, in 1990, to make 40 recommendations, the first and most important of which was to develop a coordinated international response by enforcement agencies, world-wide, and their legal jurisdictions.

Hong Kong hit the ground running, formulating the first Drug Trafficking (Recovery of Proceeds) Ordinance, Ch. 405, enacted on 01-DEC-1989. Police investigators from the Narcotics Bureau (CID NB) had, in the '70s and '80s, been increasingly successful in interdicting criminals who were trafficking in dangerous drugs on the international stage. But apart from confiscating cash seized as exhibits, alongside quantities of illicit drugs, it had never been possible for Hong Kong's enforcement agencies to go after the *hidden* assets of the convicted traffickers that they had put behind bars.

To give the reader an idea of the sort of money involved, G-7 countries, plus Australia, already had forms of legislation enabling their courts to confiscate the proven proceeds of crime. In 1986 the US Drug Enforcement Agency (DEA) arraigned 12 Colombian drug barons and, under their so-called Ricoh Statutes, they were able to freeze US$482 million in banks in five countries, including Hong Kong. But if you thought that was good, it was peanuts compared with a combined international law enforcement agency case, led by the DEA in '87. In that operation 367 aircraft, 72 boats, 710 vehicles and just short of 1,000 buildings, all purchased with the profits of drug trafficking, were confiscated in seven countries around the world. Not to mention a total of five tons of cocaine and other illicit drugs seized in over 50 raids. But the drugs trade didn't stop there and traffickers, adept at staying one step ahead of the police, using ever more sophisticated means of money laundering, were able to defeat the best efforts of investigators within the constraints of their jurisdiction's laws.

Thus it was, in '88-'89, that a team of government lawyers, led by senior crown counsels Michael Lunn and Bill Boucaut, sat down, with their police counterparts from CID NB; chief staff officer David Hodson and myself, then a detective superintendent; utilizing the experience of law enforcement agencies in Hong Kong and from overseas. They studied the legal successes and failures of major drug trafficking prosecutions with a view to incorporating the salient features in Hong Kong law.

The imperative was to provide the Royal Hong Kong Police with the teeth to investigate money laundering; to hold banks and other financial institutions to account and to enable the courts to freeze the assets of crime pending confiscation. More importantly, to create reciprocal agreements or channels of legal co-operation with foreign jurisdictions whereby external orders for the freezing and confiscation of the assets of crime can be implemented at the behest of another country. This took time but as the number of these agreements with 'designated' countries and states proliferated, so money laundering avenues for the criminals were closing off. And Hong Kong's ground-breaking anti-money laundering laws, the most effective in the world at the time of inception, were spear-heading the war.

Hong Kong has always been a consumer market for dangerous drugs, supplied by the big cartels such as Khun Sa's (1934-2007) Golden Triangle opiate empire (950,000 sq. km in Thailand, Myanmar [Burma] and Laos) and the South American, mainly Colombian, cocaine cartels. There are no such drug lords in Hong Kong; none of the hedonistic life styles of fortress houses, expensive cars, lavish living and high-rolling gambling. At street level, gangs operating under the old triad banner, were heavily involved in drug trafficking. But at the 'wholesale' level of the trade, the principal traffickers were not triads and were smart enough not to draw the attention of police by using them or by flaunting their wealth. But having said that, Hong Kong, with its comparatively low tax regime and international banking status, attracted, and continues to attract, the drug money laundering business, world-wide.

So it was with some fanfare, in legal and enforcement agency circles anyway, that Hong Kong's Drug Trafficking (Recovery of Proceeds) Ordinance came into being. And the new laws were retrospective in effect! At the same time CID NB unveiled its Financial Investigation Group (FIG), which had already been at work in police headquarters since 01-SEP-1989. That team of 30 detectives, specially selected by the commanding officer, myself, who was given *carte blanch* to retain experienced detectives, began their work with a bang, having half-a-dozen investigation files on Hong Kong drug traffickers, already in train. Also some international investigations, in collusion with CID NB, were underway by Australian, Canadian and American enforcement agencies. And, because the legal onus was now on bankers and other financiers to identify and report money laundering activity through their portals, the FIG were conducting very well-attended seminars for those professionals on their compliance with the law.

By year's end, the FIG had 29 investigations open and six of them, local drug traffickers, were up before the courts of Hong Kong, their illegal assets frozen. Roughly 60% of those assets were cash deposits, easily traced, 15% in investments, 10% in ready cash and 5% in vehicles. The remainder, miscellaneous. The largest single asset among them, restrained by court order, was a Chinese sea-food restaurant worth about HK$17 million (HK $32.1 million in 2021 money). In another case a total of HK$161 million (HK$220.3 million in 2021 money) was confiscated in multiple forms of assets.

From 1989 onwards, traffickers in illicit drugs, in Hong Kong and abroad, were on a steep learning curve in the ways and means of hiding their assets, often being advised by legal, financial and accounting professionals who, when questioned, claimed unwitting innocence.

It soon became clear that, in Hong Kong, many small businesses had been set up or purchased by criminals, needing to clean their ill-gotten gains, because their principal revenue was from cash transactions. These businesses included coffee shops and restaurants, newspaper/magazine/tobacco vendors and mobile 'phone outlets. They provided the first layer of legitimizing the proceeds of crime. But as fast as the criminals learned, so did the detectives, adding their experience and knowledge to training materials for the future.

In February, 1990, the NB FIG were in a position to take on the biggest wheel in Hong Kong's drug scene, Chan Kin-man (not his real name) and associates. He lived an unpretentious life with his family in the quieter climes of Hong Kong's New Territories; a village house in Saikung; yet his business connections, investment and property portfolios encompassed the USA, Australia and several Asian cities. The height of his extravagance, locally, was membership of the Clearwater Bay Golf Club and his daughter attending the Horse Riding School at Pokfulam, on the island.

Detective Chief Inspector Kenny Ip was the officer in charge of this case and evidence soon came to light that Chan Kin-man's money laundering activities were exceedingly complicated; extensive and wide-ranging across the spectrum of international finance; requiring professional accounting knowledge to unravel it. Government accountants were called in but could not devote their energies full-time to police investigations.

Cue local accountants Deloitte Ross Tohmatsu (DRS) [now Deloitte Touche Tohmatsu] and their forensic accounting team headed by Jim Wardell; partner and court-accredited expert; and Fred Leung. The latter moved himself and his team into the FIG offices and thus began five months of gruelling paper work, sifting through a global spider's web of intrigue and deception designed to legitimize the ill-gotten gains of the drugs trade through multiple channels and instruments. As caches of drug money were exposed so the figures mounted, reaching spectacular sums; deposits of US$84.3 million plus HK$60 million into just one particular branch of the Bank of Credit & Commerce International Ltd (BCCI) in Hong Kong alone.

On Thursday, 7th December,1989, at Kai Tak airport, Hong Kong, Chan Kin-man was arrested for drug trafficking by the FIG whilst he was waiting to meet his wife and children off a flight from Sydney, Australia. Thus began our biggest drug-money laundering investigation and, subsequently, in the early hours of 19-DEC-1989, a large scale police operation, mounted by the whole of CID NB. It netted most of the other principals in Chak-man's organisation. One of those principals who evaded capture was Sybil Chan Wai-wah, Kin-man's sister. Within hours of her brother's arrest she was implementing an emergency plan to liquidate all banked and invested assets through her contacts in the BCCI and other companies. It is estimated that, within 48 hours she had rescued, from the clutches of the law, HK$50 million, at the very least, and, a day two later, was on her way to a safe haven in the Caribbean Islands. By the time Crown Counsel got their act together, obtaining restraining orders from the High Court 12 days after the arrest, Sybil, with her rescued hoard, had long gone.

Extradition proceedings were immediately mounted in Hong Kong by the USA's DEA, to have Chan Kin-man returned to New York to face a variety of drug trafficking and money laundering charges alongside his associates already arrested in America. Kin-man, realising the weight of evidence against him was overwhelming, entered into plea-bargaining with the DEA. At trial he pled guilty and for his co-operation received a discounted gaol term in the USA of four years. Evidence led by Kin-man against his cohorts included, in 1987 alone, at least 420 units (approx 316.5 kgs) of pure heroin, with a market value of US$24 million, being 'moved' by Kin-man from Thailand to New York. Evidence exhibited in court included a yellow notebook in which Kin-man had hand-written some of his drug trafficking transactions. For example (hand-writing in italics):-

"*Bought 60 units* [of heroin] *at USD60,000- each.* [The total investment cost, including transportation, would have been about US$3.6 million]

"*After mixing* [The purity level of the 60 units when shipped was in the order of 95%. After mixing; diluting with other substances; there was enough to make 70 units at the lower purity of 80%] *consignment of 70 units sold* [to local criminal gangs in New York] *for US$85,000 per unit. Net profit US$2,350.000-* [in a single day].

The three years of Chan Kin-man's proven heroin trafficking activity in America generated vast and unwieldy amounts of cash that needed to be extricated from the US and laundered. To arrange for this he used numerous tactics, such as:-

- employing a New York remittance company 'Piano' to set up the nominee 'Wallon Trading Co' under the control of Kin-man's mother, sister and brother. 'Piano' then funnelled remittances through the BCCI to 'Wallon Trading';

- organising a service for old people queueing up at the HSBC, Hang Seng Bank and China Bank branches in New York's Chinatown who were invited to purchase up to nine gift cheques of US$1,000- each, thus not reaching the STR reporting threshold of US$10,000-. The usual handling charge of 3% was paid to the syndicate and bundles of these cheques were then posted to agents in Hong Kong who deposited them into Kin-man's nominee accounts;

- sending Chak-man (the younger brother of Chan Kin-man) to Singapore to set up a nominee company to receive remittances from New York; and

- again sending his brother to Tokyo, Japan, setting up another nominee company to receive remittances from New York.

A useful brief of the case against Chan Kin-man and associates is provided by Hong Kong's highest Court of Appeal. It presided over the final decisions made in a number of judgements during a 12 month period between January and December, 1996. In the course of these trials, ten High Court judges ruled in separate proceedings against all of the accused.

The following High Court judgements, paraphrased, reveal how the judges rationalized the evidence before them:-

"On 7 November 1996 this court dismissed the applicants' [Chan Kin-man and his brother Chak-man] *appeals against conviction* [for] *assisting another to retain the benefit of drug trafficking...we now* [16 December 1996] *deal with the applications to appeal against sentence. In the* [Supreme] *court below, the judge sentenced each of two applicants to 12 years' imprisonment. In respect of Chak-man* [a 27 years old hairdresser by profession] *the judge also ordered him to pay HK$1 million towards the costs of the prosecution.*

Where the judge referred to this case as the "worst case situation" he was, as counsel submits, clearly focussing upon the activities of the drug trafficker Chan Kin-man, who, in the three years commencing December 1986, laundered a "tidal wave" of drug money through his various nominee accounts; some US$84.3 million plus HK$16 million."

"...but having regard to the history of proceedings and other mitigating factors already referred to, we feel that some discount must be given...applicants (Chak-man and another) are sentenced each to a term of imprisonment of seven years."

Another judgement goes on to mention the part played by Kin-man's brother Chak-man and three more accomplices in the money laundering 'tidal wave' aforementioned.

"Chan Kin-man had scores of accounts with banks and other financial institutions; the majority with the BCCI, all in the names of relatives, friends, associates, nominees, offshore companies and even fictitious names. Many of these accounts were opened with no proof of identity and with false documentation. Many of the accounts with the BCCI were operated only by the application of a chop [Chinese seal]. *As regards the funds in investment companies and in BCCI accounts belonging to three named accomplices of Kin-man, a tracing exercise completed by DRS* [Deloitte Ross Tohmatsu] *accountants*

showed funds in very substantial amounts moving into and out of the scores of accounts controlled by Kin-man in bewilderingly complicated fashion: short term fixed deposits would be rolled over for a few months and then merged with other accounts; cash would come in and go out. When movements of moneys between accounts in different names were made, false documents would be created to show cash withdrawals and cash deposits: to disguise the provenance of the money.

"Chak-man speculated in shares, on his own account, and lost heavily. In October, 1987, at the time of the [global] stock-market crash, he had to be "rescued" by his brother with a loan of US$1 million.

"[In the period 1987 to1989] Chak-man was the nominee shareholder and director of several Chan Kin-man companies. In such capacity he signed many documents, sometimes in front of bankers and solicitors. He also signed account-opening forms, agreements for the operation of nominee accounts, company resolutions, tax returns, etc. In relation to a Chan Chak-man investment company, Valoria, he signed a letter to Banker's Trust nominees which stated "It is co-beneficially owned by me". There was much evidence before the jury to indicate Chak-man's close relationship with Chan Kin-man's financial affairs. In October 1987, Chak-man went with a BCCI group manager to Singapore. This was in relation to another Chan Kin-man nominee company, Bismark, in which Chak-man was a nominal shareholder and legal documents had to be signed in Singapore, in front of solicitors."

"In 1988 Chak-man attended a meeting with [a director of] Banker's Trust concerning shares held in his name. He signed documents at that meeting. In 1989, he attended a lunch meeting organised by the senior director of a Japanese investment company with whom he had opened a margin account for the purpose of trading in foreign exchange transactions. Chan Kin-man was also present at said meeting together with another of his "manager" associates.

The following four judgements relate to parallel cases in the series of Chak-man trials.

"For years yet another "manager" had a desk in a Chan Kin-man controlled company. One of his functions was to input the amounts held on fixed deposits into the office computer. Seized records show that sums in the millions of HK$ were transferred between the BCCI and Kin-man's companies.

"Chan Kin-man's sister, Sybil Chan Wai-wah, played a pivotal role in his affairs. It was she who, within hours of Kin-man's arrest, master-minded the operation to safeguard the drug money, contacting, directly and indirectly, the key managers in the BCCI, having the sums in the various accounts controlled by her siblings, in various branches of said bank, withdrawn and placed out of reach of the Hong Kong authorities. She also instructed the directors of Kin-man's foreign investment companies to liquidate all positions held in Chak-man's accounts and others.

"The inference that Chan Kin-man's [associates] *had grounds to believe that he had carried on drug trafficking was not hard for the jury to draw.*

"By the nature of the activities concerned, direct evidence of Chan Kin-man's drug trafficking in the United States [of America] *would have been virtually impossible to obtain. As it was, there was testimony before the jury* [from one of Kin-man's hired traffickers] *covering part of the year 1987. His first dealings with Kin-man commenced in December 1986 when, on the instructions of his "boss"* [another Hong Kong Chinese drug trafficker] *he personally handed to Kin-man two suitcases with US$300,000 cash in each, in a New York restaurant. There were other occasions in 1987 when large sums in cash were handed over to Kin-man. ...the object of handing over the money to him was for the purpose of "laundering". ...there was evidence before the jury that Kin-man had within his control, at various times...right through to December, 1989, when he was arrested, the proceeds of other people's* [his employed traffickers] *drug trafficking...*

"The prosecution established at trial, through the DRS accountants' pains-taking tracing analysis of the accounting documents seized by the FIG, that "tidal waves" of money did indeed sweep through Chan Kin-man's accounts for three years, commencing December, 1986. The amounts involved were enormous: US$84.3 million [US$1.9 billion in 2021 money] *plus HK$60 million* [HK$78 million in 2021 money]. *Since the direct evidence from one drug trafficker alone showed that Chan Kin-man was drug trafficking on a huge scale, the inference was irresistible that the greater part of the "tidal waves" sweeping through his accounts represented the proceeds of his own drug trafficking: though, somewhere within the huge flow of funds, there would have been the proceeds of the drug trafficking of others. But in the murky world in which Chan Kin-man operated, who precisely were his accomplices, and what were their proceeds, were matters on which no evidence could reasonably have been forthcoming"*

In the Australian courts prosecutors, acting on the evidence adduced in Hong Kong and American courts, seized and secured the confiscation of several properties and other assets belonging to Chan Kin-man, including an entire commercial block in Sydney. We don't have an exact figure but the approximate value of Chan Kin-man's property portfolio in Sydney alone was AU$1.4 billion. All of that has been successfully confiscated.

As of November, 2021, what has happened to the principal players in this case?

After release from Gaol, Chan Kin-man returned to Hong Kong and is presently engaged in business between Shenzen and Hong Kong.

Chak-man had his 12 year sentence in Hong Kong reduced to seven years after taking mitigating circumstances into consideration. He lives in Hong Kong.

Sybil Chan Wai-wah remains at large. Warrants for her arrest remain extant and an Interpol Red Notice (wanted) is still in force against her. It is believed that she is living in the lap of luxury on a remote island in the pacific where there is no extradition treaty with America, Australia or Hong Kong.

The BCCI went into liquidation on 18th November, 1991, after serious irregularities were uncovered by both the police and the banking regulators, as well as a number of its senior personnel being arrested and charged with criminal offences.

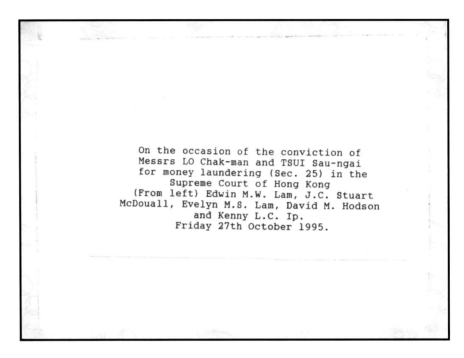

"A celebration. Edwin Lam, Stuart McDouall, Evelyn Lam, David Hodson and Kenny Ip."

Detective Chief Inspector Kenny Ip and Detective Inspector Evelyn Lam received the Governor's commendation, with the right to wear a red lanyard in uniform. Kenny was later promoted to Chief Superintendent of Police and then, upon retirement, headed up security for a major bank. Since then he has been teaching Enhanced Competency Framework in Anti-Money Laundering and Counter-Financing of Terrorism, both professional-level courses with Hong Kong university and the School of Professional and Continuing Education. Of him I wrote in his record of service that, "...if there is such a thing as the *Super Sleuth*, then it is Kenny Ip."

David Hodson retired as asst. commissioner of police, awarded the Queen's Police Medal and went on to work in Hong Kong university as an associate professor in social sciences. Health-wise he's had two near engagements with the hereafter and, as of today's date is, increasingly, in and out of hospital with old age issues.

I was awarded the Colonial Police Medal for Meritorious Service in 1995. Normally there is no citation but one was written by David Hodson 'For leadership and professional ability of a high order in commanding the Financial Investigation Group of the Hong Kong Police Narcotics Bureau between January 1989 and March 1992.' I retired in 2005 as a senior superintendent. Now living in England.

Of the other inspectorate officers in the FIG, from the same era, two were promoted to the giddying heights of commissioner rank. Five more were promoted to senior rank and/or left the police force to work at high levels in the offices of banks and credit card companies.

Michael Lunn, QC, was elevated and became the lead crown prosecutor in all of the high and appeal court hearings in the Chan Chak-man case. Both he and Bill Boucaut are now retired.

Jim Wardell has retired and Fred Leung runs his own accountancy company in Hong Kong.

SHATTERING THE GLASS CEILING

Evelyn LAM Man-sai, QPM, BA, PMSM.

"Evelyn Lam Man-sai in retirement"

This chapter has been amplified from my one-page CV, augmented with lots of anecdotes and a few vignettes into hidden thoughts. Although parts of this chapter will, indeed, read like a CV, lacking the dramaturgy of a novel and the S&V formula that makes for a page-turning thriller, I would ask that you stick with it because my story represents an intriguing window on the comparatively recent history of the emancipation of women at work in Hong Kong.

So I'll start at the end of my career in 2016, when I saw, on the news, Hillary Clinton at the US Democrat convention in Philadelphia, telling a wildly cheering crowd that she was going to shatter the glass ceiling; to be the first female President of the USA; I willed her on, thinking I've been shattering glass ceilings all my working life. Of course, not nearly as high as hers; the presidential-hopeful's ceiling.

In putting together this chapter I am conscious that I'm blowing my own trumpet but those who know me will forgive me. I'm not the shy and retiring type!

My early years. I was born in 1961 in Kowloon, Hong Kong, the last in a family of four children, one boy, three girls. Our 200 sq.ft. flat on the 4th floor of a crowded 1930s tenement block, designed like a concrete bee-hive, comprised a single room with kitchen and toilet partitioned off at the balcony end. There was no garden to play in, just the busy street outside. There was no television, just a plastic radio. In the background the constant buzz of about 400 people, living cheek-by-jowl, in close proximity with us.

I have practically no memory of my father, just a few black and white family photographs to look at, for he left us to work overseas. My mother scraped a living, working long hours every day in a nearby factory, often returning home after our bedtime, when she would wash and iron our school clothes, do some cleaning and hum a folk tune as she worked. I remember there was much fun and laughter in our family. Sometimes Mum would bring home a treat for us, a steaming bowl of beef noodles, and we'd all crowd round the table, chopsticks at the ready! At festival times, Christmas and the Chinese New Year holidays, we'd buy roasted chicken wings; ten cents for one; and think how lucky we were.

We children did our best to help out in the house, keeping the flat tidy, making our beds and doing some of the chores. There were rats and cockroaches in those old buildings and we took this for granted.

We all went to the same school in our locality and made friends with our neighbours. My sisters and I looked for ways to earn some money after school and during the school holidays. When I was eleven years old Mum let me take up full-time jobs in the summer holidays. In the early '70s these were in small, family-run factories soldering wires in radios, gluing hair for wigs, cutting cloth to make jeans, assembling component parts for plastic toys and flowers; all primary industries producing goods bearing the ubiquitous stamp 'Made in Hong Kong'.

The pay was low for such gruelling work; up to ten hours a day; and occasionally there were injuries. For me, I remember dropping a soldering iron in my lap, leaving a burn-scar that I have to this day. I was crying and two of my work-mates each gave me a dollar and took me out for a simple buffet lunch which really meant a lot to me considering their monthly salary was HK$320-. I have never forgotten that kindness and, there and then, resolved to emulate it. All of us were from the same sort of background and I was happy, slowly saving up my precious dollars, enough to buy my schoolbooks and stationery. Although the teaching was free we had to provide our own exercise books and equipment.

I continued working in my school holidays, into my teens, in a wide variety of jobs, which was fun. But, for the first time, I also witnessed harassment and bullying in the work place; the girls employed in factories being treated badly, even molested. Within my limited means I tried to help some of them who had been reduced to tears. These experiences reinforced my altruistic commitment.

I was 16 when I left school. My Mum took me to a festival banquet for people from the Chiu Chau region in China at which every guest was given a lucky number. And my lucky number won the first prize which was a state-of-the-art HK$3,000- colour television set. Given that the monthly salary of a factory worker was HK$400- this was wealth beyond my wildest dreams, and I lost no time in realising the cash value of it, sufficient to enrol myself in a UK college for O- and A-level studies, even paying for the airfare over. I went there in 1978 for two years during which time I paid my way with part-time work for a Chinese restaurateur. My hours were long, from 16.00 to 02.00 hrs, six days a week. My boss was good to me, even allowing me to accompany him after work to his regular casino where he gambled and I ate my fill of free steak and chips.

My academic grades were good enough to get me into Essex University where I embarked on a three-year Bachelor's degree course in policy-making and public administration. I took out a student loan and augmented that with part-time work in Chinese restaurants. In the long summer vacations I flew to New

York, on the cheap 'red-eye' flights, where I made comparatively good money working for jewellery stores on Mott Street. I graduated from university with a 1st class in one subject and an overall 2-1.

Upon graduation I headed back to Hong Kong after an absence of five years and the home-coming was ecstatic, as you may imagine. My mother was was still working in the factory and my older brother and sister had both left home and got married.

Now into adult life. I've never been one for letting the grass grow under my feet and I immediately set about looking for gainful employment, wanting to pay off my student loan as soon as possible. I answered an advertisement for a managerial post with an advertising company and they took me on. It was a 9-to-5 job which left me free to take on some evening work teaching English and banking studies. I lived with my Mum, paying my way. Out of my monthly wage of HK$1,800- I gave my Mum $600.00 and started paying off my student loan at $300- pm. That left me enough for lunches and a cinema ticket.

Looking around me I could see that working for the government *aka* 'the golden rice bowl', as it was known, was better remunerated, with more attractive conditions of service such as housing, than anything I was likely to get in the private sector. Accordingly, I prepared my first *Curriculum Vitae* and began applying for government service. I received positive replies to my first few applications and one of them was from the Royal Hong Kong Police (RHKP). As an inspector, I stood to earn four times as much as my day and evening jobs, combined, were paying.

And so it was, on 10th September, 1984, that I embarked upon my police career.

I began my basic training at police training school in Aberdeen, on Hong Kong Island, as a member of a probationary inspector squad comprising ten men and myself. I was the only one with a university degree. At that time the women police cadre, numerically less than 10% of the RHKP, was not doing all the duties of male officers. We wore police uniforms, had a similar rank structure to our male counterparts and had equal pay, but that is where the similarities ended. Our duties mainly involved handling women and juvenile-related enquiries, dealing with missing-person cases, domestic abuse and assisting in crime investigations where women were involved. We did not carry arms and we had no role to play in anti-riot duties.

I found the basic training tough. In my squad there were men who had been promoted through the ranks to probationary inspector and who already had a lot of policing knowledge and experience under their belts. I struggled with the physical training and the strict discipline and there were times when I thought I can't go on; I'll be one of the few who don't make it through. But I did. I passed my standard I professional exams and, on completion of my basic training, I passed out with a shiny new pip (military star) on each shoulder.

My first posting was to Tai Po police station in Shatin district, starting out in my career in the place where I was eventually to end up although I didn't know that then. In my first year, I was a patrol sub-unit commander in charge of 50 policemen. I had three station sergeants who were my deputies, each highly experienced and who became mentors to me. In my new role I was eager to learn, never shying away from responsibility. While I have many happy memories from that time, there were also some unpleasant duties when I had to supervise at the scene of every dead body found, be it a violent or natural death. In an eight hour shift I usually had at least one such case.

In Summer 1986 I was seconded to divisional CID in Tai Po when a vacancy for a detective inspector (DI) arose in one of the investigation teams. By this time I had passed my standard II exams and was looking forward to my confirmation in the rank of inspector. I was given that vacancy for a DI. Each team worked a shift, rotating through morning, evening and night, taking every crime report that occurred during that duty time. I remember that crime was rife, including a lot of triad activity; intimidation and blackmail, assaults and woundings. My team and I investigated robberies, gang fights and choppings (beef knives, meat choppers and triangular files were the weapons of choice), rapes and murders. The latter two categories of crime were passed on to district crime squads who were better equipped for lengthy and complicated investigations.

A robbery that my team was called out to one morning, in the early hours, was my first big success story as a DI. The criminals had tied up and gagged the watchman of an industrial premises and got away with HK$6 million in electronic goods. When we interviewed the watchman he was able to describe the getaway vehicle *and* recall part of the registration plate number. Armed with that information we spent hours trawling through vehicle records, ending up with a short-list of possibilities which we immediately acted on.

One of the leads I followed was a residential address where a woman told me that her husband, a delivery driver, had gone to work at 2 am that morning. We fabricated a delivery job for him to our local hospital and laid ambush there. Our target walked right into our trap and, in his vehicle, we found part of the loot we were after. Under questioning, the driver admitted his part in the robbery and gave us the identities of his two accomplices. We arrested them in short order and recovered all of the stolen property. For that I was awarded my first commanding officer's commendation. A rarity for a CID rookie and, even more so, for a woman DI.

In 1987, having been awarded early advancement to senior inspector and having passed all my standard III professional exams, I was transferred to Sham Shui Po division, in Kowloon, heading up one of their CID investigation teams. Same duties as in Tai Po but the nature of our work was different in that the local crime scene was heavily influenced by the presence of a sprawling and crowded Vietnamese refugee camp housed in a recently relinquished British army barracks. There were all sorts of crimes being committed in and around that camp and the pool of Vietnamese language interpreters, on contract to the police, were making a good living! It's an ill wind that doesn't blow somebody some good. And then, in early 1988, it was off to six weeks of CID training school for me.

My first real break came later in 1987 when I received a 'phone call, out of the blue, from CID headquarters, Narcotics Bureau (NB), asking if I would like to join the newly created Financial Investigation Group. I could hardly believe my ears, the elite CID NB looking for me! The superintendent, Stuart McDouall, had seen my record of service and marked me as a likely candidate.

We were a small, tightly knit group with one superintendent, two chief inspectors and four investigation teams, each headed by inspectors. Our offices were hived off from police headquarters in a nearby commercial office block and we immediately embarked upon the highly specialised training. It was impressed upon us that we were the professionals, dealing with lawyers and bankers on a daily basis, and must look the part. Suits and ties for the men, smart dress for the ladies.

And it wasn't long before we began our first and biggest investigation, Mr Chan Kin-man (not his real name) was a long term target of CID NB and a major Hong Kong-born drug trafficker on the international scene, with a vast stable of couriers and a global financial network. He, the *de facto* chief executive, was adroit at escaping the clutches of the law and so it was decided to tackle him through his finances. CID HQ employed two forensic accountants to work with us full time on his case.

Alongside that investigation each of our teams were running smaller-scale cases against drug traffickers, chasing their money trails, linking them to the criminals and then prosecuting them under the new drug money-laundering laws. We were spectacularly successful in those early years, catching many of our suspects off guard.

I was fortunate enough to be leading the team, under detective chief inspector Kenny Ip, in the hunt for the assets of Chan Kin-man and his partners in crime. At times it was nerve-wracking work, knowing the possibility of having contracts put out on us with such vast sums of money at stake. Sometimes...no, often, we worked late into the night with our civilian accountants, piecing together the web of money-laundering transactions to complete the evidence against our targets.

And then came the arrests, the charging and the High Court case. Our two principal targets, the master-minds, were sentenced to ten and twelve years apiece and HK$165- million (about US$412.5 million or £41.25 million in 2021 values) in drug trafficking assets was confiscated. Confiscation orders for similarly large assets were executed in Australia and the USA. For that result I was the first woman police officer to receive the Governor of Hong Kong's commendation. *Nota bene*: To this date of publication no single case in Hong Kong has netted so much in the confiscated proceeds of crime.

In amongst my hectic life in the police, often working anti-social hours, I still found time to get married and start a family.

In 1993 my boss, Supt. McDouall, put my name forward, in the periodic selection process, for the post of assistant aide de camp (ADC) to the Governor of Hong Kong, the Hon' Chris Patten. At the final interview, chaired by the Governor himself, I was selected. Another first for a woman police officer. It was a part-time post to be carried out as and when required, in addition to my day-to-day duties elsewhere.

The first week-end after my selection, I was invited to an evening pool-side barbecue at the Governor's residence in Fanling, in the New Territories, hosted by the permanent ADC to the Governor, Supt. Lance Brown. It was a formal dress occasion and I had bought a fine wardrobe especially for it. So you may imagine my chagrin when the ADC unceremoniously picked me up bodily and jumped into the pool, which was the signal for the other twelve Asst. ADCs present to jump in as well; all of us fully clothed. That was my initiation! In the end I held that post for five years during which time I was privileged to receive and escort many dignitaries including royalty and visiting ministers of state.

Also in 1993, I was promoted to Chief Inspector, still in CID NB but, in 1995, I found myself back in operational districts where I was put in charge of a district CID group tasked with serious crime investigations. This was very different work, investigating the full gamut of serious crime. And it was full-on; on call 24/7 and working anti-social hours more often than not. I had three teams under me and took personal charge over the really serious and complicated investigations.

I remember one challenging case where an early-morning dog-walker had reported finding a human leg in the undergrowth. Forensic examination revealed a small leaf, stuck to the leg, which was out of character with the surrounding flora. The pathologist also told us that the murder victim, whom we needed to identify, was a middle-aged lady. Painstaking enquiries into people reported missing came up with an address which, when we searched it, resulted in the discovery of a pot plant of the same variety of the leaf that was found stuck to the amputated leg. So, with the murder scene established, it didn't take us long to identify our suspect who was, at that moment, heading for the border with mainland China. We caught up with him, in a helter-skelter chase, at the Chinese border crossing point and found, in his possession, a quantity of jewellery that he had stolen from his victim. Got'cha! Although he was convicted of murder, the victim's leg was all we were able to find of her.

In 1996, just a year into this job, my asst. district commander for crime, was transferred out and, for want of an immediate replacement for such an important role, I was made acting detective superintendent in his place. I was the first woman police officer in that post.

In 1997, the year of the hand-over of Hong Kong back to China, I was promoted to the gazetted officer rank of superintendent. With my CID background I was posted to the New Territories border district as the asst. district commander for operations and crime. This turned out to be another first for a woman police officer. And it wasn't difficult to see why for the physical challenges in working in that comparatively inhospitable environment could be tough. Investigations sometimes took me into the surrounding thorn-covered hills that were home to mosquitoes, swamp leeches and a variety of reptiles, some venomous.

In my position, I was required to liaise with my police counterparts on the Chinese side of the border especially where cross-border crime such as smuggling and illegal immigration was concerned. I was keen to keep them on side and our meetings usually culminated in a meal; lunch or dinner; when the Chinese wine flowed in toast after toast to our continuing cooperation and friendship. Fortunately, in previous postings, I had learned to hold my liquor in social events and, I like to think, I acquitted myself, and the Hong Kong Police Force, with aplomb.

In 1999, it was time for a move to new pastures and I was given command of a company in the Police Tactical Unit (PTU). This really was a 'wow' moment, another triumph for women police. The PTU is Hong Kong's riot deterrent, its front line of last resort. This bastion of male superiority had rarely seen a woman in its ranks, never mind a commander of comparatively small stature and weaker physique. But I'm pleased to say that my strong character, self-confidence and no-nonsense discipline carried me through with flying colours, voted best company under training! Mind you, I had some jolly good officers working for me and it was a great team effort.

That posting was for a year and we were involved in a few difficult situations where law and order had completely broken down. There was a serious riot in Hei Ling Chau prison, on a populated outlying Island, where the inmates overran the officers and guards. I planned an all-out assault but, fortunately, the rioters saw sense, negotiations succeeded and we were able to stand down without a violent confrontation.

One of the more sensitive issues that we dealt with was a clearance operation against illegal squatters that had got bogged down in threats of violence and suicide if the government didn't back off. I took the initiative, dressed in my full riot gear, and parleyed with their leader, a bad-tempered, ugly man, who I eventually overawed by my femininity, sweet-talking him into submission. He caved in without a murmur, and a tense situation was diffused.

At the turn of the millennium, I was offered the post of staff officer (superintendent) in charge of training for the PTU. I took it and, in doing so, was the first woman officer in *that* role. It was at that time that the PTU was undergoing a wholesale revamp of its tactics and I engaged with some of the world's leading authorities in that arena, discussing strategy, tactics and equipment.

I was transferred away from that post in 2002, at the outset of the severe acute respiratory system (SARS) epidemic. I went to work with the government's health bureau, setting up a command and control centre and linking up the police and other government departments in a coordinated effort to contain and mitigate the epidemic. The government flew me to Atlanta, Georgia, in the USA, to study their tried and proven systems at the centre for disease control and prevention.

Back in Hong Kong, I sat in committee with relevant department heads and was able to draw up what became known as the infectious diseases contingency plan, which included periodic exercises involving some 20 government departments, and which is still in place. It has been utilized in controlling the 2002 avian flu H5N1 viral epidemic and also in the recent covid 19 pandemic of 2020-22, resulting in plaudits from the WHO. A spin-off from that was the upgrading of the Hong Kong police command and control centres.

In 2004 I was promoted to senior superintendent of police and went back to headquarters, this time as deputy head of the Police Operations Bureau. This was just in time for planning the policing of the 2005 World Trade Organisation (WTO) ministerial conference held in Hong Kong for the first time. It was in the middle of a lot of violent anti-globalisation protests happening right across the world. The threat assessment was high and a working group of senior officers was set up to manage it.

I was the only woman officer in that group. My remit was to set up and run the command centre. Obtaining technical support, I was able to link in road traffic cameras, helicopter communications and establish the first e-log recording system for all police and emergency units, including fire and ambulance, over 7,000 links on the ground. During the WTO conference there were violent skirmishes between protestors, both foreign and local, and our anti-riot police. But with technical support and all systems in train, we never lost control of the situation. I received the Commissioner's commendation for that one – the first woman officer to bag both the Governor's *and* the Commissioner's commendations.

After all that excitement it was back to CID NB, my first love in my career, this time as the deputy head. And yes, you've guessed, the first woman officer to hold down that job. By this time, in 2006, the first Financial Investigation Group had morphed into the much bigger, better equipped and, by now, renowned CID Headquarters financial investigation hub for *all* crime, not just drug trafficking. This in conjunction with the newly formed world-wide Financial Action Task Force based in Paris. *And* I was able to renew some of my old contacts in the Chinese police; quite like old times as we planned and executed cross border drug trafficking and smuggling joint investigations. When I was promoted out of that post in 2007, the head of China's drug enforcement force came down from the capital to host a dinner for me, more toasts with Chinese wine, this time leaving me just a little the worse for wear; age catching up on me! Not feeling quite so bright the next morning!

Now a chief superintendent, I had a short spell in Personnel Wing before going back into uniform as the boss of Wanchai police district. Police headquarters was on my patch and I was not only the first woman officer in charge but was also well aware that quite a few former commissioner's of police had been in command of Wanchai district before me. But, deep down, I knew better than to even think about such a possibility for myself; one glass ceiling too far. But, one day, a woman police officer will shatter it, I'm sure.

Wanchai is regarded as being one of the most testing district commands in the force. Hardly a month goes by without a mass march or demonstration, some of world-news importance, taking place. I also had police responsibility for the Hong Kong Convention and Exhibition Centre where national celebrations take place and international commercial events and performances by world famous artists are staged. And where do all these famous people, including heads of state, stay? Some of Hong Kong's best hotels are in Wanchai, also posing challenging security issues.

I was in Wanchai for three years when, in 2010, the Complaints and Internal Investigations Bureau (C&IIB), in police headquarters, needed a new head. When I was asked to take up that office it was a bit of a wrench as C&IIB was definitely not a glamorous or popular posting, lots of contentious issues as you might imagine, and interminable wrangling with the civilian Police Complaints Commission which had oversight of the bureau. I think the gods must have deliberately sought me out in order to see how the first woman chief would tackle *that* command.

Of all the complaints that came across my desk, an odd one sticks out. A woman chief inspector inspector lodged a complaint against a fellow officer for sexually harassing her; biting an ear; on a social occasion. That brought back an old memory of something similar happening to me when I was yet a youngish superintendent. That was at a dinner-dance when a male police officer, who had asked me for a dance, was hugging me, then nipped my ear with his teeth. I remonstrated with him at the time but did nothing further about it well knowing, in those days, that *my* character would be brought into contention if I made such a complaint. Anyway, cutting a long story short, that offender, seven years on, happened to be on my staff as one of the superintendents in charge of complaints for a police region. What a coincidence! I called him in with his senior superintendent and, sure enough, it was the same ear-biter, a 'Me too' moment! Needless to say, after I'd finished with him, his feet hardly touched the ground as he was ushered out of the door. He quit the force soon after.

In 2014, in my last years before reaching retirement age, I was transferred back to my first stomping ground in Shatin Police district. A lot of water had flowed under the bridge in the 30 years between times.

When I joined the force in 1984 Shatin was a sleepy farming village of less than a hundred people surrounded by paddy fields and duck farms. Upon my return in 2014 it had a fast-growing population of over 700,000. Shatin town was a brand new shining metropolis with half-a-dozen high-rise (average 60 storeys tall) housing estates, umpteen schools, a few classy hotels, a business park, shopping malls, a big hospital and lots of green park-land with recreation facilities. And, of course, all the usual law and order issues that go with such a conurbation. And, yes, I was the first woman to take charge there.

My district police station was a modern one and I had some 700 officers under my command, plus all the civilian back-up. Hugely important was our relationship with the townsfolk and I chaired numerous committees and sat on various boards for this and that. Almost of equal importance was all the socialising I had to do; taking up a lot of my weekends. But I like a good party. In addition to those duties I found time to inaugurate a few community initiatives of my own, mainly for youth and under-privileged families.

While I was in Shatin, shortly before my retirement in 2016, I received a surprise; I thought it was a joke at first; when the Federation of Women in Hong Kong, which is a government funded organisation, nominated me for their award of Hong Kong's 'most distinguished woman' which takes place every five years. Normally this goes to famous socialites on the charity scene, or the CEO of a bank. But a little old police officer...was I chuffed? Of course! Headlines in the newspapers, '**First woman police officer crowned**'. On the stage with me were seven female philanthropists, politicians of note and high-flying businesswomen.

My next 'posting' was retirement but, like I said at the beginning of this chapter, I wasn't going to let the grass grow under my feet. Sure enough, a job opportunity came my way, vice-president for global security of a major credit card company. And that is where I am now. It's no sinecure I can tell you! I am in charge of 13 global markets across the Asia pacific region. The first woman to hold that office down!

I think I was lucky, piggy-backing on the equal-rights-for-women movement. At the start of my career the emancipation of women was in its nascency. In the early 1990s it was gaining traction in male dominated institutions but with particular success in the police force. By 2010 equal rights was becoming a feminist *war-cry* and employers were listening. By then my career with the Hong Kong police had almost run its course and I like to think that I helped shape those societal changes. I did it *my* way! And despite my senior years now, I'm still going strong.

Editor: Stuart McDouall

---------- End ----------

"The Freemason's Square and Compasses emblem"

FREEMASONRY

Right or wrong?

The rights and wrongs of freemasonry are one of the world's most enduring debates. By no means the least enervating subject matter it has, for centuries, been cropping up in the news, like a dormant volcano waking up for a while, before subsiding into its preferred inconspicuousness until the next scandal features in a centre-page spread.

I recall several such episodes in my life time including the Italian P2 scandal, which broke in March, 1981, involving Freemasons and the mafia. Then there was the criminal infiltration of the Metropolitan Police in 2002, linked to freemasonry and highlighted in Operation Tiberius and, last but not least, the 2007 publication of Stephen Knight's pot-boiler, The Brotherhood, lifting the lid on just about every imaginable anti-social and criminal enterprise with alleged masonic involvement.

The bedrock of freemasonry is its universality. There are only half-a-dozen countries in the world where freemasonry has never been represented in society, either by the opening of a lodge or just by an enterprising individual bringing to bear his masonic principles and ethics in his activities. There are, however, more countries where freemasonry has been sanctioned or banned outright, principally in despotic states or atheistic cultures. Freemasons, alongside members of other organisations deemed by some countries to be anti-social or politically anti-establishment, are subject to arrest if their actions are deemed seditious. And there are religious faiths which discourage their adherents from joining freemasonry; primarily the Roman Catholic church but also other Christian sects and Islam.

Freemasonry has many different branches, all stemmed from the one trunk, known as the Craft, the foundations of which lie in King Solomon's temple. Masonic pedagogy centres around the principal tenet of a belief in one God; a supreme being; with its attendant theological values of faith, hope and charity. This alongside the ancient cardinal virtues of mind and character, namely prudence, justice, fortitude and temperance. Thus it is that members of our world's principle faiths are qualified to be Freemasons.

In medieval times, dating back to the 11th century, Roman Catholicism was the dominant faith in all of Europe, including Great Britain. After the Norman conquest of England stone masons came across from Europe and so began the construction of edifices in stone; forts and castles, walls and towers, churches and cathedrals; some of which still exist today.

By the beginning of the 12th century there is evidence of loges or lodges being formed by itinerant masons, carrying the tools of their trade and their goods and chatels with them, from building site to building site. These lodges were organised in a hierarchical, communal system and, having accepted a contract, would move to the selected site and erect their own commune in wood and stone; dormitories, kitchen and dining facilities, office, work and storage space and, most importantly, their own chapel, dedicated to God.

And in ancient documents, relating to the existence of these stone mason's lodges, we know that the Holy Bible was always the central piece of furnishing in their places of daily worship. In 1531 King Henry VIII established the protestant faith, now known as the Church of England, setting in train the gradual decline in the stone mason's trade. By the close of the 17th century operative stone masons lodges had all but disappeared for want of business but resourceful masons, financed by their former patrons, turned around their old way of life, becoming speculative or free masons. This new non-operative freemasonry soon became popular in wider society, presenting a system of morality, veiled in allegory and illustrated by symbols, re-enacting the old mason's ideals and Christian beliefs. In 1717 the first Grand Lodge of England was formed by four of these non-operative Freemason's lodges. In 1750 there was a schism resulting in the institution of a rival grand lodge which continued until 27th December, 1813, when the two grand lodges came together in one United Grand Lodge of England (UGLE).

After unification freemasonry also became cosmopolitan, admitting to their ranks men of the Muslim, Jewish and other faiths espousing the existence of one God. From this time freemasonry began to spread across the world. The Holy Bible, and books sacred to other religious faiths, took on a secondary nomenclature, in lodge, as The Volume of the Sacred Law. This enabled a lodge, whose membership was not Christian, to have eg the Koran, the Torah or the Bhagavad Gita as their central furnishing.

These innovations, in the mid 1800s, came at a time when religious conformity in Great Britain was thought important; many activities in society being restricted to Christians, including freemasonry. Some masonic orders (not the craft) were established for Christians only. These included Rose Croix (the 18th degree), the Knights Templar, the Red Cross of Constantine, the Royal Order of Scotland and even the highest 33rd degree. This was not deliberately and consciously prejudiced in favour of Christians to the exclusion of other Freemasons. Indeed, as time has moved on, such anachronisms have been made null and void.

Everyone joining Freemasonry goes through the first three craft degrees of initiation, passing and raising. After these come the Mark Master and the Royal Arch degrees, which expound upon the craft, based on the history of the Old Testament; the First Book of Kings and the Second Book of Chronicles. Next is the Royal Ark Mariners which is derived from the ancient biblical story of Noah and his ark. Then we start climbing the ladder of the esoteric degrees, to Rose Croix which is the 18th degree, known in the Americas as the Scottish Rite, the Knights Templar, and others in a line of 33 degrees to the top. Offshoots from that line are numerous; hundreds of orders; spawning membership in the thousands of Freemasons world wide.

Most vitriolic in its condemnation of the Craft has been the Roman Catholic Church with Pope Clement XII, in 1738, publishing his *In eminenti apostolatus specula* or papal bull, banning Catholics from becoming Freemasons. That came about as a result of political rivalry between the Jacobite (pro Stuarts) and Hanovarian (Whig or protestant) masonic lodges of the time, the first owing fealty to James Stuart, living in Rome and masquerading as James III of England, and the second, to Cardinal Andre-Hercule Fleury, chief minister to King Louis XV of France. The latter, alarmed at the success of the Stuarts in attracting large numbers of Europeans to their banners, persuaded the pope to forbid Roman Catholics joining freemasonry on threat of excommunication. Being politically astute the pope worded his bull from a purely religious standpoint, so as not to antagonize Britain, writing:-

> *"But it is in the nature of crime to betray itself by its attendant clamor. Thus these aforesaid societies or conventicles have caused in the minds of the faithful the greatest suspicion, and all prudent and upright men have passed the same judgement on them as being depraved and perverted. For if they were not doing evil they would not have so great a hatred of light."*

In 1983 the Vatican issued a further declaration that:-

> *"...the church's negative judgement in regard to masonic association[s] remains unchanged since their principles have always been considered irreconcilable with the doctrine of the church and therefore membership in them remains forbidden. The faithful who enrol in masonic associations are in a state of grave sin and may not receive holy communion. It is not within the competence of local* [Roman Catholic] *ecclesiastical authorities to give a judgement on the nature of masonic associations which would imply a derogation from what has been decided above..."*

The Church of England [C of E], as a whole, has never been proscriptive of freemasonry, preferring to allow their clergy to make up their own minds on whether or not to condemn or condone it. In the heyday of stone-mason's guilds; the 15th and 16th centuries; the C of E was supportive of these builders of churches and great cathedrals. It was only in the mid-17th century, when operative mason's lodges were being disbanded and modern-day freemasonry was in its nascency, that criticism found a voice.

However, it wasn't until 1926 and again, in 1987 that the C of E church synod felt obliged to take a stand on freemasonry. However, not finding any doctrinal conflict, the church forbore to condemn. But that didn't stop the Rev. C. Penney-Hunt BA publishing his pamphlet entitled "The menace of freemasonry to the Christian faith". Not to put too fine a point on it, that publication was an uninformed diatribe reminiscent of the ignorant and insidious railings of the clergy against witchcraft in the 16th century, condemning so many innocent souls to the burning stake. In 2008 another C of E priest, the Rev. Walter Hannah, took up the cudgels, writing a book titled "Darkness Visible" which is still in print. Though more circumspect than the Rev. Penney-Hunt was, Hannah still indulges in flights of fancy where he is factually wrong, drawing erroneous conclusions which, to the uninitiated reader, can sound logical.

Between 2014 and 2019 I was the convenor of the senior fellowship group of St. Mary's C of E church, Chesham, Buckinghamshire. Once a month, in the early evening, we convened in the church hall for a talk or show and between 20 and 30 elderly parishioners would attend. On one occasion I proposed that I would give a talk about the compatibility of freemasonry with the Christian faith. Our chairlady and the committee agreed and I duly gave the talk, illustrated with my aprons and collars. Afterwards there were questions but none critical, followed by the usual round of applause. After my talk one man in our congregation told me that he was a Freemason though no longer attending and one lady told me that her father had been a Freemason "*I recognise the uniform*" she said.

Three days later, after the Sunday nine o'clock service, our rector advised me that he had received complaints from two ladies of the congregation about using the church hall for a "blasphemous" talk. In discussion with him, I gained the impression that he may have read Hannah's book at seminary. I understood that that was the sum total of his knowledge of freemasonry. With that sort of tuition it is no wonder that the C of E continue their traducement of freemasonry, fortunately without definitively proscribing it.

The Church of Scotland also weighed into the debate on the conformity of freemasonry to the teachings of the church, commissioning, in 1987, a panel of five distinguished theologians and priests to put the Grand Lodge of Scotland to the test. The grand master at the time, Sir Gregor MacGregor of MacGregor, 6th Baronet, his deputy and wardens, plus two past grand masters gave their full cooperation to the C of S panel. But, unfortunately, they were not equal to the task, apparently intellectually incompetent in proving freemasonry's case that

- freemasonry is not a religion;
- the supreme being is a title commensurate to God in the world's major religions;
- the name of Jesus Christ is not deliberately suppressed in masonic ritual;
- the element of secrecy in masonic ritual has nothing to do with religion and is not unchristian. Masonry is theist rather than gnostic in its nature;
- the prohibition on discussing religion (and politics) at meetings is not aimed at preventing members' expressing their beliefs but simply to allay the contentions that these topics of discussion often propagate; and
- the gospels have not been, either intentionally or unintentionally, allegorised exclusively into a system of morality.

As a consequence the C of S, in 1989, officially denounced freemasonry to its congregations.

In these two examples of church diametrics it seems to me that the clergy would do well to cogitate on the teaching of Christ in the gospel according to St. Mark, 9: 38-41 where those who are not of a particular church but whose deeds are done in the name of God will not speak ill of Him.

> [v.40] *"For the one who is not against us is for us.* [v.41] *For truly, I say to you, **whoever** gives you a cup of water to drink because you belong to Christ will by no means lose his reward."*

Notwithstanding, I personally have two good friends who are practising Catholics, three more who are devout Muslims and literally dozens who are C of E. All of them are dedicated Freemasons who see no conflict of interest in practising their religious faith or in their political affiliations. And there are some big names in the nominal records of freemasonry who surely can't all be wrong? I list just a few of them below:

The clergy: Rev. Dr. George Oliver DD (1782-1867), Geoffrey Fisher, Arch Bishop of Canterbury (1945-1961). Bishop Jonathan Baker of Ebbsfleet and Cathedral chaplain. Rev. John Chynchen of Hong Kong. Rev. (C of E) Neville Barker Cryer (1924-2013) Chaplain to the United Grand Lodge of England (UGLE). The Revd. Dr. Simon Thorn, grand chaplain to the UGLE from 2024-.

Scientists: Sir Alexander Fleming (1881-1955) Penicillin. Edward Jenner (1749-1823) Smallpox vaccine.

Architects: Sir Christopher Wren (1632-1723) and Christopher Haffner (1936-2013).

Authors: John Bunyan (Pilgrim's Progress), Dr. James Boswell, Rider Haggard, Mark Twain, Jerome K Jerome, Sir Arthur Conan Doyle, Rudyard Kipling and Jonathan Swift of Gulliver's Travels.

Poets: Robert Burns (1759-1796) the Scottish Bard, Rudyard Kipling (1865-1936).

Philanthropists: Sir Cecil Rhodes (1853-1902) of South Africa, Sir Thomas Lipton (1848-1931) a tea merchant.

Politicians: Elias Ashmole, Sir Winston Churchill, George Washington, Theodore Roosevelt, Abraham Lincoln, Mustafa Kemel Ataturk, Pandit Nehru.

British nobility: George VI, Edward VII and VIII. Prince Michael, Duke of Kent. Prince Philip, Duke of Edinburgh. Patrick McDouall (1706-1803), 6th Earl of Dumfries, Grand Master of the Grand Lodge of Scotland. (My ancestor).

Engineer: James Watt (1736-1819) the steam engine.

Military: Lord Kitchener, General Ralph Abercrombie.

Musicians: Ludwig van Beethoven, Johann Christian Bach, Johannes Brahms, Wolfgang Amadeus Mozart, Nat King Cole.

Sportsmen: Sir Ralph Ramsey (1881-1955) a football player, Arnold Palmer (1929-2016) a golfer.

Explorers: Roald Amundsen (1872-1928) NW passage, Neil Armstrong and his crew of Apollo 11. (The moon, July 1969)

Comedian: Peter Sellers (1925-1980) of the goon show.

Actors: John Wayne (1907-1979) of western movies. Jack Nicholson (1937) of horror movies.

My masonic career

Freemasonry has played a prominent part in my life since my initiation into Lodge St. John, No. 618 on the roll of the Grand Lodge of Scotland, under the aegis of the District Grand Lodge of the far east, holden in Hong Kong, on 13th May, 1980. That was 14 days prior to my 30th birthday. By that time I had been serving in the Royal Hong Kong Police (RHKP) for nine-and-a-half years and was a newly promoted chief inspector.

I wrote my usual Sunday letter to my parents and mentioned that I had just been initiated into freemasonry. On 8th of June my step-father, Major John Bryden, wrote one of only three letters that I received from him. Normally it was my mother who replied to my regular letters home.

At that time I knew that both my father and my grandfather had been prominent masons and that my step-father had been connected with freemasonry but I had no detailed knowledge of his membership as he had never talked about it to my brothers and I. In his letter he wrote:-

> *"I'm glad to hear that you have come into the Craft, following in your father's, grandfather's, great uncle's (the Baron) footsteps to say nothing of your step-father's.*

> *"Zetland Hall sounds very well organised, as one would expect* [in the Far East]. *The lodge I used to visit in Malacca* [a British army posting with the Scots Guards in Malaya] *had a Chinese master who sounds just like yours* [Bro. Aun-e Han], *memory and sincerity and ritual perfect but pronunciation sometimes a bit odd.*

> *"I think the lodge that I belonged to in Munster* [Saxony lodge No. 842 under the United Grand Lodge of Germany] *made a masonic record in having a Dutchman as master in a German lodge working in English.*

> *"I think that freemasonry abroad has got much more to it than in England or certainly in London. My mother lodge in London* [Connaught Army and Navy Lodge 4323] *seems to have become little more than a dining club. Admittedly I was probably spoilt by joining or visiting lodges in Germany, Malaya, Borneo, Sharjah and Jamaica.*

> *"Anyway, I'm glad you are in. Wish I could be there for your 3° which is the most impressive of all."*

"W.Bro. J.H.A. Bryden, PM 842 EC, in his regalia, and his wife (my
mother) Mrs D.A. Bryden at a Ladies Night dinner"

John Bryden was a Freemason of the 'old school' that held the so-called secrets of freemasonry sacrosanct, abiding by the old stricture of never imparting any knowledge of the organisation to an outsider and never overtly inviting anyone else, even kith and kin, to join. The initiative has to come from the enquirer.

My proposer and seconder into the Craft were Bob Wiggins of the Hong Kong Customs & Excise department and Gordon Jack of the RHKP. I knew of Bob Wiggins, having met him at social events, but did not know he was a Freemason. It was Gordon Jack, who was a superintendent in the RHKP and with whom I was serving at the time, to whom I first talked to about freemasonry. He showed me a list of members of his lodge, St John 618 under the Scottish constitution, and asked if I knew any of them? Bob Wiggins' name was there. So I approached him and he volunteered to be my proposer while Gordon Jack was my seconder. A few years later Bob Wiggins suddenly left Hong Kong amidst rumours of being part of a gold smuggling racket to India. That was the last I heard of him.

Lodge St. John's membership was comprised of businessmen, professionals and government servants. Among our number were six local Chinese, four local Indians, two Pakistani Muslims and a Jew from Israel. The rest were expatriates, mostly British. There were some 50 members in total. The two oldest members were a doctor, Professor PH Teng, retired director of Hong Kong's medical & health services and Colonel Joseph Kelso Reid, a decorated war veteran who was captured by the Japanese invaders in 1940. Other society notables were Hindu Gary of the Harilela hotel & trading empire, and Gerry, boss of Wharf Godowns and a legislative councillor.

The following list of occupations of our membership reveal the diversity of our lodge in my time. A doctor (gynaecologist) ex-RAMC and one-time District Grand Master of the Scottish lodges. A retired American journalist of some renown and a prominent member of the Foreign Correspondent's Club. A retired car salesman who owned and ran a molten-lead printing press and played the organ at church and during our lodge ceremonies. A solicitor who became a magistrate and another from Sri Lanka in private practice. Two electrical engineers on the staff of Hong Kong Electric Co. Two HK telephone company engineers from Scotland. Three senior firemen coming from England's southern counties. Myself and two others were policemen. We had a member from Hong Kong's Independent Commission Against Corruption. Another was a Presbyterian minister. One owned his own quantity survey firm and obtained the beautiful stained glass windows from a defunct chapel, installing them in Zetland Hall. Two were managers with Jardine Matheson Co. Three were all Scotsmen; senior accountants with Price Waterhouse and four were captains with Cathay Pacific Airways.

Our local Hong Kong brethren included Andy, a self-made businessman and property developer, Ted, the first accountant for the Cross Harbour Tunnel, Then another Ted of the Hong Kong Stock Exchange and Noorie Razack, a Muslim and itinerant salesman. I just loved the eclectic mix of our lodge, much reminding me of Rudyard Kipling's famous poem 'The Mother Lodge' which lauds the universality of freemasonry. I only mention all these people because they are forever etched in my memory. They come from all walks of life, religion and politics, yet espousing freemasonry and one God.

On the 13th of October, 1981, I was made a master mason and it was a 'double third', my self and the Rev. Kenneth Anderson being the candidates. In the succeeding year I volunteered for floor work; reciting ritual; at each of our monthly meetings. A wordly-wise and masonic doyen of our lodge, Scotsman Harry Lavery, took me under his wing and advised me that the best way to learn freemasonry was to put it into practice. My memory retention was good and I soon gained a reputation as a reliable lecturer in our degree ceremonies or, in common parlance, floor-worker. In December 1982 I was asked if I would take over the office of secretary of the lodge as Tony was finally downing his quill after six years in the role. I was bemused by the invitation, knowing that the lodge secretary was an eminent post and that, up until that point, only past masters of the lodge had filled that office. But I agreed to take it on.

To begin with I copied my predecessor assiduously in all aspects of my secretarial responsibilities, on the premise that what worked for him would work for me. Quite quickly I got the hang of things, gaining confidence, and by the end of my first year I was fully conversant and comfortable in my duties. The nature of the secretary's duties meant that he possessed personal information about every member of the lodge. He held all the detailed records of every meeting; lodge committees and our regular ceremonial meetings. He prepared the summonses for every meeting, He was also correspondent for the lodge with the Scottish District in Hong Kong and the Grand Lodge of Scotland in Edinburgh. Whenever questions arose on protocols and directives from on high, it was the secretary's domain to reply. He became the *de-facto* authority on the administration and, to a large extent, the running of the lodge. The pen was indeed mightier than the sword.

In 1984 so enthralled was I with our effulgent lodge; the premier Scottish lodge in the District of the Far East as we dubbed ourselves; that I proposed to start an annual magazine that would not only encapsulate all of our ceremonies but also our social activities for posterity. Our district grand master at the time, Bro. Alex Purves, wrote in his foreword:

> *"Lodge St. John was the first* [in 1878], *and for many years the only, Scottish lodge in Hong Kong. It could not have been easy to maintain and uphold the traditions of the Scottish Craft in such circumstances, particularly as the remainder of the lodges in Hong Kong were all of the English constitution and the lodge relied heavily on the non-Scots to keep it alive. But maintain and uphold*

those traditions it certainly did and still does, as those who visit the lodge at work these days well know. Lodge St. John helped two other Scottish lodges [that had to leave China], transferring from Shanghai to Hong Kong in the 1950s, thus keeping alive Lodge St. Andrew in the Far East and Lodge Cosmopolitan, both still in existence."

The "Letter From Hong Kong" as the magazine was titled, continued to 1992 when, after ten years in office, I handed over the secretaryship to another brother.

What started off as a pastime soon began to stretch into a career in freemasonry, and I was not alone in that way of thinking; many of my fellow Freemasons were doing the same, to a greater or lesser extent. It was a self-perpetuating engagement, spurred on, firstly, by a curiosity to know how each degree developed into the next and, secondly, by senior Freemasons recommending new and higher orders in masonry to their juniors. They used to say, *"Don't worry, we only meet four times a year"*.

To cut a long story short, by the year 2000, I had taken my 30th degree and was a member of 14 different masonic entities in the Craft and orders, in three different constitutions. I was made Honorary Grand Sword Bearer of the Grand Lodge of Scotland, Past Master L.929 in the Irish and Past District Grand JW in the English. I was attending lodge at least once a week, often twice a week and, on a couple of occasions, in lodge installation season, I'd be up at Zetland Hall five days in the week.

Freemason's are well known for their altruism, giving substantial sums of money to all sorts of causes, often to non-masonic charities. One of those is children's orphanages and every year orphans are invited to a Christmas party at Zetland Hall where a suitably attired mason plays Father Christmas and hands out presents to each one. There is also a masonic tenet that charity begins at home and, in that regard, every lodge has an almoner whose duty it is to give succour to members who have fallen on hard times and to widows and children of deceased brethren. Where monetary grants are required almoner's draw up a petition, known as a prayer, to the umbrella Masonic Benevolence Fund Corporation. Out of about a thousand masons who frequent Zetland Hall, their committee scrutinize somewhere between 20 and 30 such applications every year, a few requiring monthly grants in the thousands of dollars. For three years I was the secretary to that corporation. I have heard it said that Freemasons are nepotists in looking after their own first. But having looked after them, our largess to non-masonic charities far exceeded our internal giving.

So it was, in the millennium year, that my wife took stock of the time I was spending on masonry and confronted me with an ultimatum, our marriage or freemasonry. Actually it wasn't as stark and sudden as that; it had been brewing for a while and I was blind to the indicators. Unwittingly I was busy making a second profession, alongside my police career, of freemasonry. The words 'profession' and 'freemasonry' are certainly not compatible.

One Freemason, who was a very good friend of mine in Hong Kong, took that incompatibility far further than I, treating it as a vocation, chasing degrees and promotions in every possible order and even setting up a new order in HK, the Allied Degrees, off his own bat. He was a long-haul pilot and often, too often, didn't go home after a flight, working on his freemasonry to the neglect of his wife and young family. In his old age he told me, ruefully, that he used to buy gifts for them by way of compensation. For him, and a few others I knew, freemasonry actually became an obsession, more compelling than other life commitments.

Without any hesitation my choice was, of course, my marriage and my family. We discussed a continuation of freemasonry, limiting my attendance at lodge to an average of twice a month. The question was where to make those cuts but that didn't take me long to answer. My favourite masonic activity centred around the craft lodges and so it was that I wrote eleven letters of resignation to the secretaries of the higher and esoteric orders that I was a member of. Among them was the Royal Order of Scotland which I had joined at the invitation of my mentor Harry Lavery. It was a privilege to be a member of this masonic elite which expounded on a composite of masonic degrees. When Harry learned of my resignation he quietly made known his displeasure and, crest-fallen, like a chided school boy, all I could do was apologise.

But I was happier. And I was able to concentrate on my craft lodges of which I was in all three constitutions. After I had completed my year in the Chair of Lodge St John in 1990 I applied to join our mother lodge, the Zetland Lodge No. 525, under the English constitution and, in March 1992, I became a member, going straight into the vacant chair of junior warden. In 1994 I was installed as master of that lodge.

Another of my pastimes was the scouts. I joined the scout movement of Hong Kong in 1985 and, by 1995, I was the group scout leader for the 36th Hong Kong at St. John's Cathedral. A year later Arthur Gomes, Grand Inspector of Irish masonry, knowing that I was a scout leader, invited me to be a founding member of a new scout lodge under Hong Kong's Irish banner and I agreed. In April, 1996, I was the first senior warden of Baden Powell lodge No. 929 and, the following year, I was it's master. Twelve months later I handed the gavel of the lodge to Gary. He was an exceptionally busy man, and of the eight regular meetings in his year, he was absent for five. So I became de-facto master. And I really enjoyed my two years at the helm. I remain a member of all three of those lodges and, in my retirement, on trips back to Hong Kong, I try to coincide my travels with their lodge meetings.

I have been asked a few times which of the three constitutions do I value or rate the best? That is too wide a question to answer in a word. However, if we just ask which constitution has the most interesting working in each of the first three craft degrees there is an aphorism among masons that the Irish 1st is the best, the Scottish 3rd is the best and the English are left with their 2nd. If I am specifically asked which of the three constitutions I like working in the most, it is the Irish. The Irish rituals are the most self-explanatory, employing theatrical illustration. Their ritual was learned by word of mouth; not written down; until the early 20th century. Even now minor deviation from their script is allowed with a view to *teaching* the candidate the landmarks, as opposed to indoctrinating him. While the Scottish adhere to the script they are flexible in format, make allowances for variations on a theme and are exegetic. The English are orthodox, demanding ritual verbatim with a modicum of theatrics for illustration.

Now, in retirement, I am a member of the Zetland and Hong Kong Lodge, 7665, holden in London under the Metropolitan Grand Lodge. There are only four meetings a year. This lodge is the daughter lodge of the Zetland Lodge in Hong Kong of which I am a past master. Most of the members of this London lodge are or were living and working in Hong Kong. I joined in 2014 and, since then, have acted as treasurer (one year), director of ceremonies (four years) and conjointly, as almoner (six years).

It is this last post that has given me the most satisfaction, able to be of assistance to the widows of deceased members as well as to our sick, frail and elderly lodge members. It entails regular contact, mostly by 'phone, with the widows, ten in number at present, monitoring their welfare and, occasionally, organising financial assistance. I try to visit our elderly members if possible, otherwise it's contact by 'phone or e-mail. Every quarter I prepare a detailed report for the members. In September, 2024, I was surprised to learn that I will be honoured with London grand rank, mainly, I think, on account of regular attendance over ten years and offices held in that time. At the age of 74 I have no further ambitions for office. The back-benches beckon. Indeed "One of the many pleasures of old age is giving things up". *Malcolm Muggeridge.*

Finally, as to the question of Freemasonry, right or wrong? My answer is unequivocal, It is right.

NOORIE RAZACK

A Eulogy

In my years of friendship with Noorie, I came to know him well. But it wasn't until the early 1980s, when Noorie was falling on hard times, that we met often and I started taking notes of his interesting life and times. This eulogy is a distillation of those notes, transcribed in the first person as Noorie spoke. When I eventually delivered this eulogy at Noorie's memorial service, I prefaced it with the statement "It *will take about 37 minutes, but what's that in a lifetime of 97 years?*".

My name is Noor Mohammed Razack. My friends call me Noorie. 'Noor' means 'light' in Arabic. I was born on 16th November, 1924. I'm a third generation Indian Muslim in Hong Kong and the eldest child in a family of six; my parents, myself and my three younger sisters.

My family were well off. I don't know when my grandfather, Mosa Abdul Razack, a devout Muslim from northern India (now Pakistan), came to Hong Kong but I believe it must have been around 1850-60. I know he was a member of the Hong Kong stock exchange and he eventually became its chairman. Grandfather also became a Freemason in Hong Kong, initiated into Lodge Naval and Military, 848 SC, though I didn't know of this until the late '70s when I read a book by a Hong Kong Freemason, the late W.Bro. Kit Haffner, in which he mentions my grandfather, M.A. Razack.

Grandfather bought a mansion in the Mid-levels where my father, Ahmed Razack, was born. He was a son of the first of grandfather's five wives. My father was educated at a missionary school on Hong Kong Island, one of the best schools at that time. When he finished his education he went to work in the government dockyards, becoming the quartermaster, a position he held until the fall of Hong Kong in the Second World War. When he married, my grandfather helped him buy a property in Leighton Hill, above Happy Valley. And that's where I was born and brought up.

I was sent to a kindergarten near where we lived and, at age six, graduated to the primary section of that school. The medium of education was Cantonese and, at that time, as was the Chinese custom, I was given a propitious Chinese name Shek Yue-man. I was quite good at my lessons and gained a place at the famous St Joseph's secondary school in Kennedy Road. There, as a school activity, I joined the scout troop; the 1st Hong Kong. I was in Form IV when the second World War II came to this colony in December, '41. I was 16 years old at the time.

Meanwhile my father and mother moved the family to a spacious flat in Fort Street, North Point. It was from there, in the months before the war, that I, being a boy scout, signed up with the Hong Kong Regiment of Volunteers. After one week of basic training, I was posted to the Despatch Corps with the title '*Desptach Rider (Bicycle)*'.

When the Japanese invaders started shelling and bombing the northern shores of Hong Kong Island, in the week before they landed in North Point, I was assigned to the Air Raid Post (ARP) at Quarry Bay school. I borrowed a bicycle from the bike shop in nearby Chun Yeung Street and rode, in my ARP uniform, all the way there. I did my duty, as despatch rider, for five days, without respite, until my commanding officer gave me permission to go home and see my family. And that just happened to be on the eve of the landing by the Japanese army on the island.

Early the following morning, when it was still dark, I awoke to the sound of heavy fighting about half a mile away, in the direction of the North Point power station. I was wearing my ARP uniform when I walked outside and down the street to Fortress Hill Road. From there I could see lots of people milling about, some obviously panic-stricken, shouting "They're coming!".

Realising that my uniform and helmet might make me an enemy target I hurried back home, got changed and threw my uniform, helmet, gas mask and leather satchel down the well in the yard of the building we lived in. My parents, who had already brought in some extra food, decided to barricade the flat, securing the front and back doors, backing furniture against them. I remember my sisters being in tears with fright.

Within the hour the enemy arrived in our street, armed soldiers mainly of Korean and Taiwanese nationality under the command of Japanese officers. One of our neighbours, living in the same block of flats as us, was a doctor (GP) of Indian nationality and I saw him attempting to drive away in his car. I think he was going to his clinic, as he did every morning. But he was stopped and questioned by soldiers. After a few minutes they dragged him out of his car and marched him back to his flat. We all heard screaming and shouting. Not long afterwards the soldiers left and there was silence. Soon word began to go round our building that the good doctor had been beheaded. To this day I don't believe that happened though I didn't see him again.

Around mid-day all the residents of Fort Street, that was a few hundred of us, were ordered out into the street where we were roughly herded, at gun point, into one long line; Portuguese, Chinese, Eurasians, Indians and even a few white British. One of our neighbours spoke Japanese and went on his bended knee to plead with the Japanese army captain for our lives. That seemed to work for the officer warned all the residents "Go back home" he shouted. "Stay home. Don't come out on pain of death." So all of us turned and rushed home. The captain stationed several of his soldiers on guard duty in the street and then left with the rest of his men.

As darkness fell on that first night of captivity everyone locked their doors and windows against intruders. The soldiers on guard outside began to visit the residential blocks, presumably looking for food and any valuables they could carry away with them. Not every household was targetted and my family was one of the lucky ones. But we were terrified when we heard a couple of guards, apparently Korean by their language, forcing entry into the flat immediately above ours, on the first floor. It was the home of a Chinese family, with three teenage daughters, that we were friendly with. We heard shouts and then screams but it wasn't until the next morning, when all was quiet, that my Dad dared to go upstairs to see if he could help, and there he found the parents hog-tied on the floor and their two eldest daughters in their bedrooms having been raped. At least they had survived.

Within just a couple of weeks relative peace was restored under Japanese rule and, thereafter, a daily routine in our neighbourhood began to emerge, one dominated by fear. The necessity for food and water, as well as medicines, became a daily torment as myself, and others, ventured outside looking for food or just trying to get to work. We had to be alert to the presence of soldiers wherever we went, ready to bow before them or risk being beaten. On one such expedition I learned that lessons in the Japanese language were being given free at local schools, sponsored by the military. I decided to enrol on a three-month course thinking, by doing so, that I could curry favour with the occupation forces and, hopefully, be in a better position to help my family in desperate times.

Up Fortress Hill Road, only a few hundred yards away from our home, there was a government rice-rations outlet manned by civilians, lackeys of the Japanese, but with soldiers marshalling the queues of the hungry. Long lines of people of all ages stood in an orderly manner while troops watched them closely. It could be hours before one reached the head of the queue and, particularly in the hot summer sun, people fainted. The soldiers never helped anyone. I remember one time when one of my sisters came back home crying. She had witnessed a Korean soldier pulling a rather fat Chinese man from the queue ahead of her, cursing him loudly and then, in his anger, sticking his bayonet into the man's belly. That poor man was left to die in the road.

News from other theatres of the world war was sparse and unreliable. Very few people had radios in our neighbourhood. But late in 1943 we didn't need a radio for we all heard and saw American bombers flying over Hong Kong, the first glimmer of hope that the allies might have the upper hand at last. But that presented another immediate danger, adding to our already impossibly rigorous lives, and that was of being killed by allied bombing. My parents had contacts and our whole family quietly slipped away one dark night, heading for Macau. The journey was fraught with difficulty and danger but, hiding in the engine room of a motorised junk, we made it to the British Consulate in Macau and registered as refugees.

In the succeeding two years, '44 to '45, I was able to attend St Louis school, in Macau, that was run by the Catholic fathers of Wah Yan college. In that time I picked up a reasonable grasp of the Portuguese language. A classmate and good friend of mine was Edwin Wong Man-wai who, later, qualified as a doctor at Hong Kong university. And many years later I discovered that he was a Freemason and member of Lodge St. John, 618 SC (Scottish Constitution).

When the war ended my whole family returned to Hong Kong and I went looking for work, finding a job in Chan Brother's ship's chandlers. It was one of the partners there who advised me to change my Chinese name to a more lucky one, Shek Ho-man, which I did. Grateful for the job, I worked hard and was promoted to a position of responsibility, being made ship's chandler to the hospital ship 'Maine' permanently moored in Victoria Harbour. My job was to engage Chinese crew for her and for visiting ships of the British Navy Auxiliary Fleet. I also arranged the repatriation of Indian and Chinese crews.

In 1947 I was given a special assignment which I carried off successfully. My employers were so pleased that they gave me a letter of commendation which I have kept ever since. It reads, in part:-

> *"An outstanding case he attended to was the reception of a Japanese ship's company of about forty men who sailed the 'Carmen Moller' to Hong Kong on her rendition to the British Government. This was a ticklish job requiring the disembarkation of the Japanese crew at Tai Kok Tsui, transporting them to Queen's Pier and then handing them over to the military who took the sailors in, pending repatriation. Mr Razack intelligently carried out the instructions given to him in this affair with credit to himself and satisfaction to all concerned."*

In those years with Chan Brothers I spent much of my time in and around the Hong Kong dockyards along the foreshore from Murray Building (then on the waterfront) all the way to Arsenal Street in Wanchai. It was during that time that I met Jim Barber, an ex-navy officer, who befriended me and told me something of freemasonry *"...It's a society where you learn to be a good man."* Jim impressed me but I thought it was a club for expatriates only and took that subject no further. Once again, it was only later that I discovered he was a member of The Zetland Lodge, 525 EC (English Constitution).

In 1953 I left the Royal Navy dockyards, looking for other ways to improve my lot. I went to visit a Chinese fung-sui-lo (geomancer) who told me that my birth elements were *gold* and *wood* and that I should change my Chinese name to Shek Yiu-fai. This I did; my third name change. I quickly found new employment, joining Moller's Shipping. And it was on 20th June, 1953, that I left Hong Kong for my first overseas trip aboard a cargo passenger ship, the MV Soochow. I wore the uniform of ship's purser with the label 'No. 1 Writer' on my breast pocket.

The MV Soochow plied between Hong Kong, New Guinea (Port Moresby) and Australia (Sydney) and in each place I spent a few days ashore. I did a couple of these voyages but decided that the ocean-going life was not for me. I was home-sick. I missed my family and wanted to settle back into Hong Kong. I resigned on 19th November, 1954. I was presented with a glowing reference from the ship's captain in which he wrote:-

> *"...Purser Razack has been a loyal and dedicated crew member. 100% reliable in the execution of his duties and, above all, trustworthy. He has shown initiative and team spirit, keeping good time and always with a smile."*

And it wasn't long, after leaving Moller's Shipping, that an assistant manager in Swire's Shipping, John Bremridge, contacted me, offering the post of ship's purser with Swire's. Not wanting to go back to sea I politely turned him down. Sir John Bremridge later joined the Hong Kong government, becoming financial secretary. And I think he might have been a Freemason though I never found out if he was.

On 1st September. 1955, I found a position with Metro Cars (HK) Ltd, part of the Dodwell group, who were the sole agents for Austin Motor Cars. Starting as a sales representative in the *Personnel and Export Department (Home leave sales)*, it wasn't long before I was made a senior sales rep' and I made the acquaintance of a departmental manager, Roger Pennels who was, though I didn't know it at the time, a member of Lodge St. John, 618. He had come out to Hong Kong as a young man and married a Malaysian lady named Wazira. The three of us got on well and became life-long friends.

With my linguistic talents I was made responsible for expatriate customers and always wore a suit and tie to work. I sold them cars for their use while they were on tour for a year or two in Hong Kong. I even arranged to ship their cars for them back to their country of origin if they so wished. Sometimes old clients would return to Hong Kong for work and I would help them get their car shipped out with them. I provided this service over and above my normal duties. In 1963 I was voted top salesman in the company, an achievement that was rewarded with the gift of a new Austin Mini and a written citation.

It was in 1958 that I met my life partner, Linda, a divorcee with two children, a boy and a girl, by her first marriage. She was a Chinese beauty; a part-time actress and model. I kept magazine photos of her, displayed under the glass top of my coffee table, to show guests at my home. In 1959 we decided to buy a property together, a flat in the then newly built Causeway Bay Mansions. My sisters did not approve; us not being properly married and she not being a Muslim; actually having no religion. When her children grew up they never amounted to much. Her son went to live and work on the mainland but whenever he was short of money he'd come to see us in Hong Kong and scrounge some cash. Even now.

It was also in '59 that I became a member of the Indian Recreation Club (IRC) in Soo Kon Po, proposed by my then ailing father. It was he, once a top player in the Hong Kong Lawn Bowls Association, who had long been coaching me in the game. A fellow member of the IRC was one David Roads, a well known American foreign correspondent. We met occasionally at the bar. Many years later we met again as members of Lodge St. John, 618 SC.

I stayed with Metro Motors for ten happy years; from '55 to '66. But I got itchy feet eventually and, on leaving the company, I was given a letter of reference written by senior manager Roger Pennels. The following quote is taken from it:-

> "..has been a faithful employee, always giving of his best and with the best interests of the company at heart. He is honest and hard-working. His customers are mostly British; They all like Mr Razack because of his pleasant manner and desire to be helpful."

Shortly after I left, my friend, Roger Pennels, moved to Zung Fu (Mercedes) as their senior manager.

On the lawn bowls circuit I was becoming well known as a good player and was approached by two friends who happened to be members of the Craigengower Cricket Club (CCC) in Happy Valley. They persuaded me to become a member and join their lawn bowls team. At that time membership was cheaper than the IRC and the club house was better situated at the Causeway Bay end of Happy Valley, nearer to my home. Later, in 1980, I was approached by Harry Turner, the President of the HK Lawn Bowls Association. I didn't know it then but he was also a Freemason and a member of Lodge St. John, 618 SC. He offered me the post of Chief Coach. I accepted the offer and was then re-elected, year on year up to 2004, when I became ineligible for that post be reason of age.

When I was 73, myself and a lady friend, Lydia Yang, partnered with my masonic and lawn-bowls friend, Paul Foster and his wife, entering the Hong Kong National Mixed Fours Championship. The final was held at the CCC and we won. It was my first and only National Championships win.

In May, '66, I moved to Kian Gwan Company (China) Ltd, a *rice hong* but with a side line in cosmetics. Starting off as a salesman in the cosmetics department I was promoted, in '67, to the vacancy of sales manager. In that capacity I got to know the managing director of Kian Gwan, an Indonesian by the name of S.G. Liem who was married to a Dutch lady and domiciled in Holland. On his bi-annual inspection visits I was his assistant, usually taking him to lunch at the CCC.

It was in casual lunchtime conversation with him that freemasonry was mentioned. Liem told me it was *not* an exclusively expatriate club and that, if I wanted to join, I only need ask my old friend, Roger Pennels. From that I was given to understand that not only Roger Pennels but Liem, himself, was a Freemason and, as I later discovered, also a joining member of Lodge St. John, 618 SC.

While I was with Kian Gwan I was invited to take up the agency for 'Rimmel' Cosmetics in Hong Kong, I did so and worked from home until leaving Kian Gwan in March, 1970. That same month I joined 'Henry David (HK) Ltd', an import and export company dealing mainly in cosmetics. I was their general manager and brought 'Rimmel' with me to my new employers.

I still met up with Roger Pennels every now and again and it was in '72 that I asked him if I could become a Freemason? Roger seemed pleasantly surprised and straight away agreed to propose my membership. He found a seconder by the name of Si Min, a Chinese Malay friend of mine from the IRC who I didn't know was a member of Lodge St. John. I duly attended a lodge enquiry committee meeting and then was asked to wait for a whole year before I could be initiated. That was in 1974 when fellow Indian Gary Harilela was in the chair of Lodge St. John, 618 SC. It was only then that I chanced upon many acquaintances of old and wondered at the coincidence of how they had all played a part in my life.

Leaving the employ of Henry David (HK) Ltd in '73, I tried my hand at yet another line of work, in the legal field. I was taken on by Hastings & Co. Solicitors in Central District as a clerk. In '74 I was given the job of office manager, a post I went on to hold for ten years, 'till my 60th birthday in November, '84. That was when I met solicitor John Glass, later a magistrate, also a member of Lodge St. John, 618. In '84, I wasn't ready to retire and went on to work for another solicitor's firm, Susan Liang & Co, eventually and finally retiring from gainful employment in 1989.

Having said that, I found out about a marketing enterprise in cosmetics where there is no shop, as such. One just buys-in products to sell on to one's friends and acquaintances. So I started doing that from home. My friends told me it was pyramid selling. I didn't think there was anything wrong with that except that I never made much of a profit because I kept giving my products away to friends. So finally I retired and started attending public lectures, mainly on health and welfare issues. I liked those, making more friends. Sometimes I invited them to have lunch with me at the CCC where we enjoyed good local cuisine and a chit-chat well into the afternoon.

Freemasonry now played a big part in my life. I soon got a reputation for not missing a single one of Lodge St. John's nine meetings every year. My party-piece was the north east corner lecture or charity charge in the entered apprentice degree working. I never needed a prompt. I also attended the socials, bringing my Linda with me to the annual ladies night, all dressed up. In later years I couldn't afford those grand dinner dances but a few of my dear brothers used to club together and pay for Linda and I. In 1985 came what I call my crowning achievement in life when I was elected to be the right worshipful master of Lodge St John, 618 SC. After my installation, at the banquet, all of my brothers there, about a hundred of them, stood to sing the master's song for me. I was so humbled and elated that I cried unashamedly.

Soon my meagre savings began to run out and, in the millennium year, finding that I would not be able to afford the management fees for the building Linda and I lived in, I had to ask my masonic brothers if they could help me out. It was Bro. Stuart McDouall, the almoner in Lodge St John at the time, who wrote the prayer on my behalf to the Far East Masonic Benevolence Fund Corporation which came to my aid with a grant-for-life in exchange for a first charge on our flat. Linda was suspicious of the mason's intentions but not me. I completely trusted them and am happy that the masons should be reimbursed for looking after Linda and I for the rest of our lives. That generous monthly grant kept Linda and me, and then only me after she died, in board and lodging up until now.

After my Linda was taken ill and put into a care home, which the masons paid the fees for, I lived for a while on my own. I visited her everyday in that tiny, windowless room shared with another elderly lady. She remained there for five years. In the last two years she never left her bed, hardly talking and wearing gloves made with strips of bamboo for the fingers, wired together so that she couldn't itch herself involuntarily. During that time I was glad I had my Lodge meetings for the comfort and friendship of my brothers, Bro. Raymond Teng in particular, used to pick me up from home and then drive me back home after the meeting. Very kind.

I remember one time when Bro. Sarath Disanyaka, the RWM at the time, arranged, through Linda's care home, for the hire of a private nurse for Linda. Nothing came of it but, at about the same time, my monthly grant from the masons went up by about twenty thousand dollars which I thought very generous and I used it to entertain my friends. But about a year later those extra funds suddenly stopped so I couldn't do so much entertaining but it was nice while it lasted. I was never any good with bills and banking but Bro. Stuart used to sort-out the home bills and bank statements for me.

[It was for nearly a year that the Masons's gave the money to Noorie to pay a nurse to look after Linda part time. Noorie had not understood his instructions and never did hire a private nurse]

When Linda passed away, I was finding it very difficult to look after myself. Some strangers from the mainland, involved in cross-border illicit trading in tins of baby milk powder, pretended to look after me but actually they invited themselves in to use my home for business or leisure purposes, sleeping on the sofas and occasionally taking cash from my wallet. There was a man, who said he was a professor, who came to stay and I liked talking to him. He and his friends used to accompany me for meals at the CCC and I always ended up paying the bill. My short-term memory was really bad and I couldn't remember the names of all my visitors.

Shortly after my Linda died, her son came back, refusing to pay for his mother's funeral *and* still looking for cash but fellow lodge members Henry Aun and Raymond Teng told him he had no call on me any more. Bro. Henry and Bro. Raymond supported me all the way, helping and looking after me. It was they who eventually found me the excellent care home that I am now living in. I am one of the few men there. Most of the residents are widows with whom I like to chit-chat and occasionally make up a mahjong foursome.

Post script: On 20th November, 2021, Noorie had his 97th birthday. A picture was taken of him grinning like a Cheshire cat!

Eight months later, at 11.10 hrs on Thursday 28th July, 2022, Bro. Noorie Razack died peacefully at the care home in Shaukiwan, Hong Kong, where he happily spent the last few years of his monumental life.

- End -

THE REPATRIATION OF HONG KONG TO CHINA.

The inner cordon.

As a British crown colony and dependent territory, Hong Kong ceased to exist at the stroke of mid-night on Monday 30th June, 1997. The ceremony of the repatriation of Hong Kong to the People's Republic of China (PRC) took place in the newly built Convention and Exhibition Centre (CEC) in Wanchai district, on the waterfront of Victoria Harbour. Present were heads of state, government and royalty (HRH Prince Charles on behalf of HM The Queen) from China and Britain, accompanied by 66 'internationally protected persons', as per UN convention; the largest and most prestigious gathering of world leaders in the history of Hong Kong. I was an acting chief superintendent at the time and was allocated the secure inner cordon as my sphere of responsibility.

By way of background, Hong Kong became part of the British Empire, ceded by Imperial China in the Treaty of Nanking, June, 1842. When the Union Jack was first planted on the island, in November, 1841, Hong Kong was little more than a barren rock. In 1860 the then flourishing colony successfully augmented its land-mass, at the conclusion of the first Opium War, to include the Kowloon peninsula and Stone Cutters Island. Then, in 1898, still flourishing and outgrowing its boundaries, Britain obtained for Hong Kong a 99-year lease of what became known as The New Territories, northward of Kowloon. And, at the end of that lease, in June 1997, came the end of 155 years of British rule.

The preparations for the repatriation actually began in December, 1984, 13 years before the end of the 99-year lease, when the British prime minister, Margaret Thatcher, visited Beijing and formally signed The Sino-British Joint Declaration with her Chinese counterpart, Premier Zhou Ziyang. The Joint Declaration agreed that the PRC would "...*resume the exercise of sovereignty...*" over the whole territory of Hong Kong with effect from 1ˢᵗ July, 1997. In the same document the *"One country, two systems"* principle between Hong Kong and China, which was the brain-child of President Deng Xiaoping, was enunciated. The agreement was that the socialist system of the PRC would not be practised in *"...the Hong Kong Special Administrative Region"* (HKSAR) and that Hong Kong's previous capitalist system and its way of life would remain unchanged for a period of 50 years, ending 30ᵗʰ June, 2047. This inspired strategy created the time buffer necessary to gently, over time, facilitate parity between the countries in matters of law and order, economy, politics and culture.

From about the same time, and gathering momentum as the years ticked by, the dominant subject of conversation in Hong Kong became the repatriation. And it changed lives. The more it was discussed the more uncertainty came to the fore, raising many *"what if"* questions that didn't seem to have an answer in the Joint Declaration.

Policy decisions on the long term future were made at the highest level in government and in the private sector which, when journalists heard of them, fuelled increasing concern among society-at-large, over a sustainable outcome after the repatriation. This despite government assurances that all would be well.

Four particularly high-profile plans did nothing to allay fears. These were:-

1. The Hong Kong government, aware of the potential for discontentment, announced that a new British National Overseas (BNO) passport, approved under the auspices of the British Government, would be created. The intention was to provide registered Hong Kong citizens, who either did not wish to live in the territory after the repatriation or who just wanted a safety net available should there be troubles at some time in the future, with a bolt-hole. This would entitle the holder to citizenship in the UK if, and whenever, he/she wished to exercise that right. The Chinese side quite justifiably queried the necessity for such a safety measure.

2. In the police force it was promulgated, quite early on, that any officer serving in Special Branch; the political and highly sensitive wing of police work in which officers were all positively vetted to top secret level; would be given early retirement in the years and months before the repatriation, with financial incentives to leave Hong Kong and start a new life overseas;

3. On the corporate front, Simon Keswick, chairman of Jardine Matheson & Co, Hong Kong's most enduring 'Hong', said they were *not* pulling out of the territory, *but*, as a contingency measure, were setting up a new holding company in Bermuda; and

4. The Hong Kong Shanghai Banking Corporation (HSBC), which has a global network, likewise decided to move their headquarter operations to London.

And so it was, as the date for the repatriation drew nigh, that some of my peers in the police force decided to leave Hong Kong, expressing a disinclination to working under a communist regime. And there were more in the community, particularly expatriates, dismayed or even alarmed at their future prospects, who packed their bags and headed home. But the numbers were not large; not a mass exodus by any means.

For me, I was fortunate enough to be selected for the HK Civil Service senior command course held in May, 1996. During that fortnight symposiums and lectures were conducted and given by top officials and leading lights in society including government directorate, the president of the Legislative Council, the Chair of the Law Society, the Chair of the Basic Law Committee, the deputy to Lu Ping who was head of the HK and Macau Affairs Office of the state council of the PRC, the senior manager of the Bank of China of HK and, lastly, the Vice Chair of the Democratic Alliance for the Betterment of Hong Kong who was Mr. TAM Yu-chung. By the end of the course I felt justified, when returning to my duties at Police Training School, in assuring my fellow officers that there was absolutely *no need* to fear any misfortune after the repatriation. Some, I know, did not heed my advice. Others had already made their mind up.

It was against this backdrop of doubt and baseless rumour-mongering that the repatriation was held. There was a dress rehearsal on the 25th of July for all the organising parties, with actors playing the principal roles. My rehearsal, as commander of the inner cordon, went according to plan and I was not aware of any glitches in other venues and aspects of the event.

Monday the 30th of June dawned with a dismal weather forecast of clouds and rain spanning the entire day. And there was no possibility of inclement weather even delaying the repatriation ceremonies for one moment, never mind postponing the event.

At 15.00 hrs I reported for duty, in full uniform; at the control room set up in the CEC. The dep. dir. of operations was present and he gave an update of the latest threat assessment which was, thankfully, all clear at the two ceremonial venues. One minor, peaceful political protest was being mounted by pro-democracy advocates outside the Legislative Council building in Central district.

At about the same time the out-going governor, HE Christopher Patten, was treated to a personal farewell ceremony by all the staff of Government House. It was organised and led by his aide de camp, police superintendent Lance Brown, dressed in full regalia, wearing his plumed pith helmet and girded with ceremonial sword. The Union Jack was lowered for the last time from the flag pole in the forecourt as the Last Post was played by a police bugler. The flag was then folded and presented to Chris Patten, who was dressed in a plain suit and tie, for him to keep. The ceremony ended with two RHKP pipers playing the heart-stirring tune 'Highland Cathedral'. His family watched from the sidelines, a few tears I think.

By 17.00 hrs all duties were in place at both of the ceremonial arenas; first at the harbour frontage to the British Forces head quarters building known as HMS Tamar and, second, at the CEC, some 300 metres eastward, along the water front. The first venue was for an entirely British ceremony, Prince Charles and Chris Patten bidding farewell to Hong Kong. The second venue was for the political ceremony presided over by PRC President Jiang Zemin and guest of honour Prime Minister Tony Blair.

Light rain was falling at 17.30 hrs when President Jiang Zemin and Premier Li Peng arrived in Hong Kong, having flown down from Beijing to Shenzen in an Air China Boeing 747, with an entourage of some 30 officials. They were escorted directly by car to the Grand Hyatt Hotel in Wanchai.

At 20.00 hrs guests began to arrive at the CEC, minor officials first and then, by 21.00 hrs, the pace had quickened as more senior officials, foreign dignitaries and distinguished guests arrived, showing their passes and being escorted by staff to the cocktail reception being hosted by the Hong Kong Government for 4,000 guests in all. And, as that was happening, a total of 500 vehicles of the People's Liberation Army (PLA) were being driven across the Chinese border into Hong Kong. They disbursed among four former British garrisons, the fourth being HMS Tamar itself.

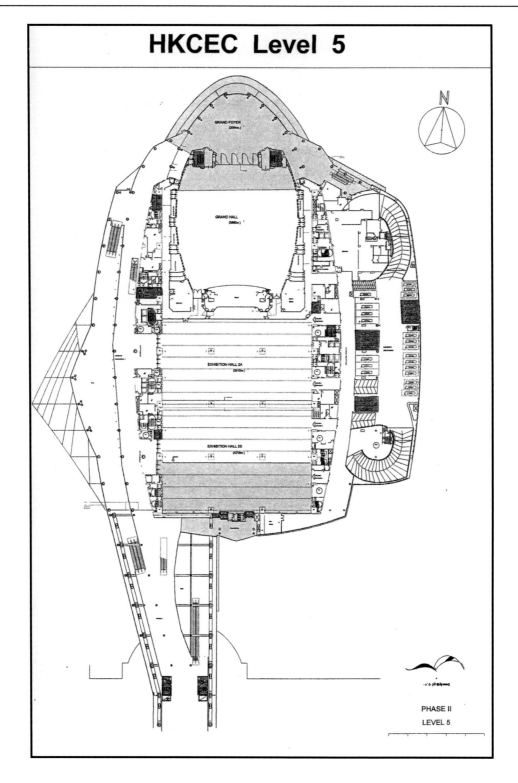

"Floor plan of the inner cordon at the Hong Kong Convention and Exhibition Centre"

At 23.00 hrs all the guests for the repatriation ceremony at the CEC were ushered through my *cordon sanitaire* and into the main hall for the ceremony to begin at 23.45 hrs. At this time it was raining hard all along the harbour waterfront. From my vantage point above and to one side of the main entrance of the big hall I could see, through the enormous glass walls of the CEC, the grand stands in front of HMS Tamar and the temporary parade ground on the harbour frontage. It was well lit and hundreds of spectators in all their finery were getting very wet before the ceremony started, even with umbrellas up. There was a roof over the stands but it looked like a giant venetian blind laid horizontally above them. The huge, slightly curved slats, about 12" apart, were literally channelling rain water straight into laps below. Not particularly insightful of its designers.

At 23.40 hrs ceremonies in both venues began. In front of HMS Tamar a regimental guard of honour paraded and then Prince Charles, as guest of honour at the British event, dressed in the uniform of Admiral of the Fleet, British Navy, gave his speech, exuding hubris and good cheer. He lauded the achievements of Hong Kong people and thanked the out-going governor for his sterling work and fortitude during his period of office.

In the CEC, the raised stage for the VIPs at the front of the huge auditorium, facing the four thousand strong audience, was all in red; the carpets and the seating; and hanging from the ceiling above them were the two flood-lit flags of China and the UK. In the forefront of the stage were two lecterns bearing the English and Chinese emblems, and to the right and left of the stage were two flag poles, that on the right with the Union Jack raised and that on the left, empty. Beside these, two military guards of honour, each 15 strong; one from the PLA and the other comprising a mix of British army, navy and airforce officers; lined up on the left and right respectively. In comparing the two line-ups, I was thinking they looked like something out of a Monty Python show; the Chinese side immaculate, all 6' tall soldiers, splendid physique, not a uniform crease out of place. And then the British side all of different heights, short and fat, tall and thin, different uniforms and couldn't even dress in a straight line. The British delegation, led by Prime Minister Tony Blair, sat on the right while the Chinese delegation, led by President Jiang Zemin sat on the left. Tony Blair made the first speech and was effusive in his praise of the success of the bi-lateral talks that had led to the mutually agreeable promulgation of the basic law. Next, President Jiang Zemin, solemn, in a dark suit and tie, took the rostrum and launched into a spirited, at times strident speech in Putonghua (Mandarin) lasting over ten minutes. Not being a Putonghua speaker I understood none of it and had to wait until the following morning before I saw the English transcript.

"President Jiang Zemin greeting Prime Minister Tony Blair at
the conclusion of the ceremony of repatriation"

And having read it I was nonplussed. On the one hand irritated by what was, in my humble opinion, a slightly high-handed speech; a little insensitive to the feelings of the people of Hong Kong. But, on the other hand, satisfied, well knowing that the President had every right to stamp his authority, and justice for the Chinese people, in reclaiming the territory that was wrested from their forbears by the British empire which had enforced the unequal treaties in the first place.

My observation, kept to myself, was that the British were handing back a peaceful, thriving and economically viable territory; a going concern; where there was only a barren rock at the start of their occupation. One might have thought, if only in the interests of *entente cordiale*, that laudable mention might have been made of this fact, but no.

Back at the HMS Tamar venue, HE the Governor, Chris Patten, took the stage after Prince Charles had sat down, and delivered what sounded distinctly like a eulogy to HK which, in effect, it was. And as he finished with a final "Good bye" the Hong Kong Philharmonic Orchestra, off to one side, played Elgar's popular 'variation', Nimrod, a fitting and emotive musical signature at the end of an era. Chris Patten sat in his chair, head bowed in both hands, with Prince Charles leaning across and briefly patting his shoulder in consolation.

Exactly one minute before midnight the flags of the United Kingdom and the British Hong Kong Flag, flying before HMS Tamar, were lowered by two parties of three perfectly-drilled Hong Kong police officers while the Last Post was played. Then the British National Anthem was played by the orchestra with all the sodden spectators singing lustily. At the same time, in the CEC, a British military flag party ceremonially lowered the Union Jack and, on the dot of mid-night, a flag party of the PLA raised the Chinese flag, on the other flag pole, to the proud notes of the Chinese national anthem and with an emphatic flourish. There was a minor hiatus, which I heard over the secure radio, that the English National anthem was played at Tamar 12 seconds before the Chinese national anthem was played at the CEC. No one but the meticulous time-keepers were concerned, or even noticed.

And that was the end of the ceremony of repatriation. Doors to the main hall in the CEC were flung open and the 4,000-odd spectators began to file out. The doors closest to where the great and the good had been seated opened and first out was President Jiang Zemin, escorted by Premier Li Pang exiting ahead of British Prime Minister Tony Blair who was accompanied by British Foreign Secretary Robin Cook. Then came several Hong Kong legislative councillors, one of whom was pro-Beijing, Mr. TAM Yu-chung. And he, on recognising me standing to one side, tipped me a wink as he passed by. All appeared to be in jovial mood. Then came a few more British politicians, no doubt enjoying the free party. In their midst, accompanied by body guards, former Prime Minster Margaret Thatcher, dressed fetchingly in blue and white, plus matching hat, walked by, somehow looking lonely and decidedly weary.

It took a full 40 minutes before the doors to the main hall were closed after the last person therein had left. And there was silence in the huge glass-walled atrium overlooking the harbour. I took a solitary walk over to the side of the atrium opposite HMS Tamar, my steps echoing loudly in the void, and watched the royal yacht, HMY Britannia, gracefully heading out of the harbour, southward. This was to be her last official engagement before being laid-up in Glasgow.

Leaving the CEC at about 01.30 hrs, I took a taxi home and noted, with some wonder, how packed the streets, the pubs and the restaurants all appeared to be; parties everywhere; some celebrating and some, no doubt, commiserating.

The newspapers in the morning were, of course, full of the events of the night before. The Royal Observatory published a screen shot of the Hong Kong weather map taken at 23.30 hrs the night before. It was coloured in contours of light blue, dark blue and a single blob of green right over HMS Tamar; light rain, heavy rain and torrential rain respectively. And the superstitious were arguing the omens, giving their verdicts; either the promise of great wealth because the Cantonese word for water, *sui*, is also a euphemism for riches. Or tears for the funeral of a loved one.

--------- *End* ----------

NOT QUITE RETIRED

A container ship, a teacher and a private detective

My retirement date was set by the Hong Kong Government for my 55th birthday, 27th May, 2005. With ten months to go I received a memorandum from Civil Service Branch advising me of said date, as if I didn't know, and giving details of a pre-retirement week-long course, at which my attendance was invited, on how to manage retirement. And so began the wind-down.

At that time I was second in command of Kwai Tsing District, a fairly busy post, for which a detailed hand-over report to my successor was necessary before leaving. This document is a comprehensive compendium of all the duties for which the post is responsible for. It includes security responsibilities for civil installations in the district; container terminals and the petroleum and dangerous goods storage for Hong Kong. Within the police station details of the administration and budgeting, occupational safety and health issues, internal discipline, state of manpower, the state of police equipment including vehicles, on-going projects, the police canteen, organisation of social and sporting events, morale among the troops, and more.

As well as writing the hand-over report it was also necessary for the retiree to start planning his own future. At the age of 55 quite a few retiring officers, still reasonably fit and healthy, consider looking for gainful employment in other occupations and that is what I did. Having a penchant for teaching, nurtured during my time as a police course instructor and, latterly, commandant of Police Training School, I decided to enrol for a diploma in teacher training. That achieved, I was hired by a secondary school run by the Hong Kong University Graduates Association where I taught English and History for a year, and started up a scout group.

The HK government treasury department wanted to know how I would like my pension paid. There were several options and I chose to have 50% of it in a down-payment, as a capital investment, and the remaining 50% to be paid out monthly for the rest of my life. When that money came to hand I had enough liquidity to buy a small flat in a high-rise residential block, which my wife and I promptly did. Our new property, the first I had personally owned, was in a big high-rise block on a verdant hillside above Kennedy Road, in Wanchai District, Hong Kong Island. A few days after retirement we moved out of our spacious government quarters, halfway up the Peak, into our rather more compact home, down-sized by nearly half, in the middle of the concrete jungle, with no eye-catching views. But it was ours and we were happy.

Eventually the months before retirement day came down to weeks and the farewell parties began. At this stage I was was handing back stores and had signed off on my hand-over report. Pleasant was the surprise at the number of invitations that I received for drinks, lunches or dinners, not just within the police force but from legal department, friends in the Independent Commission Against Corruption (ICAC), Customs and Excise and Public Works Department *aka* the Please Wait Department as some wags would have it, all of which I had previously had dealings with in my various police postings. One of the most frequent questions asked of any retiree is his/her plans for the future. Mine was already mapped out, a school teacher for a while and, no, I was not going to be a private detective or take a job in the security industry.

Finally the last day at work came to pass. And the next morning, squinting at my disheveled visage in the mirror, I said, out-loud, "This is the first day of the rest of your life" with a big grin on my face.

One of the conditions of service that I signed up to at the start of my career, in 1970, was a government-paid sea passage, upon retirement, back to my country of origin. Accordingly, in the school summer holidays of 2005, I booked a voyage back home, not on a cruise ship but on a container ship. Neither before nor since have I heard of retiring expatriate government servants taking a cargo vessel on their voyage home, preferring the comforts of a commercial cruise ship. But having been chairman of the security committee for the container port, as part of my police duties, I knew what the conditions for passengers were like on the newer container ships; comparatively luxurious and about two thirds of the price of a standard cabin on a cruise ship.

And so it was, on 21st June, 2005, that my wife and I took a taxi to the Kwai Chung Container Port and boarded the CMA CGM Berlioz, a flat-bottomed, French owned, container ship. It was built in South Korea in 2001 to a standard design, just under 300 metres in length, 40 metres wide and weighing in at 73,157 tons. It had a fully laden average speed of 21 knots and its crew complement was just 14. The captain and his four officers were French. The head chef was also French. The remainder of the crew were Romanian.

A little known fact is that these 'standard built' container ships have four passenger cabins in the bridge superstructure. We were the only passengers and were given the owner's cabin which comprised an en-suite double bedroom, a spacious lounge *cum* reception room, complete with cocktail cabinet and well-stocked fridge, and a walk-in changing room and storage cupboard. Our reception room could comfortably entertain 12 people and we did invite the captain and his officers twice to pre-lunch cocktail receptions on the first and last Sundays of our trip. On Sundays the officers all wore their formal 'whites' with caps and badges of rank.

Below decks, above the engine room, is a space given over to keeping fit; an 8 x 4 m heated swimming pool, a well-equipped gymnasium and a table tennis court. The open deck could be walked round but no running was allowed as there were all sorts of obstructions; pipes, wires and hatches. A couple of evenings, when the weather was clear, calm and warm, Susanna and I made our way to the bows and just stood against the railings taking in the immensity of the ocean and the starry firmament above, all in complete silence. No engine noise could be heard up at the bows.

Each time the vessel put into port; never more than 24 hours in each place; the steward took his charges ashore, showed us around the locality, ordered a taxi for sight-seeing and took us to the best restaurants – for which we happily paid for his company. We never needed a visa for any country that we visited since we were on the ship's crew visa, listed as 'Super Cargo'. Between container ports we occupied ourselves. Susanna knitted prodigiously, read books and, together, we won the crew table tennis championship. For me, every day I spent an hour in the gymnasium and the swimming pool, followed by a leisurely breakfast. The ship had wi-fi connections and we were able to receive and send e-mails and follow world news.

Lunch was a sumptuous three course meal served at the captain's table, with French wines out of the ship's embargoed alcohol and tobacco locker. The menu was varied and truly at Michelin Star level. One day the captain asked my wife if she can cook Chinese food? That question led to Susanna taking the head chef round a market in Kuala Lumpur, one of the ports we stopped at, shopping for a Chinese feast. The next morning Susanna was in the galley showing the chefs how to prepare the sea food and other ingredients for five different dishes. Lunch that day was much appreciated by the entire crew. Our dinners were always privately served by the steward in our cabin, again with French wines gratis.

But all good things have to come to an end and late, one dark and wet evening, we berthed in Southampton container port, our six weeks blissful sojourn on MV Berlioz ended at the foot of the gang plank on the dock-side where we bade our steward a fond farewell.

After another six weeks in the UK we flew back to Hong Kong where Susanna returned to work and I went back to my teaching.

Shortly before the Christmas holidays, 2005, I received a 'phone call from a solicitor of my acquaintance who invited me to a lunch-time meeting with a client of his. This turned out to be a request for assistance in a case of suspected crimes committed against a local Hong Kong entrepreneur in the watch business. For over an hour I listened to a complicated tale of woe, ending with a report to the police which resulted in his lawyer being told there was insufficient evidence of the commission of a crime. The entrepreneur had lost a lot of money invested in the business and I agreed to try and help him get it back.

Over the next few weeks I spent many hours, after school, with the client, Ashley, in his offices, making copious notes and unravelling a complicated web of intrigue which had all the hallmarks of criminal activity but of which hard evidence had yet to be elicited.

Ashley turned out to be a retired government pharmacist whose claim to fame was his invention of a cheap but effective cough mixture that the government manufactured in large quantities for the masses and which became widely known as *Ma-liu* (horse-piss) on account of its colour and smell. His hobby had always been horology but, in retirement, it became his full-time business, setting up his own workshop in a rented apartment of a factory building. He had remarkable ingenuity and designed his own brand of 'hygienic' wrist watches. He spent a lot of his savings having his designs registered and parts manufactured in Switzerland. His own specially designed silicon straps and fastenings, all part of the hygiene principle, were produced in China. And the completed ensemble became the first 'hygienic' wristwatch in the world; one that could be washed in disinfectant, used safely in surgeries and apothecaries and which could be put through rough handling, so clean and solid was it's make.

But Ashley did not have the funds necessary to comprehensively advertise his watches, not even locally, never mind internationally. It was this shortcoming that doomed his creation to obscurity and which propelled him into the hands of unscrupulous agents in the business. Buying a stake in a local, commercial watch business with interests in China, he hoped to use their platform for his own brand. Initially all went according to plan until his business partners began to make demands for more money and that he give them a stake in his sales. Ashley was also aware of and, by association, complicit in what he believed to be underhand deals and deceptions being practised by his partners with other watch brands. Becoming alarmed he decided to pull out, demanding that his investment, nearly a million HK dollars, be returned. And that is when things became nasty. His personal computer was hacked. Then he received anonymous threats which he believed to be made by triads hired by his partners. He became scared of physical reprisals against him and/or his family.

To cut a long story short I was able to piece together evidence of criminal intimidation and a conspiracy to defraud Ashley of his investment in the business. I showed Ashley's statement, together with some documentary evidence, to a superintendent in the police Commercial Crimes Bureau (CCB). But I knew the case was weak; one man's word against another's; and was advised that a civil suit was the best way to continue. So it was that Ashley sued his business partners and won a judgement for the return of most of his investment. But they laid a counter suit and the partners produced false witnesses stating that the subject investment was legitimately used to settle contracts in which Ashley was partner to and for which he still owed them money. Ashley believed that even the paper-work must have been falsified. But he could not disprove it.

The only good to come out of the whole sorry saga was that, despite the loss of money, there was no more aggravation. What's more, he did achieve some fame in horological circles when the British Museum's Department of Horology displayed his hygienic watch design as a unique innovation in horology. I left off teaching and took up part-time work in Ashley's watch business, becoming good friends with him and his family, and remaining so, even now.

Hot on the heels of that case came an investigation of a totally different nature and which had a more satisfactory outcome. It was a local solicitor of Sri Lankan nationality, an acquaintance of mine, who called and asked me to help out a client of his.

The story was that someone unknown had stolen HK$8.5 million over a period of about three weeks, from the coffers of an Indian diamond merchant whose offices were in a high security factory building in Hung Hom, Kowloon. A report had been made to the police and detectives from the CCB had visited the scene. After several interviews and studying the finance systems of the company they had been unable to find any evidence of criminality beyond the fact of a black hole appearing in the company accounts. They had put the accountant and his office under the microscope but found nothing incriminating. The company directors also vouched for their accountant as a kinsman from the same village. The company was nepotistic in its staffing.

After interviewing the directors of the company, including the company secretary, it appeared to me that the answer to the mystery had to be in the company's banking arrangements. The company secretary made an appointment for himself and me to meet the manager of their bank to a) verify the company accountant's version of events and b) to assess the bank's security instructions and policies for safety and confidentiality. That mission highlighted one interesting security feature which was their requirement for personal authorization, by 'phone, with any client making a transaction with the bank. I spent a whole day in the bank's comms room, assisted by one of the bank staff, listening to telephone recordings authorizing transactions made by our diamond merchant's company over the previous month. We knew the total amount of money we were looking for and we had the dates and times of legitimate transactions. What I was looking for were illegitimate transactions, not recorded in the company records.

In the several days that I was working out of the diamond merchant's offices I was invited to lunch with the company directors, every day, to a Jain restaurant in an adjacent factory building. You'd never know it was there unless you'd been told about it. The food was delicious and the place was well patronised too, apparently all from India and all of the Jain faith. The diners all seemed to know each other. It was explained to me that, like Jewish people being associated with banking and finance, so Jains are associated with diamonds. And they weren't the only diamond merchants in Hung Hom.

Back to the case in hand, I noted down the details of 12 transactions originating from the diamond merchant's company, all in the hundreds of thousands of dollars and not officially accounted for. The company secretary listened to those 12 recordings and verified that it was the voice of the company accountant authorizing those transactions. The chairman of the board of directors was informed and he couldn't quite believe it. He, himself, came to the bank to listen to the recordings in question. He listened to the first recording and stepped back a pace, visibly shocked. This was his relative and a trusted employee.

The very next day I was invited to attend a board meeting in the company offices, together with their solicitor. It turned out to be an informal inquisition of the accountant who was seated before a semi-circle of the directors and senior management. I was asked to lead the questioning. I simply laid out the evidence against the accountant. The latter, looking very ill at ease, kept on saying and even swearing by his deity that it wasn't him. But when the chairman himself told him that he had listened to the bank's recordings, he went quiet, saying nothing, looking straight ahead of him.

The Chairman rounded on the accused, his relative through marriage, with undisguised contempt for one who had betrayed the family trust. The latter began sobbing, explaining his indebtedness over love affairs. The Chairman demanded to know if he could repay the money and his silence was negative. The accountant was told to go home, escorted by one of the senior management. After he'd left, the solicitor advised that I be asked to submit my case investigation to the police but the Chairman of the board refused. In the subsequent discussion, in which I took no part, a consensus was reached that the public embarrassment to the company, not to mention a possible loss of clientelle, did not make prosecution through the courts, with likely press interest, worthwhile. The company would handle the matter themselves.

The following week the solicitor called again, asking me to meet him in a Wanchai coffee shop for a chat. There he handed me a handsome cheque for my services to the diamond merchant's company. The other news from the solicitor was that the accountant had gone missing from his flat the very next day, reported to the company by his wife as only taking his passport, some cash and a few documents with him. As for the accountant's whereabouts, the solicitor said that the family was looking for him, suspecting that he was returning to India where he would go to ground.

Another month passed before I had a chance meeting with the solicitor in the street. I enquired of him for news of the accountant and he said he didn't know. But he also surmised that the family wouldn't rest till they found him and, in that event, he didn't give much chance for his survival.

For me, the only sequel to that case investigation was a crate of Alfonso mangos from India, in the month of July, for the ensuing three years. They are the best, the biggest and the juiciest I have ever tasted.

I undertook just one more request for assistance from a small chain of restaurants wanting advice on increasing their physical security against triad or gang extortion; literally blackmail. The owner said he had heard stories from other owners of restaurants and cafes and was frightened that he might be targeted. All I did was advise him to make a note of any approaches that were suspect, to have a recorder ready to use on the telephone lines in his restaurant, to instal CCTV in his restaurants and to inform the local police station of any threats received. For that I made no charge.

Finally, full retirement.

EXPLORING CHINA

The holiday of a life time

In January, 2012, my wife Susanna and I set forth on what Victorian society used to call 'The Grand Tour'. Our son Jack was living and working in Beijing and welcomed us to use his flat as our springboard into China's wealth of historical sights, an open-ended tour with a flexible itinerary. In the space of five months we covered around two thousand miles of road, rail and river, criss-crossing the vast landmass from our Beijing nexus. We'd go away for a couple of weeks before returning to our hub for a shower and change of clothes (I jest) and then set off again on a different compass bearing. When we decided to call it a day, we felt that we had hardly scratched the surface of all that China has to offer.

China has a remarkably well-connected and efficient public transport infrastructure. The railways are its backbone, reaching every corner of the country; cheap, fast and reliable. Between cities six-lane highways, in immaculate condition, stretch for hundreds of miles. Within the cities, trams, buses and taxis are plentiful. We used all these forms of transport, mingling with the masses of humanity on the move day and night. We didn't look old and infirm yet we often encountered genuine social awareness when our fellow travellers, young and middle-aged, offered us their seats on crowded vehicles. Many times pedestrians solicitously asked us if they could help us with directions or map-reading. When we were carrying luggage up steps young men and women approached us, wanting to carry our bags. And on occasions, when we asked passers-by for advice, not once were we cold-shouldered.

Fortunately, in those winter months, the weather was mostly dry and the days sunny. But the one issue we had was with air pollution, particularly in the cities. Some mornings we woke up, finding it unexpectedly dark outside, and realised that it was the effects of pollution; the sun reduced to a dimly-glowing, brown orb barely penetrating the pervasive smog. We visited towns and villages where the residents, not having central heating, were burning briquettes of powdered coal to keep warm and do the cooking on.

And we put up with some anti-social habits such as people clearing their throats and spitting carelessly around them, inside or out. Littering was clearly a problem with everything from cigarettes to empty polystyrene food boxes discarded in gutters and drains. And smoking was endemic, anywhere and everywhere, in lifts, in restaurants, on buses and trains.

Government is aware of these unhygienic nuisances and one sees rubbish bins, signs and warnings, hygiene notices in public places and an army of road-sweepers out early, every morning.

Apart from the wonderful sights and sounds of ancient and modern China open to tourists there is also the fascination of what living and working in China is like today. The highly ordered and regimented way of life is anathema to western thinking that endorses freedom of speech, capitalism and the right to vote and participate in politics. When one thinks of the logistics of feeding, housing, educating, employing and looking after the health and welfare of 1.3 billion people (2012 statistics) living on 9.6 million Km^2 of land I, for one, can't propose any better solution for maintaining peace and stability other than by authoritarian government. No matter how unpalatable some may think it, it works.

I am not an apologist for China. On our travels we talked to many people, from different walks of life, and it became apparent to us that none of them feel that they live in a repressive society. Indeed, quite the opposite for the older generations who appreciate the wholesale improvements in life compared with what it was in the 1960s and before. The collective conscience in the younger generations seems to be just as optimistic. Unemployment in 2012 was practically nil; all able-bodied adults in gainful employment. Even now, 2024, it is still lower than in the Americas and in Europe. There are very few homeless people; beggars few and far between; in a society where medical aid and social welfare is freely available. Yes, especially in such a vast country, there are bound to be societal differences which have led to public friction with government. But from our humble perspective these are not as disturbing as they are in many western societies.

We arrived in Beijing on the fourth day of the Chinese New Year holidays and unpacked ourselves into our son's high-rise flat. As night settled over the city the fireworks began, lighting up the residential estate around us in flashes of yellow and red, to the sounds of battle. There were long ribbons of small red fire-crackers, touched off at one end, exploding with the rat-a-tat-tat of a machine gun. The windows rattled in the blasts of rocket explosions. It wasn't until past mid-night that peace and quiet descended. The following morning Susanna and I went for a walk in the adjacent park and discovered a hawker stall with a vast range of pyrotechnics on sale, from hand-held sparklers to rockets standing three feet tall. Nowadays, in 2024, fireworks are banned throughout China, the place where gunpowder was invented, on account of the alarming mortality rate, not just through accidental 'bangs' but also the occasional factory, manufacturing them, blowing up.

Being in the grip of winter we decided to make our first foray to the northern city of Harbin to see the famous ice-sculptures festival. For the three days that we were there the temperatures were minus 10 C at night, rising to minus 7 C during the day. The main street had a few benches made of ice and there was a shelter with sofas inside, also made of ice. Arriving at the Sun Island theme park we were all agog at the incredible ice-carving display. There was a working indoor cafe with a counter and half-a-dozen tables, a full-size replica of Moscow's triumphal arch, a life-size team of boatmen hauling a barge up the rapids of the Volga river and a big fish tank with fish swimming among the fronds of weeds, all made of ice. Walking on down the line of ice sculptures we viewed a vast seascape with tall waves billowing around flying seagulls; all in still-ice motion. Lastly, a ten metre tall bottle of Harbin beer, lit from the inside as if the bottle was full of beer, complete with bubbles, and ice-cold of course.

The Ming [Dynasty] tombs or necropolis, sited in the beautiful valley of Tianshan Mountain, hosts the mausoleums of 13 emperors and their consorts, buried there between 1368 and 1644. All of the tombs have been the subject of archaeological examination with the mummified remains and the fabulous artefacts found with them placed on display in the museum complex there.

Another highlight for us was the hanging temple of Hengshan. From the car park in the valley below the mountain, one looks up at it's soaring, sheer face to a line of traditional Chinese temples, ancestral halls, pavilions and 15 joss altar spaces, with linking corridors, hugging the rock face 75 meters above ground level. In 491 AD a Buddhist monk, Liao Ran, led his followers up the gorge and decided that he would build his monastery up there. It must have been a huge leap of faith for him but he persevered, building bit by bit, materials all fashioned out of timber. It is a feat of building engineering that even today would present a major challenge.

Suzhou province is home to one of China's most spectacular nature reserves, including many gardens; in reality works of art; and a peninsula that has been dubbed its 'little Venice'. Ancient Chinese villages, scattered along a web of waterways, remain as they have been for hundreds of years. Government regulations forbid modern developments and provide for the maintenance of the whole area. We spent several blissful days there, taking sampan rides down the picturesque 'lanes' and ambling around four of the most famous gardens that Chinese nobility built for themselves between 1600 and 1800. Another claim to fame that Suzhou province has is its reputation as the home of China's most beautiful ladies. I'm afraid to say that we didn't particularly notice that.

And then there was Nanjing, proclaimed the capital city of China in 1911 by Dr. Sun Yat-sen. Now it is a vast urban conglomeration of factories, residential estates and all the infrastructural trappings of modernity. But at its heart remains the original walled city. At 33.7 km long, 21 metres tall and 14.5 metres thick at its base, it is the biggest city wall in China and built entirely of bricks, including the 13 garrison blocks over each gate. We hired a tandem bicycle and rode right round the walls, passing numerous Ming dynasty cannon and other artefacts.

Altogether we encompassed 48 historical sights, ranging from a single hutong house in Beijing to the garden province of Suzhou. At the end of that I compiled my diary entries and the hundreds of photographs that I took into a book that I called 'All agog in China' published in 2013. It is a record of how well China has looked after its heritage.

GATHERING THE CLAN

Edinburgh, 2018.

In 2011 my wife Susanna, and I, made the move from Hong Kong to our newly purchased house in the township of Chesham, snuggled in the pristine Chess River valley of England's rolling Chiltern Hills. Chesham is in London's outermost zone nine and it is the last station of the London underground's Metropolitan line on which its residents can make it all the way to King's Cross Station in just over an hour, if there are no delays. A big 'if' as we soon found out.

Hot on our heels arrived a container truck carrying our green-painted China Shipping Lines 20' container with all of our wordly possessions in it. Out of the cab stepped three burly men who busied themselves with breaking the seals on the double doors, opening up and hauling out the contents. The first item taken out was a piece of rosewood furniture, a broken-legged chair. Fortunately it turned out to be the only damage in the container. It was fairly obvious that UK Customs had broken it when they searched the container for a 'long bladed object' that their x-ray machine had picked up on the screen. Of course they denied that and released the container once they had ascertained the object in question was an RHKP ceremonial sword. *Nota bene*: If it had been a scimitar rather than a ceremonial sword it would have been impounded as an unlicensed weapon.

Also unloaded from our container was an old tin trunk chock full with ancient correspondence and family documents dating back to the 1700s which had been gifted to me by my uncle (once removed) John Crichton McDouall (1912-1979), formerly Secretary for Chinese Affairs in Hong Kong, and by two of my great aunts Margaret 'Mardie' Leslie nee McDouall (1907-1998) and May 'Maisie' McDouall (1892-1998) of Australia.

It was Rev. William McDouall (1775-1849), Canon of Peterborough and Prebendary of Luton, England; my great x2 paternal grandfather; who started the collection of family correspondence. He avidly collected correspondence from his father, John McDouall of Glasgow (1733-1803), his uncle Patrick McDouall, 6th Earl of Dumfries, his siblings, other uncles, aunts and his own nine children, plus an assortment of letters from his friends and associates. All tied in neatly labelled bundles were a sum total of 2,100 items in the one battered tin trunk. On top of that lot I had a few bundles of my own correspondence from my living family, never mind 30 years of diary entries of my own. Hoarding must be in the genes!

Back in 1969-70 I visited my uncle John McDouall, aforementioned, in his home in Oxford, where he had been busy, in his retirement, working on the McDouall of Freugh family tree and associated history. He had a head-start with the family tree because the McDouall of Freugh lineage is published by both De Brett's and Burke's 'Peerage and Baronetage' on account of our family having married into British nobility[1] in 1725. Through that medium and other historical references it has been possible to trace our direct ancestry to Fergus (1096-1161), 1st Lord of Galloway.

It was also uncle John McDouall of Hong Kong who collaborated with Dr. Herbert Crichton McDouall (1860-1947) of Sydney, Australia, and I have some of their correspondence in which the two compared notes on a *whose who* of the McDoualls of Freugh, building up a picture of our ancestry and their lives. Dr. Herbert, particularly, purchased ancient books[2] on his couple of visits to London and typed out pages of notes referring to the McDoualls. Meanwhile John McDouall made a number of research forays (masquerading as holidays) into McDouall heartlands of Dumfries and Galloway; their haunts and grave yards.

Thus it was that I began the task of sorting out the bundles of correspondence and, in trying to read some, I quickly realised that the vast majority were not easily readable. To cut a long story short, in 2014, I talked to my twin brother Philip about the task of transcribing this incredible cache of historical correspondence and he needed no second bidding. As it happened he had a planned visit to England, coming up and, staying with us. For his return to Canada, I was able to fill his suitcase with a goodly number of the Rev. William's packages.

I had more help in the person of Dr. Heather Swanson *nee* McDouall, a historian at Birmingham University and an expert calligrapher; reading and transcribing ancient script. Pre-20th century there were no photo-copying facilities and business correspondence was copied long-hand into business-letter copy-books, each of 100 pages measuring 24.5 x 36 cm. We have three such letter-books owned by John McDouall of Glasgow (1733-1893) dated 1759 to 1761, 1761-1764 and 1764 to 1768. They contain his trading correspondence and accounts as a merchant in the profitable tobacco trade.

The three of us spent some five years doing copious transcriptions. Most of the correspondence, aged 100 years or more, is on what has become become flimsy, dried-out, discoloured-with-age paper, written in black ink, now all sepia. Unfolding, spreading out and re-folding of such fragile material has to be carefully done. The style of writing on them is copper-plate, as was taught at school in those times. But whereas perfect copper-plate is easy to read, that which is written by the adult hand, either too quickly or without sufficient care, becomes very difficult to decipher; the letters of the alphabet losing form and closing up in the shape of a concertina, sentences commonly lacking punctuation and missing conjunctives.

A four page letter, written on four sides of one sheet, where the ink has often blurred through the thin paper from both front and back, took me a few hours to accurately transcribe. Even more difficult were the letters completed in cross-hatch in order to save precious writing paper. This came about by the original correspondent writing to the addressee on all four pages, back and front. Then the addressee replying to the correspondent on the same four sides of paper but at 90 degrees, ie cross-hatch, to the original writer's lines. Those ancient letters can take days of patient work to decipher, holding the paper up to lighting of differing intensities, trying to high-light the layers of writing and using a powerful magnifying glass as a reading aid. Make no mistake, this art is a forensic science in its own right.

But it was all worth while. The stories that those crumbling letters exuded, like vapours from dusty antiques, have revealed the wraiths of past lives. Our painstaking transcriptions have animated them into reality, rescuing them from obscurity. Even more fascinating was the time taken for these letters to be delivered in the days of sailing ships. Much of the correspondence between Australia and England in the 1850s took three to four months to reach their destination. The reply coming back could be another four months. So the originator of the letter read the reply to him/her after an eight-month time lag. Time must have seemed to stand still for those anxious correspondents.

By 2016, Philip and I were in a position to piece together chunks of the jig-saw puzzle that each piece, each letter, provided us with. That information, when merged with the family tree and the names and dates of our ancestors, transformed them into living beings, fleshing out the skeleton so-to-speak. We knew, for the first time, the full extent of our wider family and we were contacting them by spreading the word from one to another to another. I forget whether it was me or Philip who suggested we should organise a clan gathering or if it was a mutual understanding. Whatever, Philip produced the first of many bulletins transmitted by e-mail to an ever increasing mailing list of clan members. The response was terrific.

At the same time we decided that the McDouall's of Freugh really should have their own tartan and give up the McDougall tartan that my father, JCS 'Jack' McDouall 'borrowed' and began wearing when he was a young man, keen to identify with his Scottish heritage by wearing the kilts, buying a crummock (which I still have) and going on walks in the green and pleasant lands of his forbears.

When my brother and I came of age and substance, sufficient to afford the kilts, we likewise borrowed the McDougall Clan tartan the dominant colour of which is red. It is an unusual tartan, for the pattern is spread over an 18" square whereas the usual tartan pattern covers one quarter of that size. I decided that our own tartan should incorporate that same feature in gratitude to the McDougall clan. Philip designated the colours as befitting those of the land of our forebears, dominant light and dark greens with faint lines of yellow for the gorse, light blue for the sky and darker blues for the sea. And finally thin lines of vermilion red for the clan's secondary motto, the fearsome *Vincere vel Mori*, meaning Victory or Death. I sent our application to the Scottish Register of Tartans which was accepted. A while later I received through the post a certificate announcing to all and sundry that *"This is to certify that the following tartan has met the conditions of registration set out in the Scottish Register of Tartans Act, 2008"*.

Our tartan certificate, framed and hanging on a wall in my house, is signed and waxed-sealed by the keeper of the register and there is a notation that our registration number is 12,180. I thought that must be a mistake for there are several hundred known Scottish clans, not even a thousand, let alone 12,000. I looked up the Scottish tartan register on the internet and you may well imagine my surprise at who has officially obtained a registered Scottish tartan. Here are a few of them:

> Mohammed Farooq of Morocco, Personal Category. Ferrari Racing, corporate category. Little Frogs of Massachusetts, family category. Royal Australian Air Force, military category. Yamaha Marine of Japan, corporate category. Burberry Grey, fashion category. French Freemason's Pride, fashion category.

Not one of them a Scottish a clan.

At £70.00 per registration (and there is no VAT) the Scottish Registry is clearly sitting on a gold mine, never mind the Scottish Kilt makers firms who charge anything from £250.00 to £800.00 for each bolt of cloth made in a newly registered tartan. I reckon this business is one for the Monopoly's Commission too look at, as well as our chancellor of Exchequer, Rachael Reeves. She could be taxing them rather more than she is, helping to fill the £20 billion black hole discovered, after the July 2024 parliamentary elections, had been left by the Tories.

By July 2017 Philip and I were in the throes of organising the first world-wide gathering of our clan members, those bearing the McDouall name, those who had at least one parent or grand-parent who is/was a McDouall of Freugh and, of course, the spouses of those claiming McDouall genes. And as the replies came in to our invitation, the family tree grew exponentially larger, and larger.

We set the dates for the gathering as 17th to 23rd August, 2018, to take advantage of the famous Edinburgh festival and the expected fine summer weather. Philip took on the role of administrator and accountant while I looked after operations; designing and planning the programme, booking accommodation for 100 pax, engaging transport, reconnoitring the routes and consulting and bargaining with those responsible for places to be visited.

I can't remember ever having to work quite so hard, for a whole year, in organising such an extravaganza for so many people. Hotel accommodation in and around Edinburgh during the festival is always in short supply and many of the group bookings, such as ours, are made a full year beforehand. Thus it was that I found it difficult to muscle into the big hotels. The higher the star rating the less chance I had of booking the 60 rooms I needed. My imperative was to keep everybody together, not disbursed in several hotels. I hastily booked at the lower end, obtaining a reasonable price at the Trouble Lodge. And it was indeed troublesome as hotel rates and other charges changed at the whim of the owners. We also needed hotels in Dumfries and Galloway and there we had to split into smaller groups, our coaches shuttling between different hotels.

The fun part of my assignment was arranging all the tour sites, the first two days being in Edinburgh. I made an early block booking of 105 seats for an evening performance of the Royal Edinburgh Military Tattoo on the esplanade of Edinburgh Castle. I made another group booking for the National Museum of Scotland which, fortuitously, had an exhibition on the 700-500 BC Crannogs or lake dwellings where McDouall ancestors subsisted. And the last and most important booking was for the final Burns Supper night at the five star Caledonian Hotel. I booked their grand state room.

The remaining bookings, away from Edinburgh, were comparatively easy. I was able to book a tour of the splendid edifice of Dumfries House, the seat of Patrick, the 6th Earl, and which Prince Charles, now King Charles III, saved from ruination at the hands of the 7th Marquis of Bute, John Crichton Stuart *aka* Johnny Dumfries (1958-2021) who ran down the family fortunes having dropped out of school to go car racing and neglecting all but the Mount Stuart estates. He sold Dumfries House to the Prince's Trust in 1976, presumably to recoup some of his losses.

The glamorous Edinburgh Tattoo proved to be very popular. We had a whole block of seating in the centre of the grandstand and, at the start of the event, the master of ceremonies made a public announcement that the McDouall of Freugh clan were present. Mass cheering erupted from the centre stand. Of all the different performances from many countries, the massed pipe bands of Scotland stole the show, ending with the solitary piper up on the battlements of the castle, an emotional moment. The fireworks extravaganza then began as the audience flooded down the Royal Mile, heading for the ancient and historic pubs for a nightcap.

Sunday 19th morning saw a number of our younger generation boarding the coaches, finding a seat and promptly crashing out. First stop was the Highland Games in Perth where we were given a right royal welcome by the chieftain of the games and invited to participate in them. No one attempted to toss the caber but many of us spent some time in the whisky tent.

After a picnic lunch we drove back to Dumfriesshire to view Sweetheart Abbey, the ruins of which are in surprisingly good condition. This once flourishing abbey was built by Lady Dervorguilla circa 1250 and run by the Cistercian monks. Her husband was John Balliol, one time King of Scotland who was taken prisoner by King Edward and banished to France where he died. It is said that their hearts were entombed together under the high altar of the abbey. The connection with the McDoualls is with John Balliol's ancestry.

The final stop was in Dumfries town where we were shown around their museum and then granted the honour of Freedom-of-the-Town for a couple of hours. Dinner that night was at Hetland Hall, the only five star hotel in Dumfries, and the entertainment was a talk by Australian McDoualls about the ancient Australian McDoualls.

The next day our coaches took us all the way to the western coasts of Galloway and the isthmus where the famed Logan House botanical gardens lie. Because of the warming influence of the Gulf Stream there are palm trees and other plants normally associated with much warmer climes. I presented our clan shield to the owners who hung it in pride-of-place in a greenhouse. We visited the old district of Freugh where there is now a Ministry of Defence research station occupying an old wartime airfield. Just one ruin of an original village house survives. We were met by the head of station who boarded the lead coach and directed our tour of the old airfield. We saw the remains of house foundations in the grassy verges and that was all. But one interesting tale we heard was of how the famous Dambusters of World War II trained with their bouncing bombs from this aerodrome, flying their Lancaster bombers across the adjacent bay, doing their target practice.

Another place of interest was the family church of Stoneykirk, only a couple of miles away from Freugh. This church was built in 1740 and was the first in Scotland to have a circular congregational seating design with the altar placed at the eastern circumference of the circle. This Church of Scotland is now decommissioned and derelict, the surrounding grave yard rank with weed and bush growing riot. When we visited in 2018 the doors were padlocked and windows boarded up. We were told by a villager that a builder's firm used it for storage and that the furnishings had long since gone.

When I made my first visit in 1976 it was still a working church and, wandering through the darkened old wooden pews, I discovered the family names and their heraldic shields carved into the pew-ends, McDouall's mostly, a few variant spellings thereof; McDowall and McDovall; and a couple of Maxwells. And it was the same in the grave yard, at least 50 stones and grander monuments, some upright with ivy growing up them, many tilted this way or that and some fallen flat and broken. Where I was able to read inscriptions most were former occupants of those polished wooden pews aforementioned. Sadly it didn't occur to me take some photographs for the sake of posterity.

Leaving Stoneykirk, the day was very well rounded off with a visit to the Annandale Whisky Distillery, newly re-built in 2012 after years of decay and ruin. In 2018 the only whisky available was their immature distillation aged six years. But one could sense the promise in the owner's venture in the excellent guided tour of the distillery.

On Tuesday 21st our coaches dropped us off at Dumfries House for a tour, a Scottish dance class, a presentation to the trustees and a luncheon laid on for us. The house is run by the Prince's Trust, now the King's Trust, and it is a museum *cum* apprentice training college set up by the then Prince Charles as a business that runs a first class museum depicting life in the 18th century and exhibiting the world's largest collection of Chippendale furniture and furnishings.

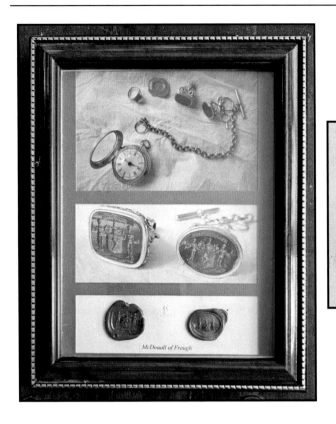

The gold Pocket watch, chain and and seal
of Patrick McDouall-Crichton of Freugh,
6th Earl of Dumfries.
Also the seal of Countess Margaret of Dumfries
and a memorial ring containing a
lock of the Earl's hair.

Loaned to Dumfries House on 21st August, 2018,
by John Crichton Stuart McDouall.

At the time of our visit there were 52 young, paid apprentices from local towns and villages, learning half-a-dozen different trades including those of electrician, plumber, farmer, builder, carpenter, cook, curatorship and material restorer. During the tour we visited the opulently furnished study of the 6th Earl, complete with estate ledgers, stationery, blotters and his library of leather-bound books. Added to the Earl's desk-top now is his gold seal and his gold pocket watch that I presented to the trustee on behalf of our clan. Next we staged a quadrille dance for four couples in the dining hall. The four couples, all members of our clan, were dressed up in late 18th century period costume, and taught their steps by a dance expert in the baroque period from the 17th and 18th centuries. The quadrille came from the court of King Louis 14th of France and became fashionable in Georgian England. We know from letters of Eleanor McGhie, sister to Patrick McDouall, 6th Earl of Dumfries, that this dance was one of the evening pastimes in Dumfries House. And last, but not least, a lavish lunch was served.

The last day of the gathering arrived and 104 clan members, including children, dressed-up for the grand finale Burns Supper, turned up at the famous old Caledonian Hotel, renamed the Waldorf Astoria. The piper played the head table in. John McCormick, son of Madge, the matriarch of the clan (103 years old in 2024), gave a stirring rendition of the Selkirk grace and the broth was served. After that came the full haggis ceremony, complete with a lively performance of Robert Burns's *Ode to a Haggis* by my younger son Patrick McDouall.

As the Chieftain of the Burns Supper, I gave the toast of the evening and announced that we hoped to arrange these gatherings of the clan every four or five years. As we all know, in 2019 the global covid pandemic hit, putting all plans on hold for the ensuing three years. However, the embers of the first gathering smouldered on and finally burst into flame again for the second gathering in April 2024 in Australia and New Zealand.

[1] British Nobility: John McDouall of Freugh *aka* Castle McDouall (1700-1757) married Lady Elizabeth Crichton Dalrymple, daughter of Penelope, Countess of Dumfries in 1725. Their first son and heir was Patrick McDouall (1726-1803) who became 6th Earl of Dumfries and married Margarate Craufurd. Their only child, Elizabeth Penelope McDouall (1772-1797) married Viscount Mount Stuart, eldest son of the 1st Marquis of Bute. Upon the death of the 6th Earl, the 1st Marquis of Bute unilaterally seized Dumfries House and lands on behalf of his daughter-in-law.

[2] ancient books purchased by Dr. Herbert, most pre-dating De Brett's and Burke's peerage books: Buchanan's history of Scotland, Vols I-II published 1722. History of Dumfries & Galloway by Sir Herbert Maxwell, Bart, published in 1834. History of the Hereditary Sheriffs of Galloway 1330-1747 by Sir Andrew Agnew, Bart. History of Scotland Vols I-IV by Patrick Fraser Tyler, FRSI, published in 1869. British family antiquity Vols I-VIII by William Playfair Esq, published 1811. A system of Heraldry Vols I-II by Alexander Nisbet, published in 1816.

Printed in the United States
by Baker & Taylor Publisher Services